Football, Community and Sustai]

A lack of 'sustainability thinking' is evident at the heart of many of the problems that football faces today; from the huge amounts of money that clubs seem compelled to spend on what are often short-term gains – and the speculation, debt and market-centred ideology that goes with it – to the not unrelated deep disenchantment experienced by many football fans for a game that they still, despite it all, remain determined to love.

Sustainability here is more broadly conceptualised than focusing on environmental issues. It encompasses social and economic sustainability, albeit with a critical eye on the interdependent, often contradictory, relationship between what the United Nations regards as the three 'pillars' of sustainability (environmental, social and economic).

Fittingly, this book is the result of an international collaboration between an interdisciplinary network of academics and football industry practitioners, brought together by the Centre for the Study of Football and its Communities (CSFC), based at Manchester Metropolitan University, UK. The critical insights collected here focus not just on football's problems, but also how clubs, authorities, players and fans in a range of local contexts are positively tackling the challenges of surviving and thriving in the contemporary global game.

This book was originally published as a special issue of *Soccer & Society*.

Chris Porter is based at the Centre for the Study of Football and its Communities, Manchester Metropolitan University, UK. His research explores the links between football fans, class-consciousness, neoliberal ideology and globalisation.

Anthony May is based at the School of Marketing and Management, Coventry University, UK. His research explores the relationship of sport with a range of social and political issues, including austerity, sustainability, and political campaigning, as well as with other forms of culture.

Annabel Kiernan is based at the Centre for the Study of Football and its Communities, Manchester Metropolitan University, UK. Her research interests cover public sector reform and the role of football in local service delivery and community identity.

Sport in the Global Society: Contemporary Perspectives

Edited by Boria Majumdar, *University of Central Lancashire, UK*

The social, cultural (including media) and political study of sport is an expanding area of scholarship and related research. While this area has been well served by the *Sport in the Global Society* series, the surge in quality scholarship over the last few years has necessitated the creation of *Sport in the Global Society: Contemporary Perspectives*. The series will publish the work of leading scholars in fields as diverse as sociology, cultural studies, media studies, gender studies, cultural geography and history, political science and political economy. If the social and cultural study of sport is to receive the scholarly attention and readership it warrants, a cross-disciplinary series dedicated to taking sport beyond the narrow confines of physical education and sport science academic domains is necessary. *Sport in the Global Society: Contemporary Perspectives* will answer this need.

For a complete list of titles in this series, please visit https://www.routledge.com/series/SGSC

Recent titles in the series include the following:

Football, Community and Sustainability

Edited by
**Chris Porter, Anthony May and
Annabel Kiernan**

R **Routledge**
Taylor & Francis Group

LONDON AND NEW YORK

First published 2018 by Routledge

2 Park Square, Milton Park, Abingdon, Oxfordshire OX14 4RN
52 Vanderbilt Avenue, New York, NY 10017

Routledge is an imprint of the Taylor & Francis Group, an informa business

First issued in paperback 2019

Copyright © 2018 Taylor & Francis

All rights reserved. No part of this book may be reprinted or reproduced or
utilised in any form or by any electronic, mechanical, or other means, now
known or hereafter invented, including photocopying and recording, or in
any information storage or retrieval system, without permission in writing
from the publishers.

Notice:
Product or corporate names may be trademarks or registered trademarks,
and are used only for identification and explanation without intent to
infringe.

British Library Cataloguing in Publication Data
A catalogue record for this book is available from the British Library

ISBN 13: 978-1-138-08366-0 (hbk)
ISBN 13: 978-0-367-22984-9 (pbk)

Typeset in TimesNewRomanPS
by diacriTech, Chennai

Publisher's Note
The publisher accepts responsibility for any inconsistencies that may have arisen
during the conversion of this book from journal articles to book chapters, namely
the possible inclusion of journal terminology.

Disclaimer
Every effort has been made to contact copyright holders for their permission to
reprint material in this book. The publishers would be grateful to hear from any
copyright holder who is not here acknowledged and will undertake to rectify any
errors or omissions in future editions of this book.

Contents

CONTENTS

Citation Information

The chapters in this book were originally published *Soccer & Society*, volume 17, issue 5 (September 2016). When citing this material, please use the original page numbering for each article, as follows:

Introduction
'Thinking long and wide': which communities have a future within the global game?
Chris Porter, Anthony May and Annabel Kiernan
Soccer & Society, volume 17, issue 5 (September 2016) pp. 661–665

Chapter 1
One rule for one: the impact of Champions League prize money and Financial Fair Play at the bottom of the European club game
Steve Menary
Soccer & Society, volume 17, issue 5 (September 2016) pp. 666–679

Chapter 2
Chao Amigos! Hello Thailand: football, migration and sustainability in Thailand
Carolina Brill and Chuenchanok Nin Siriwat
Soccer & Society, volume 17, issue 5 (September 2016) pp. 680–691

Chapter 3
Football clubs as symbols of regional identities
Adriano Gómez-Bantel
Soccer & Society, volume 17, issue 5 (September 2016) pp. 692–702

Chapter 4
Football and community empowerment: how FC Sankt Pauli fans organize to influence
Mick Totten
Soccer & Society, volume 17, issue 5 (September 2016) pp. 703–720

Chapter 5
Easton Cowboys and Cowgirls: anatomy of an alternative sports club
Will Simpson
Soccer & Society, volume 17, issue 5 (September 2016) pp. 721–731

Chapter 6

Ten years of Supporters Trust ownership at Exeter City AFC: an overview
David Treharne
Soccer & Society, volume 17, issue 5 (September 2016) pp. 732–743

Chapter 7

Fighting strategic homophobia in football
Roy Krøvel
Soccer & Society, volume 17, issue 5 (September 2016) pp. 744–758

Chapter 8

Sustaining health improvement activities delivered in English professional football clubs using evaluation: a short communication
Andy Pringle, Daniel Parnell, Zoe Rutherford, Jim McKenna, Stephen Zwolinsky and Jackie Hargreaves
Soccer & Society, volume 17, issue 5 (September 2016) pp. 759–769

Chapter 9

Football and its communities: the celebration of Manchester United FC's Ability Suite
Juan Luis Paramio-Salcines, Phil Downs and John Grady
Soccer & Society, volume 17, issue 5 (September 2016) pp. 770–791

For any permission-related enquiries please visit:
http://www.tandfonline.com/page/help/permissions

Notes on Contributors

Carolina Brill is based at the International Organization for Migration, Bangkok, Thailand.

Phil Downs is Disability Liaison Officer and Secretary of the Manchester United Disabled Supporters' Association, Manchester United FC, UK.

Adriano Gómez-Bantel is a Communications Manager and Public Relations Specialist in Stuttgart, Germany.

John Grady is Associate Professor at the Department of Sport and Entertainment Management, University of South Carolina, USA.

Jackie Hargreaves is Senior Lecturer at the Centre for Active Lifestyles, Research Institute of Sport, Physical Activity and Leisure, Leeds Beckett University, UK.

Annabel Kiernan is based at the Centre for the Study of Football and its Communities, Manchester Metropolitan University, UK. Her research interests cover public sector reform and the role of football in local service delivery and community identity.

Roy Krøvel is a Professor at the Department for Journalism and Media Studies, Oslo, and Akershus University College, Norway.

Anthony May is based at the School of Marketing and Management, Coventry University, UK. His research explores the relationship of sport with a range of social and political issues, including austerity, sustainability, political campaigning, as well as with other forms of culture.

Jim McKenna is Professor of Sport at the Centre for Active Lifestyles, Research Institute of Sport, Physical Activity and Leisure, Leeds Beckett University, UK.

Steve Menary was an Associate Lecturer at the University of Winchester, UK, and is now a freelance journalist, writer and lecturer.

Juan Luis Paramio-Salcines is an Associate Professor at the Departamento de Educación Física, Deporte y Motricidad Humana, Universidad Autónoma de Madrid, Spain.

Daniel Parnell is Senior Lecturer at the Centre for Active Lifestyles, Research Institute of Sport, Physical Activity and Leisure, Leeds Beckett University, UK.

Chris Porter is based at the Centre for the Study of Football and its Communities, Manchester Metropolitan University, UK. His research explores the links between football fans, class-consciousness, neoliberal ideology and globalisation.

Andy Pringle is Reader at the Centre for Active Lifestyles, Research Institute of Sport, Physical Activity and Leisure, Leeds Beckett University, UK.

Zoe Rutherford is Principal Lecturer at the Carnegie School of Sport, Leeds Beckett University, UK.

Will Simpson is a freelance journalist.

Chuenchanok Nin Siriwat is based at the Social Sciences Division, Mahidol University International College, Thailand.

Mick Totten is Senior Lecturer at the Carnegie School of Sport, Leeds Beckett University, UK.

David Treharne is Chair of Phonic FM, a community radio station based in Exeter, UK.

Stephen Zwolinsky is Research Officer at the Carnegie School of Sport, Leeds Beckett University, UK.

INTRODUCTION

'Thinking long and wide': which communities have a future within the global game?

Chris Porter, Anthony May and Annabel Kiernan

Sustainability is a concept with which the world of football is increasingly starting to engage, if not yet fully embracing or grasping its relevance wholly or coherently. The second Annual 'Football and Community' Conference of the Centre for the Study of Football and its Communities (CSFC) in June 2013 carried sustainability as its overarching theme, and saw academics, football industry practitioners and community stakeholders coming together in Manchester to present, discuss and debate the different ways in which football in different parts of the world is coming to terms with issues of sustainability. It is from those collective, collaborative, multi-disciplinary endeavours that this collection of papers has been brought together.

It should be emphasized that the overriding interpretation of sustainability within this collection is not one that focuses on environmental or ecological sustainability, but one that shares a concern that football might foster, nurture or facilitate more *sustainable communities*. The focus therefore is predominantly on what the United Nations refers to as the *social* and *economic* pillars of sustainable development,[1] that are conceived separately – if not independently – from their more immediately recognizable fellow pillar of *environmental* sustainability. This focus raises many questions in itself and deserves critical discussion around interpretations of sustainability, as does the important acknowledgement that processes related to sustainability interact interdependently, both within and beyond the world of football.

The often uncritical use of the term sustainability reflects similar definitional problems around the concept of community. As highlighted by Brown et al. in a 2008 special issue[2] of this publication, football like other high-profile industries often pays lip service, and certainly insufficient critical attention, to its engagement with such agendas, despite or perhaps more likely because of the ubiquitous appearance of these 'buzz words' in policy documents, corporate social responsibility claims and mission statements.

Indeed, the founding of the Centre for the Study of Football and its Communities was based in large part on a shared recognition that football clubs and authorities, particularly in the UK, were increasingly touching the lives of different kinds of community as a result of significant transformations in the scope and aims of their operations.[3] The broader social, cultural, economic and political milieu within which football exists can partially explain such transformations, but we should not overlook the active and calculated role of football's owners and guardians in wilfully embedding clubs and the game amidst the myriad flows of global capital,[4] thus both exploiting and manipulating the character of that milieu for ends that often conflict with the interests of some of football's communities, both old and new.

The contradictions therefore that exist between those different yet connected pillars of sustainability, threaten to undermine the long-term stability that can only be achieved through a more encompassing embrace of the values that underpin environmental, economic *and* social sustainability. Indeed, English football's attempts over recent decades to balance a social inclusion agenda with a prevailing free market ideology has raised serious questions around the sustainability of what Mellor called the *Janus-face* of the English Premier League.[5]

The overriding sentiment expressed throughout the June 2013 Manchester conference, as reflected in this collection of papers, is that the game of football has the capacity – financially, socially, culturally, symbolically – to be a real force for sustainable good in its interactions with its various communities. Qualifying such optimism however was a recognition that more critical focus is needed, via academic researchers, journalists and football industry practitioners themselves, on the fundamental contradictions that severely lessen the potential of football to play a positive role in making that interdependence between social, economic and environmental sustainability a cause for celebration rather than despair.

Scholars, practitioners and stakeholders

A core principle of the approach of CSFC has been to see academic research and analysis as a resource for knowledge exchange, to be shared with football industry practitioners, supporters and other community stakeholders, including journalists, community groups and policy-makers. The perspectives and insights of all these representatives of football's communities, from the UK and beyond, both complement and strengthen the understandings of academics seeking to make sense of contemporary football.

This process is deepened further when multi-disciplinary collaboration within academia is embraced, and CSFC has already benefited from the collaborative spirit that has developed between researchers representing such disciplines as sociology, politics and public services, architecture, business, human geography, literature, information and communications, art, psychology, sports studies, management and history.

The involvement of practitioners and those who have the inside track on the processes they describe is one of the key features of this collection. First-hand practitioner accounts are not a standard feature of academic journals, but they provide fresh angles upon the issues they discuss and allow for levels of inside knowledge that researchers often cannot access. Academic writing conventions have therefore been dropped to the bench at key moments in producing this collection in order to give a run out to such welcome insights.

The papers

The articles contained in this collection are laid out in three broad themes: the first examines financial sustainability and related issues in both Europe and Asia; the second looks at the sustainability of fan culture and fan-owned clubs in Europe; and the third evaluates the success and prospects for particular community initiatives launched by football clubs in the United Kingdom. This structure organizes articles in terms of broad themes, yet there are clearly overlaps between them and they can stand together as a coherent whole under the overarching theme of the sustainability of football's communities.

Steve Menary's 'One rule for one: the impact of Champions League prize money and Financial Fair Play at the bottom of the European club game' examines an important but thus far under-examined issue regarding sustainability in the smaller football nations of Europe. The award of Champions League prize money in nations like Luxembourg, San Marino and Cyprus appears to be changing the nature of domestic leagues such that once a team has qualified for European competition and been awarded the requisite money by UEFA, they are able to use that money to dominate domestic football for years to come. This means that prize money ultimately creates an unequal playing field and dilutes the competitiveness of, and ultimately interest in, domestic football.

By contrast, Siriwat and Brill broadly welcome the recent influx of money into the domestic league that they focus upon, the Thai Premier League. This relatively new competition has attracted financial backers locally and as a consequence foot-ballers from across the globe, and particularly from South America, have travelled to play in the top division of Thai football. 'Chao Amigos! Hello Thailand: Football, Migration & Sustainability in Thailand' examines the issues that face football migrants to Thailand, and is a particularly useful insight into the processes involved in migration from powerful football nations to a relatively weak one, providing an insight into a local culture that hasn't to date been the subject of much academic study in the West.

Adriano Gomez-Bantel's work examines the ways that VfB Stuttgart have been able to both foment regional identity and thrive through exploiting it. Writing from a financial point of view, the author discusses VfB's success in using an existing sense of identity in Baden-Wurttemberg for their own ends. The discussion con-tained in 'Football Clubs as Symbols of Regional Identity' also focuses upon regio-nal rivalries in Germany more broadly, and is therefore of interest both to scholars of sports management and those who examine the development of sub-national identities.

A further discussion of football culture in Germany can be found in Mick Totten's 'Football and community empowerment; How FC Sankt Pauli fans organise to influence'. This article provides a useful contrast to Gomez-Bantel's by examining the culture of a club whose appeal is multi-national but whose culture is tied firmly to locality. Totten particularly examines the political nature of St Pauli, and analyses how the now-famous sense of community associated with the club developed and is maintained by a network of activists. The autonomous and non-hierarchical organi-zational structure of St Pauli fans is examined in detail and the article also discusses ways in which fans influence politics outside of football. This demonstration of the potential of football communities to influence matters outside of the sport itself is particularly interesting from a socio-political perspective. St Pauli continue to inspire other fans to take political action at their own clubs, and Totten's article discusses this in detail.

Similarly to Totten, Will Simpson explores fan activism in his article 'Easton Cowboys and Cowgirls – Anatomy of an Alternative Sports Club'. Simpson provides an engaged, and engaging, insider's account of a club that attempts to bridge the difficult gaps between participatory club membership, enjoyable sports participation and the embrace of a more active, politicized worldview. Sustainability appears to be something that lies at the heart of what drives the Cowboys and Cowgirls, both from an internationalist perspective of social justice, solidarity and collaboration, and also from a concern for maintaining what they have created for the benefit of future generations.

David Treharne's overview of 'Ten years of Supporters Trust ownership at Exeter City AFC' offers a unique insight into his experiences as a founder of the Trust and Chair of the club itself. Those interested in the sustainability of fan owner-ship gain a complete history of Exeter's experiences as a fan-owned club. The strug-gles of the Trust to gain control of the club, and the governance issues that they faced, are examined in detail. As one of the first fan-owned clubs in the English game, Exeter City are a fascinating and extremely useful case study for those interested in fan culture and sports management. Treharne's discussion of the issues Exeter City faced is essential reading for all would-be fan activists.

A much less savoury aspect of fan culture is explored in Roy Krøvel's 'Fighting Strategic Homophobia in Football'. Krøvel examines a Norwegian case study, and analyses homophobic comments made both at matches and online in web forums. He suggests that such comments are designed to upset opposition fans (who are involved in anti-homophobia movements) and are therefore part of the anatomy of fan rivalry. Krøvel also examines the sustainability of homosexual football fans being involved in the sport in Norway, linking the broad concept of sustainability to *resilience* and willingness to deal with abuse. This understanding of the concept broadens the scope of the collection and adds a new paradigm to the study of sustainability in sport.

The final two articles in this collection cover initiatives that are run by football clubs with an aim of improving the lifestyle and experiences of their supporters. Pringle et al. in 'Sustaining health improvement activities delivered in English pro-fessional football clubs using evaluation' examine the health promotion programmes of two clubs currently competing in the English Football League. This article high-lights the importance of thorough monitoring and evaluation strategies in sustaining the effective promotion of positive lifestyle changes through football-based commu-nity initiatives.

Perhaps the most popular football club in the world are the focus of Paramio-Salcines, Downs and Gray's article on the experiences of disabled football fans. 'The Celebration of Manchester United FC's Ability Suite' provides an authoritative history of the initiative – Phil Downs was one of the driving forces behind the Ability Suite. The article suggests that the scheme provides Manchester United with a competitive advantage in attracting and meeting the needs of disabled fans, and argues that other clubs should invest in similar initiatives in order to keep pace and provide more equality of access for match-going fans.

This collection of papers brings together some of the many ways that football has a real stake in maintaining, or working towards, social and economic sustainabil-ity, and in so doing shares international reflections as well as bringing practitioner experience to the fore. This collective insight thus provides a snapshot of the chal-lenges faced at all levels of football and its diversity of communities.

Disclosure statement

No potential conflict of interest was reported by the authors.

Notes

1. United Nations, *Report of the United Nations Conference on Sustainable Development.*
2. Brown, Crabbe, and Mellor, 'Introduction: Football and Community – Practical and Theoretical Considerations'.
3. Giulianotti, *Football: A Sociology of the Global Game*; Giulianotti and Robertson, 'The Globalization of Football'.
4. Conn, *The Football Business.*
5. Mellor, 'The Janus-faced Sport'.

References

Brown, A., T. Crabbe, and G. Mellor. 'Introduction: Football and Community – Practical and Theoretical Considerations'. *Soccer & Society* 9, no. 3 (2008): 303–12.
Conn, D. *The Football Business*. Edinburgh: Mainstream, 1997.
Giulianotti, R. *Football: A Sociology of the Global Game*. Cambridge: Polity Press, 1999.
Giulianotti, R., and R. Robertson. 'The Globalization of Football: A Study in the Glocalization of the "Serious Life"'. *The British Journal of Sociology* 55, no. 4 (2004): 545–68.
Mellor, G. 'The Janus-faced Sport: English Football, Community and the Legacy of the ThirdWay'. *Soccer & Society* 9, no. 3 (2008): 313–24.
United Nations. *Report of the United Nations Conference on Sustainable Development (Rio de Janeiro, Brazil)*. New York: United Nations, 2012.

One rule for one: the impact of Champions League prize money and Financial Fair Play at the bottom of the European club game

Steve Menary

The aim of this paper is to analyse the impact of the prize money distributed by UEFA for participation in the Champions League in the early rounds and to demonstrate that the impact of this money is both disproportionate compared to larger clubs and will, under UEFA's guidelines for Financial Fair Play, run contrary to governance for larger clubs. This will show that UEFA's interest in club governance and the impact is solely focused on larger clubs, allowing a seemingly unregulated free-for-all in financial terms at the lower end of the club game, which is unsustainable and runs contrary to UEFA's own-stated ambitions in terms of fair play, competitive balance and financial governance.

The main prize

When Chelsea won the Champions League for the first time in 2012, the English club earned €59.9 million in prize money from UEFA after playing just 13 games.[1] Currency rates change, but roughly speaking that prize money is comparable to the £54.4 million earned by the club for playing 38 games and finishing fourth in the English Premier League (EPL) in 2011/2012.[2] Both sums contributed to a then record turnover for the 2011/2012 season at Chelsea of £261 million.[3] That snapshot illustrates the balance between domestic income and European prize money at the top of the game. Further down football's European pyramid, there is a significant imbalance between income generated domestically and monies earned from UEFA through playing in the Champions League. The further away clubs get from the grand prize of Champions League success, the greater this disparity appears to grow. In the same season that Chelsea won the Champions League, FC Basel – generally regarded as Switzerland's largest and most successful club – succeeded in qualifying for the last 16 stage ahead of 2007/2008 Champions League winners' Manchester United. FC Basel were then eliminated by Bayern Munich but those eight matches earned the Swiss club prize money from UEFA of €15.8 million.[4] To put that money into perspective, in the 2012 calendar year, Basel's turnover was €65 million (80 million Swiss francs), so European participation was one of the main reasons between Basel helping to drive revenue up from €55 million (68.5 million Swiss francs) in 2011 (Table 1).[5,6]

Basel's accounts cover a calendar year, so the 2011 figure includes some of the 2011/2012 Champions League run but not the income from the last 16 tie with

Table 1. FC Basel accounts and the impact of Champions League success (in Swiss francs) 6.

Year	Revenue	Profit	Transfer income	Income from UEFA/Raiffeisen Super League
2012	80.0	15.0	27.4	11.1
2011	68.5	5.5	10.0	16.7

Bayern Munich. The 2012 figures include this and also income from Basel's participation in the 2012/2013 Champions League, which ended at the play-off round. All clubs eliminated in the play-off round received a fixed allocation of €2.1 million.[7] Money for clubs participating in Switzerland's Raiffeisen Super League is low compared proportionately to the EPL and was less than 10% of the amount earned by Basel from UEFA in 2011. Although the financial and sporting years do not run parallel, typically at FC Basel a successful run in the Champions League is worth close to a third of revenue compared to around a fifth at Chelsea, which won the tournament. Consequently, when FC Basel consequently failed to reach the group stages in 2012/2013, the club sold a number of players, such as Xherdan Shaqiri to Bayern Munich, to ensure profitability. These figures may appear as abstract ones chosen at random but a line can clearly be traced through clubs that appear relatively regularly in the Champions League down to those whose appearances in the group stages is peripatetic down to clubs for whom qualification to the elite round is, given their playing and financial resources, impossible. At a time when UEFA is encouraging greater fiscal responsibility at clubs competing in European competition through the introduction of Financial Fair Play (FFP) and the penalties that lay within this new structure, little thought appears to have been given to the proportional nature of prize money from pan-European competition and just how sustainable this is lower down the food chain. This study aims to fill that vacuum and illustrate that UEFA's decision to impose the sclerotic structure of FFP on the upper echelons of the game fails to consider the impacts of prize money at a lower level and how unsustainable this is.

In part of their analysis of European football revenues, Solberg and Haugen take the case of Sweden, another country where qualification for the group stages of the Champions League is a rare occurrence. The revenue that Helsingborg earned by qualifying for the 2000/2001 group stages was €6.9 million (SEK 52 million) and helped push the club's annual revenue up by 80%.[8] That direct revenue from the Champions League comprises around half of Helsingborg's revenue, a trend that is described by Solberg and Haugen as 'uncommon in Swedish football at that time'.[9] Solberg and Haugen add: 'There are few other industries – if any – where firms of so few employees can generate such enormous revenues as the football industries'.[10] To take Solberg and Haugen's quotation one step further, there are few industries where the rewards for smaller companies participating legitimately in overseas ventures can be quite as disproportionate to their domestic income as football. In the cases of countries that do exceed the expectations of local fans and domestic finances, the financial rewards are such that the consequences for competitive balance and the sustainability of clubs that fail in these smaller countries can be devastating (Table 2).[11]

Table 2. Helsingborg's revenue in the years surrounding participation in the Champions League 11.

	One year before CL participation	Year of CL participation	One year after CL participation	Two years after CL participation	Three years after CL participation
Revenue (Swedish Krona)	60.4	109.0	64.3	59.5	63.3

Moving away from the main prize

In 1994/1995, UEFA made structural changes to the nascent Champions League in response to pressure from the G14 grouping of European major clubs, which was lobbying for a Pan-European League. Clubs from smaller UEFA members were relegated to the UEFA Cup, then allowed to return in 1997/1998, when non-champions were also admitted. These changes produced the genesis of the modern-day Champions League and the beginning of solidarity payments to compensate these smaller clubs for the impact of playing qualifying matches during what was then widely regarded as pre-season in many European countries.

Hungary is a country with a long and proud football history but one where the game has suffered from a combination of poor economic growth and an inability to match the growing commercialization of the larger clubs in Western Europe. By the 2011/2012 season, only two Hungarian clubs had ever succeeded qualifying for the group stages of the Champions League. When Ferencváros of Budapest qualified in 1995/1996, the rewards on offer were vastly different to those earned 14 years later by Debrecen. The club is from the second largest city in Hungary and the owner Gábor Szima epitomizes the type of 'sugar daddy' – an owner offering external support that would be unsustainable from a club's own resources – that UEFA is trying to mitigate through the introduction of FFP. In 2001, Szima, a prominent Hungarian businessman, secured majority control of Debrecen and four years later his club won their first Hungarian title and in 2009/2010, Debrecen reached the group stages of the Champions League for the first time. Though this brought little success on the field, Debrecen were eliminated after losing all six group stage games but this participation, which had been achieved after progressing through three qualifying rounds, brought UEFA prize money of €9 million.[12] The impact in Hungary's fragile sporting economy – a place a few steps further away again from the main prize than FC Basel and Switzerland – is substantial and produced a severe revenue spike. To put the value of that UEFA prize money further into perspective, a TV broadcasting agreement agreed in 2013 is expected to be worth around €530,000 a year to Debrecen and the other clubs in Hungary's leading OTP Bank Liga.[13] By 2011, Debrecen's annual revenue was down to just 975 million Hungarian Florints (€3.4 million)[14]; a revenue spike that is copied elsewhere amongst clubs depending on their success or otherwise in European competition.

When Michel Platini succeeded in winning an election to take over the presidency of UEFA, one of his first acts was to attempt to widen participation in the group stages of the Champions League to include clubs from smaller countries, who could then benefit from the increasing financial rewards on offer. This was opposed by the larger clubs and the initial proposals then diluted but the changes in the qualification format allowed some clubs from smaller UEFA members to qualify, such as Belarus, Bulgaria and Cyprus. In the 2006/2007 season, Levski Sofia became the first club from Bulgaria to qualify for the group stages and a year later BATE Borisov emulated this feat on behalf of Belarus. In Cyprus, a country with a population of less than 1.2 million,[15] the prospect of any local clubs participating in the Champions League once seemed distant but the commercialization of the Cypriot game mirrored an economic bubble on the Mediterranean island after the turn of the Millennium. Cypriot clubs began importing larger numbers of foreign players, particularly from Eastern Europe with some subsequently gaining residency and switching nationalities to qualify for the Cypriot national team. In 2008/2009, Anorthosis Famagusta succeeded in becoming the first Cypriot club to reach the Champions League group stages and won one and drew three of six matches in a group also including Inter Milan of Italy, Panathinaikos of Greece and Werder Bremen of Germany. Anorthosis Famagusta had justified the changes made by Platini and illustrated that Cypriot clubs were worthy of competing in the group stages. The 2008/2009 season Champions League qualification also provided Anorthosis Famagusta with €7.5 million in prize money from UEFA.[16] In 2009/2010, APOEL emulated the feat of Anorthosis Famagusta but although the club proved slightly less successful on the pitch the rewards were greater, providing €10 million, a figure that exceeded the UEFA monies won in the same season by Debrecen as APOEL had benefitted from €1.2 million for drawing three of their six Champions League group fixtures unlike the Hungarian team, which lost all six games.[17]

In 2011/2012, APOEL again qualified for the group stages and went on to reach the quarter finals of the Champions League, earning prize money from UEFA: a total of €18.1 million.[18] APOEL had to win through three qualifying rounds and played a total of 16 matches, but the sheer scale of this reward in the context of domestic Cypriot football can be illustrated by the work of Kartakoullis and Theophanous, which shows that in 2009 the total turnover of the entire Cypriot top division amounted to just €17.5 million.[19] The gross revenue at the 14 clubs in the Marfin Laiki League would certainly have risen between 2007 – the year of the survey conducted by Kartakoullis and Theophanous – and 2011/2012, when APOEL achieved a feat that no Cypriot club is likely to outdo or even match. This shows what massive impact UEFA prize money can have on smaller domestic leagues which are less commercialized. In their study, Kartakoullis and Theophanous show that revenue at the 14 leading Cypriot clubs ranged from €2.8 million down to €744,319.[20] Like the wider Cypriot economy, the work of Kartakoullis and Theophanous proves that Cypriot clubs were spending well beyond their revenue, which came from four sources: tickets sold for home matches, television rights, membership fees and financial support from friends of the clubs, and commercial activities including sponsorship. An extra source for those clubs in Europe was clearly UEFA prize money, although as the research was conducted before the recent surge in UEFA prize money and the Champions League group stage participation of Anorthosis Famagusta this omission can be understood. The survey also provides a clear insight into the working economy of a professional football league at a smaller UEFA member for whom Champions League participation could be a realistic and achievable aim. The survey showed that:

> Six clubs declared that they were expecting losses in the period under investigation; while the other eight clubs expected to have a profit;

The biggest profit to be made was estimated at Euro €640,725, and this was by a club which by the end of the season was relegated to the second division;

Paying the salaries of players, foreign and domestic, and coaches consumed 75% of every club's budget;

From the data gathered, it was clear that foreign players were paid better salaries than the domestic players;

Season tickets contributed an average of 10% of the total income for the clubs. The highest contribution from season tickets to total income was 20%, and the lowest was 1%;

The television rights for the period under examination were calculated to €934,177, which represented 5.3% of the total income of clubs.[21]

The survey also addressed the issue of competitive balance, which is central to ensuring a sustainable football competition. In smaller countries, less diversity can be expected in terms of clubs winning the local championship as there are typically fewer sizeable population centres on clubs are generally based and draw support. The Cypriot league is dominated by five clubs and only three of these clubs, Anorthosis Famagusta, APOEL and Omonia, are viewed in the study as capable of regularly competing for the title and thus securing an opportunity to qualify for the Champions League. In 1994/1995, the Champions League was in its third season since the rebranding from the old European Cup and in this period major structural changes were pushed through, including the use of four groups. The catalyst for the evolution of the modern Champions League group stages can be traced back to this season. Between 1994/1995 and 2013/2014, Cyprus were awarded 18 places in the Champions League qualifiers and between them, the five Cypriot clubs cited by Kartakoullis and Theophanous – AEL, Anorthosis Famagusta, APOEL, Limassol and Omonia – took all those places. In the year of the survey, television rights for the Cypriot league were valued at €934,177, which equates to 6% of clubs' total income.[22] Although this figure was expected to rise to 12%, any income from domestic TV income is low compared to the vast rewards that can be derived from European success. The impact of this on clubs seeking European qualification to balance their books is clearly detrimental to the overall game in Cyprus as Kartakoullis and Theophanous state:

Over a typical weekend with seven games on the national league calendar, approximately 190 players were used including substitutes during the 2005–2006 seasons. Out of those 190 players, only 75 were Cypriots. This is a trend which is increasing every year; whereby last season, there was a point where there were teams starting without a single Cypriot player in the first 11. Back in the 1992–1993 season for example, the clubs in Cyprus used to have eight Cypriot players and only three foreigners in the starting 11.[23]

In 2009, Kartakoullis and Theophanous wrote that Cypriot football was in 'crisis' and this was before the tsunami of UEFA money that would subsequently engulf the game there and the wider systemic economic failure on the island during 2012/2013. By 2014, the Cypriot league had the highest proportion of expatriate players in Europe.[24] As this research has demonstrated, the maxim quoted by Back et al. that the three major sources of income for football clubs – tickets, television rights, and commercial activities – should deliver roughly the same amounts clearly does not apply to the peripheries of European football.[25]

The peripheries of the European club game

Further out into countries where the idea of qualification for the Champions League group stages is wholly unfeasible, the impact of the money paid out for failure is equally as influential and perhaps even more capable of severe distortion. This funding can also arguably be shown to have created a footballing 'gravy train' funded by UEFA, where the sheer size of the financial rewards on offer just for competing in a few qualifying rounds is sufficient to sustain a club for an entire season, helping to create an extremely unhealthy reliance on UEFA in sustaining domestic football (See Photo 1).

In 2005/2006, F91 Dudelange became the first club from Luxembourg to win a tie in either the old European Cup or its successor the Champions League for 42 years after defeating NK Zrinjski of Bosnia & Herzegovina 4–1 on aggregate. F91 Dudelange were subsequently eliminated in the next qualifying round but in 2012/2013 became the first club from Luxembourg to win through two qualifying rounds of the Champions League. F91 Dudelange have benefitted from the same sort of investment that Gábor Szima provided in Hungary, but in the context of Luxembourg football and their own financial situation F91 Dudelange are now far more reliant on UEFA prize money. F91 Dudelange is controlled by Luxembourg businessman Flavio Becca and was formed in 1991 by the merger of three older clubs in the same town in southern Luxembourg. Like many clubs that have been artificially manufactured in this way, F91 Dudelange is viewed with a degree of antipathy locally. Over the past two decades, the club has virtually monopolized football in Luxembourg using the 'sugar daddy' model, but the initial input from private owners has been replaced by UEFA's prize money. These funds are

Photo 1.   F91 Dudelange in orange and red vs. Tre Penne of San Marino at the Stade Jos Nosbaum in Luxembourg, Champions League first round tie 3/7/2012. Credit: Steve Menary.

dependent on performance but are not, however, subject to the same governance regimes as larger clubs such as Chelsea or Basel, where UEFA money makes up less of the overall annual revenue.

In 2012/2013, F91 Dudelange beat Tre Penne of San Marino 12–0 on aggregate in the first qualifying round of the Champions League and then Red Bull Salzburg on away goals after the two legs finished 4–4 on aggregate. F91 Dudelange then lost 5–1 on aggregate to the Slovenian champions Maribor, but banked €620,000 in prize money from UEFA.[26] Annual revenues at clubs in Luxembourg is estimated to be around €500,000 a year, but F91 Dudelange won the league title (and secured Champions League participation) in 10 of the 13 seasons up to and including the 2012/2013 season and annual revenue at F91 Dudelange is estimated to be around €1.2 million a year.[27] This level of playing budget can buy a circle of domestic success that is hard to break. No club in Luxembourg has an entire squad of full-time players, but anecdotal local evidence suggests that F91 Dudelange generally have more full-time players than any other team in the BGL League. In the 2012/2013 season, F91 Dudelange were denied another triumph in the BGL league only after another local businessman Gerard Lopez began funding Fola Esch using the same unsustainable sugar daddy model of providing external funding for players' wages that FFP was set up to combat.

At Tre Penne of San Marino, F91 Dudelange's opponents in the first qualifying round of the 2012/2013 Champions League, the reward for losing a tie 12–0 on aggregate was more marked and disproportionate than any other level of the Champions League. In 2007/2008, UEFA allowed clubs from both Andorra and San Marino to compete in the Champions League and two years later a restructuring was made to the qualifying rounds with the introduction of an extra round. This theoretically gave clubs such as Tre Penne the opportunity to win a round but in reality simply reinforced a subsidy culture and a reliance on UEFA funds to guarantee help hegemony at a domestic level. At this level of European football, there is little realistic prospect that the reforms pushed through by Platini would ever enable a side to reach the group stages but there is an acceptance that UEFA's Champions League monies are having a substantially disproportionate impact. After witnessing F91 Dudelange beat Tre Penne 7–0, Luxembourg Football Federation president Paul Philipp stated:

> UEFA money can go a long way in places like Luxembourg. The guys from UEFA are studying these results. No-one is happy when a team is winning by a score like 7–0. That could be a reason for more pre-qualifying. Imagine that a team like [Tre Penne] played a major team from France or Germany, imagine the result, it could be terrible. I think that was the worst team I have ever seen in European competition; they at least have to be fit.[28]

Also in the 2012/2013 season, Northern Irish champions Linfield beat B23 of the Faroe Islands on penalties after a 0–0 draw over two legs. In the next round, Linfield lost 3–0 on aggregate to Cypriot champions Limassol and exited the Champions League with €480,000 in prize money from UEFA, yet in four matches played over these two legs Linfield had not even managed to score a goal. Tre Penne's financial reward for losing 12–0 over two legs was €340,000 and that figure in the context of Sammarinese football, where, according to UEFA's 2012 UEFA Club Benchmarking Report, average club revenue is just €86,000 a season. In the modern, commercialized football world, the Campionato Sammarinese is closer to amateur status than any top flight elite men's competition in Europe and Tre Penne that the prize money from the Champions League was used to improve facilities and invested in youth development, which would serve to attract better amateur players on one level and secure the services of stronger younger players at youth level to continue the success[29] (See Photo 2).

The impact of this distorted financial reward is clearly corrosive in terms of competitive balance as Tre Penne again took San Marino's sole Champions League place in the 2013/2014 season. Tre Penne won their home tie with Shirak of Armenia but were still eliminated 3–1 but were still guaranteed another €350,000. If Tre Penne's annual revenue is around the average figure given by UEFA for San Marino then four matches in two seasons of European participation yielded financial reward equal to eight years of annual revenue. The impact of this money will be tested further in the 2014/2015 season, when clubs from UEFA's newest member, Gibraltar, will enter the Champions League and the Europa League and the cash from participation in both will surely have a major impact on a virgin territory in football finance terms. At this macro-economic level of the European club game, there is little excitement at the prospect of clubs progressing to the Champions League group stages as recognition exists that an already damaging financial trend could lead to catastrophe. In 2007/2008, Montenegrin clubs were admitted to the Champions League qualifiers. The former Yugoslav republic has a population of just 653,474 and manages to sustain a professional league but in 2009 Ivan Radovic, the media officer at the Football Association of Montenegro, responded to the changes to the Champions League qualifying process by stating:

Photo 2. F91 Dudelange vs. Tre Penne of San Marino in white and blue stripes at the Stade Jos Nosbaum in Luxembourg, Champions League first round tie 3/7/2012. Credit: Steve Menary.

The Football Association of Montenegro believes that the reforms will give chance to smaller members clubs, which will help the development of football in small countries. It will, for sure, lower the quality level of the Champions League, at least of the group stage, but we believe it will take it a step away from the richest clubs private league that it seems destined to become. If someday one of our clubs reaches group stage there will be a big chance that it will probably dominate the domestic league for years.[30]

These concerns are reflected elsewhere in other smaller UEFA member associations where the size of Champions League payments for clubs with no chance of making the group stages is already significant. In Iceland, turnover at clubs in the leading Pepsi-deildin in 2013 according to the governing body, the Knattspyrnusamband Islands (KSI), was between €1.25 and €2.5 million.[31] KSI media officer Ómar Smárason says:

Qualifying for Europe makes a huge impact. A club playing in Europe year after year, even just in the qualifying rounds like most of our clubs do, they are in a very strong position. Should a team from Iceland qualify, we would without a shred of doubt (sic) see total monopolization of the domestic team by that league.[32]

For clubs from isolated UEFA members such as Iceland or the Faroe Islands, the domestic commercial impact of money from a single round of European competition can be watered down by being drawn against an opponent from the other side of Europe, which could generate higher than usual travel costs and less saleable television rights. However, at all levels of the Champions League, the growth in money distributed by UEFA to domestic champions has helped to produce supported long-standing periods of hegemony in places as disparate as Armenia, Latvia, Luxembourg, the Ukraine and Wales. An index showing the diversity of clubs in the Champions League over the first 20 years of the tournament illustrates the impact of increased UEFA prize money and how the diversity of the competition has been diminished to such an extent that a European League has in many ways already been created. There are clearly a finite number of clubs that could prove capable of winning their national title and entering the race for UEFA's riches, but as the size of the money being distributed by UEFA at all levels of the Champions League has grown, so the diversity of the clubs taking part has stagnated (Table 3).[33]

More money, less diversity

The Champions League Diversity Index works by dividing the total number of places on offer to UEFA members in the 20 seasons between the advent of the structural changes of 1994/1995 and 2014/2015 to produce an index number. Only four clubs from Greece and the Ukrainian clubs have played in the Champions League group stages over the period of study but Greece is the least diverse nation as the country has been offered more places in the group stages than the Ukraine. Montenegro, where UEFA money has had less time to influence club finances, is the most diverse with five clubs taking the seven places on offer since the country became eligible to take part in the Champions League. In 2011/2012, just 11 of the clubs taking part in the Champions League had not appeared in the competition since the structural changes; by the following season, the number of new entrants had dwindled to nine clubs and in 2014/2015 only five of the clubs taking part in the Champions League at all levels from the first qualifying round to the group stages had not appeared in the competition in the preceding 21 years covered by the

Table 3. Champions League diversity index.

Position	Country	Total apps	Clubs	Index
1	Greece	40	4	10.00
2	Ukraine	36	4	9.00
3	England	70	9	7.78
4	Scotland	31	4	7.75
5	Croatia	22	3	7.33
6	The Netherlands	43	6	7.17
7	Portugal	46	7	6.57
8	Italy	69	11	6.27
9	Turkey	37	6	6.17
10	Serbia	18	3	6.00
11	Spain	72	12	6.00
12	Belgium	35	6	5.83
13	Germany	61	12	5.08
14	Russia	38	7	5.43
15	France	55	12	4.58
16	Luxembourg	19	4	4.75
17	Austria	27	6	4.50
	Latvia	18	4	4.50
	Lithuania	18	4	4.50
	Moldova	18	4	4.50
21	Slovenia	18	4	4.50
22	Israel	22	5	4.40
23	Czech Rep.	30	7	4.29
24	Cyprus	20	5	4.00
	Denmark	27	7	3.86
26	Bulgaria	18	5	3.60
27	Estonia	18	5	3.60
	Malta	18	5	3.60
	N Ireland	18	5	3.60
	Wales	18	5	3.60
	Norway	24	7	3.43
32	Romania	27	8	3.38
33	Albania	18	6	3.00
34	Armenia	18	6	3.00
35	Faroe Islands	18	6	3.00
36	Finland	18	6	3.00
	Georgia	18	6	3.00
	Iceland	18	6	3.00
	Slovakia	18	6	3.00
	Poland	21	7	3.00
41	Belarus	18	7	2.57
42	Hungary	21	9	2.33
43	Sweden	21	9	2.33
44	Azerbaijan	16	7	2.29
	Ireland	18	8	2.25
46	Macedonia	18	8	2.25
	Andorra	8	4	2.00
48	San Marino	8	4	2.00
49	Bosnia-Herz.	15	8	1.88
50	Kazakstan	13	7	1.86
51	Montenegro	8	5	1.60
52	Montenegro	7	5	1.40

Notes: Where the index is the same, the country with the fewer entries is ranked higher. Liechtenstein does not enter teams in the Champions League.

UEFA members where no club qualified for Champions League group stages 1994/1995–2014/2015.

study. Often, these domestic hegemonies only end or are even interrupted by clubs developing unrealistic aspirations in terms of Europe spending on players to chase the greater rewards on offer from UEFA participation, as occurred in Wales with Barry Town, which took every Welsh Champions League place up to 2003/2004 before running into financial problems and collapsing. UEFA's flagship contribution to this sort of financial mismanagement has been the introduction of the FFP regime, which is widely regarded as flawed but necessary for the sustainability of the European club game.

Data from the CIES Football Observatory covering 2011/2012 shows that annual revenues of top clubs rose more than those of middle- and bottom-ranked ones and the CIES cautioned that:

> Without new regulatory mechanisms to improve income distribution, competitive balance will be further jeopardized through the transformation of top level clubs into global brands, [through] their regular participation in the increasingly lucrative Champions League and investments made by wealthy owners.[34]

This is evident when stripping out those UEFA members whose clubs have failed to qualify for the Champions League group stages from 1994/1995, when this structure was introduced, to and 2014/2015. There is greater diversity here than amongst the more developed and commercialized leagues and that could be because governance is arguably weaker here. Since the advent of UEFA's Club Licensing system and 2012, 49 clubs from 25 countries have been banned from UEFA competition by their national associations for failing to adhere to the club licensing criteria.[35] The largest proportion of those clubs are in countries where no club has ever qualified for the Champions League group stages.

Global club football brands are unlikely to be created in Hungary and Cyprus, let alone by semi-professional or amateur clubs in Luxembourg and San Marino, but the impact of UEFA money from the Champions League clearly has the potential to be far more influential here. In 2012/2013, clubs eliminated from the first round of Champions League regardless of performance over the two legs were awarded €340,000. According to UEFA's own benchmarking data, the average annual revenue at the nine countries in the poorest band – Albania, Andorra, Armenia, Georgia, Moldova, Malta, the Former Yugoslav Republic of Macedonia, San Marino and Wales – was €350,000.[36] Annual revenue in the next tier up, classified as 'small' clubs by UEFA ranges from €350,000 to €1.25 million and 12 UEFA members are categorized in this band: Azerbaijan, Bosnia & Herzegovina, Bulgaria, Estonia, the Faroe Islands, Iceland, Latvia, Liechtenstein, Lithuania, Luxembourg, Montenegro and Northern Ireland.[37] Of these dozen countries, only Bulgaria has produced a club capable of reaching the Champions League group stages. Should any of these dozen countries prove capable of producing a club capable of getting to the final qualifying round, in 2012/2013 this would guarantee a minimum reward from UEFA of €2.1 million plus an opportunity for further income generation from dropping down into the group stages of the Europa League and further income distribution. So a club achieving this in 2012/2013 from the countries in the small band would increase their annual revenue by a minimum of 68%, whilst should any club from the micro band manage this, the financial reward would equate to a minimum reward of six times annual revenue.

There are then 12 countries in the medium tier and of this number, only the Republic of Ireland and Kazakhstan have failed to produce a club capable of qualifying for the Champions League. At least one club from the other 10 UEFA members in the medium revenue bracket – Belarus, Croatia, Cyprus, the Czech Republic, Finland, Hungary, Israel, Serbia, Slovakia and Slovenia – have all qualified for the group stages between 1994/1995 and 2014/2015. As the size of UEFA's rewards increases, so will the potential impact at all levels of the European game but the European governing body's drive to increase financial distribution to clubs and improve governance is lacking in one key area, which has the potential to create further structural weaknesses. Clubs that can prove to UEFA and their Club Financial Control Body (CFCB) that their income and expenses are below €5 million in the two years before qualification are exempt from the key break-even clause of FFP. As this study illustrates, that includes a significant numbers of UEFA members, including those who are still capable of producing clubs sufficiently strong enough to qualify for highly profitable group stages. UEFA's explanation to this is:

> The potential exemption is only in place for the detailed assessment of the break-even rule, although all clubs will still have to submit data to UEFA and the CFCB as they have to prove their relevant incomes and expenses have been below €5 m in each of the two previous financial periods. The break-even rule objectives Article 2 (2) e)&f) are particularly addressed at the impact of individual clubs behaviour on club football as a whole and to rebalancing the spending and investing of larger clubs, which has been defined in the 2012 regulations as €5 million. In practice a club with total relevant expenses of less than €5 million a year is unlikely to have much of an influence on the sustainability of club football as a whole.[38]

FFP – where are ya?

Having succumbed to the pressures from the leading clubs for a potential breakaway, UEFA has created a system of financial reward that is both damaging the overall diversity of the Champions League and threatening competitive balance at all levels of the European game. Given the priorities that the European body set out on the creation of FFP to create a more sustainable game at the elite level, this is hardly tenable. UEFA makes annual solidarity payments to competitions where clubs do not qualify for the Champions League, which artificially create a system of subsidy not dissimilar to the European Union Gravy train that is often the focus of rightist political ire. In competition law and other areas, de-minimis rules usually apply and the cost of regulatory compliance may well be disproportionate to the overall cost base, but UEFA's approach has clear weaknesses. Unscrupulous owners could gamble on bankrolling European qualification at smaller clubs, then simply keep any rewards and withdraw, thus leaving these clubs to flounder. This sort of dangerous and untenable financial behaviour may well subsequently increase diversity in terms of Champions League qualifiers, yet does little to enhance the governance of the game at this macro-level.

A fairer system that would encourage sustainable success and help avoid an unregulated centrally funded hegemony emerging in smaller European leagues that the unsustainable sugar daddy model can break could be for the prize money that is allocated to clubs in UEFA competitions to be shared in a different format. By splitting UEFA money in half and leaving 50% with the successful club, then giving the other 50% to clubs in that domestic league this could provide a macro-economic shift that would benefit the structural diversity of European club football. Sustainability would be encouraged as appearances in the Champions League qualification system would be a success that would benefit all top-level clubs in smaller countries outside of the arbitrary €5 million FFP zone. At present, UEFA appears to have created a subsidy culture outside of the Champions League group stages leading to a two-tier economy with a bottom level simply ignored in terms of a key part of the new FFP governance regime.

Disclosure statement

No potential conflict of interest was reported by the author.

Notes

1. UEFA, 'UEFA CHAMPIONS LEAGUE: Distribution to Clubs 2011/12'.
2. Harris, 'Where The Money Went: Premier League Prize and TV Payments 2011/12'.
3. Conn, 'Premier League Finances: Turnover, Wages, Debt and Performance'.
4. UEFA, 'UEFA CHAMPIONS LEAGUE: Distribution to Clubs 2011/12'.
5. FC Basel 1893 und FC Basel 1893 AG Geschäftsberichte 1. Januar 2012 bis 31. Dezember 2012.
6. Ibid.
7. UEFA, 'UEFA CHAMPIONS LEAGUE: Distribution to Clubs 2011/12'.
8. Email response from UEFA media department to the author, November 14, 2013. Answer was 8.5 million Swiss Francs.
9. Solberg and Haugen, 'European Club Football: Why Enormous Revenues are Not Enough?'.
10. Ibid., 331.
11. Ibid.
12. UEFA, 'UEFA CHAMPIONS LEAGUE 2009/10: Distribution'.
13. 'MLSZ: marad a közmédiában és a Sport Tv-n a magyar futball'.
14. Muszbek, 'Sportgazdasági nagyító'.
15. CIA World Factbook, 'Cyprus: Population'.
16. UEFA, 'Distribution of Revenue to Participating Clubs: 2008/09 Champions League' in UEFA Direct, 6.
17. UEFA, 'UEFA CHAMPIONS LEAGUE 2009/10: Distribution'.
18. UEFA, 'UEFA CHAMPIONS LEAGUE: Distribution to Clubs 2011/12'.
19. Kartakoullis and Theophanous, 'Important Parameters of the Football Industry in Cyprus: Challenges and Opportunities'.
20. Ibid.
21. Ibid.
22. Ibid.
23. Ibid.
24. CIES Football Observatory, 'Demographic Study Now Available'.
25. Back, Blatter, and Burgin, 'Playing to Win in the Business of Sports the Pressure is on. Making Money – Not Just Popularity – is the Name of the Game'.
26. UEFA, 'UEFA Champions League Revenue Distribution'.
27. These figures are based on estimates from the Luxembourg Football Federation and other local sources given to the author during a visit to Luxembourg in July 2012.
28. Luxembourg Football Federation president Paul Philipp interviewed by the author, Luxembourg , July 4, 2012.
29. Email communication from Tommy Fantini of SP Tre Penne to the author, November 26, 2013.
30. Play The Game Diversity Index, 'New Champions League Index Shows Less Diversity'.
31. Menary, 'Financial Fair Play?'.
32. Ibid.
33. Play The Game Diversity Index, 'New Champions League Index Shows Less Diversity'.

34. Poli, Ravanel, and Besson, *CIES Annual Review*, 7.
35. *UEFA Club Benchmarking Report*, 2012, 21.
36. Ibid., 41.
37. Ibid.
38. Email communication from UEFA to the author, September 28, 2012.

References

Menary, S. 'Financial Fair Play?' *The Blizzard* 8 (2013): 149–53.
Poli, R., L. Ravanel, and R. Besson. *CIES Annual Review*. CIES/Opta Pro, 2013.
Solberg, H.A., and K.K. Haugen. 'European Club Football: Why Enormous Revenues Are Not Enough?'. *Sport in Society: Cultures, Commerce, Media, Politics* 13, no. 2 (2010): 329–43.
UEFA. *UEFA Club Benchmarking Report*. Zurich, Switzerland: UEFA, 2012.

Chao Amigos! Hello Thailand: football, migration and sustainability in Thailand

Carolina Brill and Chuenchanok Nin Siriwat

Since its establishment over two decades ago, the Thailand Premier League (or officially known as the Toyota Thai Premier League) has seen enormous growth in sponsorship, driving the league to one of the top in the South-east Asian region. Over the years, South American players have looked to Thailand for opportunities to play at the professional level. As South America is home to the world's greatest footballing heroes, South American players are in high demand, especially in Thailand, where push and pull factors have lead these football players to find better opportunities. Accordingly, the factors pushing players out of their home countries and pulling them to Thailand have created crucial migration networks that assisted the systematic flow of footballing talents. The research shows the primary push factors include: low pay, high barriers to entry and volatile playing conditions. On the other hand, a variety of pull factors draw players half way around the globe to Thailand. These pull factors include: high incomes, higher opportunity to play and a safer working environment. Considering that over 112 non-Thai players played in the Thailand Premier League in 2012 season alone, football migration has proven to be extremely important in drawing South Americans to Thailand. The paper concludes by discussing the implications of our results, with particular attention on the sustainability of the Thailand Premier League.

Introduction

The story of football development in Thailand is similar to that of other European countries, with football being tied to provincial support by fans from different local areas. For instance, Manchester United Football Club was formed in 1878, albeit under a very different name – Newton Heath LYR (Lancashire and Yorkshire Railway).[1] It was established as an activity for the workers in the railway yard at Newton Heath to indulge in their own passion for football. Similarly, the Thai football league has drawn influence from other popular leagues, with Clubs scattered and affiliated with provinces throughout Thailand. Just like the German Bundesliga, in Thailand, the football league is divided into a three-tiered system, with the Thailand Premier League (TPL) as the highest professional league. It is followed by the Division 2 League and at the bottom level, the Division 1 League. The TPL consists of 18 clubs competing every season, with four clubs relegating to Division 2 league at the end of each season. On the other hand, the top two clubs of Division 2 are eligible for promotion to play in the TPL. In the Thailand Premier League, as many as 116 players were registered in the 2012 season.[2]

The 2012 season saw an increase in the amount of foreign players. Clubs in the Thai Premier League are permitted to register up to seven non-Thai players, but only three foreign nationals and one Asian, non-Thai player are allowed to play on the field at once. With the quota of four non-Thai nationals, as opposed to the allowance of five players in 2012, during the pre-season, teams have been investing heavily in high-profile, experienced non-Thai national players. Therefore, up to 116 foreign players from 31 different nationalities were playing in the Thai Premier League in 2012, the most originating from Brazil such that up to 22 players were registered for 18 Thai Premier League clubs. With the vast amount of sponsorship pouring into the Thailand Premier League, participating teams are able to invest in signing deals with foreign players.[3]

The economy of Thai football

As with any successful business venture, the Thai Premier League must generate income. The League does so in three main ways. These three money generators include government support, private sponsorship and individual club's business activities. Accordingly, each and every fiscal year, the government allocates the biggest proportion of its sport fund to sponsoring football. In 2009, the Thai government allocated 210 million Baht (~£4,000,000) to sponsor the TPL. Furthermore, the Sports Authority of Thailand allocates up to 100 million Baht (~£1,900,000) for operation costs. It also provides the Champion with 10 million Baht (~£190,000) as prize money for the TPL.[4]

Alongside the government's financial support, the private sector has shown continuous interest in partnering and sponsoring the Football Association of Thailand. One example was 16 years ago when the League was first established. Johnny Walker funded the league with financial support of approximately 75 million Baht (~£1,400,000).[5] This money from the government and the private sector helped develop the Thai League. Recently, a Thai-owned corporation known as 'Sponsor' financed the 2010–2011 season. As a sports drink company, it solely sponsored the league with up to 70 million Baht (~£1,300,000) per season. Similarly, during the current 2013 season, Toyota Motors jumped on the bandwagon and signed a major deal to sponsor the Thailand Premier League. Now the League is known officially as the Toyota Thailand Premier League.

Although sponsorship has been important since the beginning of the league, in the past four years, there has been a dramatic increase in sponsorship. For example, in the 2011 TPL season, the television coverage of every match of the TPL provided a major incentive for large- and medium-sized companies to financially support the clubs. The increased exposure of company logos and slogans on the pitch and on jerseys provides an indirect way to further publicize businesses. Indeed, the television broadcasting rights of the Thailand Premier League have been auctioned for at least 600 million Thai Baht per season (~£11,500,000). In 2013, Siam Sport Syndicate, which oversees the Football Association of Thailand's commercial operations for the domestic competition, confirmed that the auction for television rights was conducted transparently for an estimated worth of 1.8 billion baht or approximately 35 million Pound Sterling. As a result, True Visions Cable Company was awarded the right to be the sole broadcaster of TPL matches in Thailand.[6]

In addition to sponsorship, the amount of money generated by each club's separate business activities had grown significantly. For instance, in 2011, when Buriram

PEA, now known as Buriram United, hosted Chonburi Football Club (CFC), over 23,712 spectators attended the big match.[7] The money generated from ticket sales alone was valued at around 1.83 million Baht (~£35,000). As the popularity of the League increases, the commercialization of sport has dramatically amplified. The footballing industry in Thailand depends on a systematic combination of ticket sales, concessions, official sponsorships and the sale of media broadcasting rights.

In 2010, conservative estimates of the overall worth of the Thailand Premier League suggested a total of around 500 million Baht (~£9,000,000), while in 2012, similar estimates placed its value at over 1 billion Baht (~£19,000,000).[8] With the support provided from the government, sponsors and fans, clubs are financially able to acquire better players. Accordingly, this increase in sponsorship has also enabled an endless flow of foreign players to migrate to Thailand to play in the country's football leagues.

Methods

The research was divided via two methods: interviews and bibliographic analysis. The main research objective was to discover the most significant push and pull factors that influenced the decision of foreign football players to move to Thailand. The methodology for this research included both field research and documentary research. The first method involved conducting in-depth interviews with a sample of migrant football players in Thailand.

A total of 50 interviews with foreign players, drawn from the 112 listed in the Thailand Premier League season for 2011–2012, were conducted. The interview process explored the push and pull factors while identifying the decision-making processes behind the football players' decision to migrate to Thailand. The second method involved a bibliographical analysis of various secondary resources such as books, journals, textbooks, newspaper articles, theses and reports, among others. This approach generated an underlying theoretical and academic background context for the empirical research and for understanding the theme of this paper.

Findings

Players migrate in search of better opportunities, higher salaries, more realistic chances to play and, in general, a better quality of life. Poor circumstances existing in the home country often push players out to other countries, where players search for better opportunities. The three main push factors are economic, social and political. Economic factors include lack of employment opportunity, low salaries, lack of shelter and food and low standard of living. The social factors include lack of education and health services available in the home country; and the political factors include conflicts or wars, terrorism, unfair legal systems and problems in the governmental system. However, the main three push factors according to the interviewed players are low pay, high entry barriers and volatile playing conditions.

The pull factors include the same three main categories as above: economic, social and political. The economic factors that pull people to migrate include offers for a more stable employment and higher salaries, better access to food and shelter and a higher standard of living. The social factors include better health care services, greater access to education and higher religious tolerance. Lastly, the political factors include better safety, freedom from persecution and better protection under the law.

The three main pull factors drawing players to Thailand are higher income, more opportunity to play and safe playing conditions.

Push factors

(1) Low pay

Various players in the TPL revealed that poor economic conditions at home in South America were among the main elements pushing them out of their home countries in search of better opportunities elsewhere, especially in Asia. Some originally searched for opportunities in other towns within their native countries, whereas others originally expressed the desire to play in neighbouring countries. Although many dreamt of playing professionally abroad, very few envisioned they would be in Thailand. Economic conditions were unstable, and at times rather sluggish, so players frequently searched for new opportunities.

The average monthly pay for a football player in Colombia was around $1986 USD per month, whereas the average pay for players in Ecuador was approximately $5000 USD per month. In comparison, international players in the TPL made significantly more money.[9] Several players interviewed reported that they made at least two to three times as much as they did in their home country. One player stated that he made $9200 USD as starting pay at [his] club in Thailand. Therefore, the low, unstable pay in South America pushed footballers to either change their career or seek employment in other counties.

(2) High barriers to entry

Several countries in South America are known to be home to the world's greatest football talents. Many succeeded, with a few becoming 'heroes' in the world of football. As a result, there is a large supply of players in South America, creating barriers for other players to succeed, with only the best coming out on top. Barriers to entry exist at almost every level of South American football. The first hurdle a footballer faces is simply the barrier to find a spot on a team. If a player can overcome this barrier, he then faces the barrier to have consistent playing time. After overcoming this hurdle, the player then faces the barrier of playing for a top-flight team. In the long run, the player faces physical and psychological challenges in competing with younger talents. All of these barriers push players overseas into markets where the supply of footballers is lower.

In countries such as Brazil, competition is especially fierce. Brazil is among the top five most populous countries of the world, and the vast majority of the South American players in Thailand are originally from Brazil. Worldwide, from an estimated 5 million Brazilians living abroad, 4000 alone are estimated to be football players.[10] The large supply of players in Brazil has created fierce competition for those looking for a place on the field, reinforcing why the first wave of Brazilian emigration of football players took place as early as the 1930s.[11] In this case, some footballer players are unable to find a job playing football, and unavoidably gave up on their dream career in order to support themselves through other means. Over half of the interviewed players admitted that as they aged, it became evidently more challenging to play against the younger players back home, despite the vast amount of clubs available. As Eduardo, re-called:

> It was getting much more difficult to fight and play against the young boys. They will chase you down, and try to beat you in every way to prove that they are capable ... In the end, if they are truly talented, then it makes it harder to stay on the starting line-up.[12]

He claimed it just got easier to look for new opportunities somewhere else, as it was more or less like a fresh start.[13] However, starting fresh each time was detrimental to the players' careers because they had to start from the bottom, rather than continue to advance their skills. As a result, they were unable to improve their skills and progress to better teams. Players explained that the desire to improve their skills at a more competitive level pushed them overseas. Having lived in Thailand for over three years, one player recalled his experience:

> When I was back at home [in Brazil], I played for an average club. We won trophies and championships but only within our own state-level competitions ... or at most ... let's say, regional-level competitions. But that was it. Hardly could I ever compete with clubs that were at the top, top-level. Until I met some friends who recommended me to an agent who helped find opportunities to play in Asia. I was in contact with him and told him I would love to go abroad for the first time in my life and to continue improving my professional career. Now, when I am here in Asia, I have chances to play in the Asian Champions League ... it is an amazing experience for me, as it is so far beyond what I have imagined. I tell my friends that I am living the dream as I have a chance to play against world class players who moved to play football in Asia.[14]

(3) Volatile Playing Conditions at Home

In the late twentieth century, football served as a unifying force in South American societies, as well as a vehicle that politicians, economic elites and influential gang leaders have manipulated to protect their status quo.[15] Football has inevitably been used as a tool to reinforce nationalistic, authoritarian, class-based, community and regional-based notions of identity and culture.[16] The 1969 World Cup qualification matches between Honduras and El Salvador serve as an example of violence and the destructive consequences in football. The matches triggered a war that lasted up to 100 h. The 'soccer war' resulted in over 6000 causalities over 12,000 were wounded, and 50,000 were internally displaced.[17] At the domestic level, the development of football in South America exacerbated regional tensions between professional teams from different cities. At times, the disproportionate recruitment and selection of national team players from one particular club or region also stemmed clashes among rival teams. As Bar-On states, the political harnessing of football for nationalistic ends has spawned divisive consequences, posing threats on issues of security in sports in the South American context.[18]

Moreover, football's popularity and its connection to organized crime network continue to serve as a hindrance to the overall development and sustainability of the league. Players and clubs must be responsible for their image, and more importantly clubs must ensure safety for the fans. In 2013, the Brazilian league recorded the highest amount of deaths in football-related incidents, where up to 30 fans died in one year.[19] From the sponsorship perspective, the football-related violence has prompted sponsors to withdraw their support for the clubs. In 2013, after the brawl between Atlético Paranaense and Vasco de Gama in the last round of the

Campeonato Brasileiro, Japanese carmaker Nissan decided to end its sponsorship deal with Vasco Da Gama. The lack of safety and security in the domestic leagues of South America is therefore a major push factor, driving players to migrate to Thailand in order to play in a safer environment. In most cases, after the first year of successfully playing abroad, a vast majority of the players interviewed claimed that they were reunited with their families and loved ones once again. The players' wives, fiancés, girlfriends and young children temporarily moved to Thailand, immediately after the players passed the first year threshold of playing abroad, and were awarded with a new contract.

Pull factors

(1) Higher net income

Income derived from playing abroad continues to act as an important magnet attracting foreign talents to play overseas, especially in Thailand. According to the World Bank, in 2013 alone, around 414 billion USD were sent home by migrants around the world. Brazil alone received around 4.7 billion USD in the form of remittances.[20] A portion of this remittance was transferred to Brazil by the Brazilian footballers playing in the Thailand. Migrating players are able to earn three times as much as their average salaries back at home in countries such as Brazil and Chile, making this factor a major pull attracting them half way around the world to Thailand.

Most players who had been playing in Thailand for over three years claimed they had been able to send remittances back home to their families, as their salary starts at a higher rate than at home. Such remittances constitute a key aspect of the migrant experience more or less everywhere. Others explained that the income gained from playing in Thailand had enabled them to increase their savings over the past few years. Playing in Thailand for over three years, a Brazilian player who now plays in the Division 1 League unveils that:

> It [income] is much more predictable here in Thailand. I do not have to worry. My agent and team takes care of me well. At home, I don't have an agent. Here, he helps me with everything.[21]

In recent years, foreign players have surged into Thailand, playing in all three levels of its national leagues. The higher pay pulls these players to Thailand, and a bonus is the lax tax requirements. The Thai Government has so far placed little emphasis on the need for foreign athletes to pay taxes compared to the tax demands levied on foreign nationals working in corporate offices. Of all the respondents interviewed, not a single player mentioned taxation, claiming that their respective clubs all had ways of dealing with tax payments without troubling their players.

Remittance networks in Thailand serve as a significant factor that directly plays a role in footballers' decision to move to Thailand. This is essential. Without strict tax laws on foreign players, as opposed to local Thai professional players, clubs and agents have been able to deliver to the needs of players financially. As opposed to strict law-enforcement countries like Singapore, Thailand in the recent years is still relatively relaxed when it comes to taxing foreign football players. Due to this incentive, foreign players, in general, may be more drawn to play in Thailand as opposed to a country with higher taxation and stricter implementation on expatriates. Additionally, in comparison to other competitive leagues in South-east Asia, such as the Vietnamese League (V-League) or the Malaysia Premier League (Liga Super Malaysia), TPL proves to be more attractive as the highly experienced South American agents often play a substantial role as an all-in-one agent and financial advisor to these players. With several years of experience living in Thailand, players are psychologically assured that they are not neglected by any means.

(2) Higher opportunity to play

A majority of the respondents also claimed that their move to Thailand had been strongly facilitated by the opportunities available. One reason, more opportunities are available in Thailand, is the established network existing between agents and players. This network makes is relatively easy to make migration decisions, regardless of whether a player speaks English or Thai because the agents help connect the players to interested clubs. Over half of the players interviewed took part in auditions and scouting programmes, involving Thai football Club representatives in Brazil. Chonburi Football Club (CFC) was one of the first clubs from Thailand to embark on programmes such as these in order to create a platform for players to show their skills and talents, and potentially to increase their opportunities to play in Thailand.

In 2008, Coach Jadet Milarp, former coach of Chonburi Football Club as well as the head coach of the Assumption Chonburi Football Team, flew to Brazil to draft potential players for the Club. To date, over half of those who were scouted and selected from the Milarp's initial visit are still playing professionally in Thailand. In an interview, one player revealed that:

> The trials and auditions that were opened at that time created a whole new opportunity for me. Never before did I think I would play in Thailand, as I have never even been outside Brazil before.[22]

An additional reason that makes South American players popular in the TPL is due to the strong market demands. Clubs specifically vie for South American players because in Thailand, Brazilian players are stereotyped as some of the most skilful players in the world. At the same time, the salaries of South American players are less expensive in comparison to European players. Therefore, Thai fans believe they are getting the best quality players, and the club managers know they are paying a slightly trivial price for the satisfaction of their fans. This combination of stereotype and affordability creates sustainability because the clubs are not placed in a position to overpay. Consequently, they have money to continue to acquire players in the future.

Another added benefit of having higher opportunity to play is more starting time. In some cases, those respondents claimed that playing for new leagues and new teams increased their chances of playing. Since the South American migrants saw more playing time, they were able to develop and improve their skills. As they became more skilled, these players also became more valuable to the Club. Recently being awarded with a prize by the local sports media in Thailand for his personal achievements and sportsmanship, a Brazilian defender claimed that:

> It has been a life-changing opportunity for [him] … moving to Thailand has opened up new opportunities for [his] family. [His] young siblings are all able to go to school

back in Brazil and occasionally visit [him] here in Thailand. [He] can afford to send them all to school and still spare some money to renovate [their] old home.[23]

Accordingly, all the players suggested that they were able to grow and develop 'professionally' in their careers, despite being far from home. As one respondent summarized:

> The pace of football in Thailand, or the style in general, is not exactly the same like in Brazil. But since we are the foreign quota players, a lot of emphasis has been made on us to help the team as much as possible with our personal skills. For me, it made me realize how important it is to never stop learning.[24]

With over five years of experience in playing football in Thailand, the player humbly explained that the unpredictability in the game of football is what keeps the supporters and Clubs in the long chase for success.

(3) Safe, welcoming environment

One of the more overlooked reasons why some South American football players are pulled to Thailand is due to the safe environments to play professional football in Thailand. The violent environments surrounding football at the local level are virtually inexistent. Football in Thailand is treated seriously. However, the rivalry between different clubs is not as threatening as in other leagues around the world. Many of the respondents of this research pointed out that football fans in Thailand are not as 'hardcore' as the ultra-fans in divisional leagues in Brazil. Instead, South American players in Thailand often experience the exact opposite. One migrant player recalled the first week he arrived at Chonburi Football Club:

> The Club officials drove me to go buy basic electronics for my apartment. We went to buy things for the kitchen, and I remember so well that the workers at the store introduced themselves to me and said that they were fans of the Club. They did not speak English well ... nor did I, but they were all so eager to help me with everything, which made me feel very welcomed. Small incidents and experiences like this made me realize the role of football in this place which I've called home for the past three years.[25]

Many of the foreign players included in this research shared similar views in stating that they particularly enjoy living in Thailand. They felt very welcomed, particularly by the fans in their given communities. Football, therefore, could be viewed as a form of largely non-verbal theatre, whereby the 'we-feelings' aroused through the vehicle of football has become important at the individual, local, national and international levels. Football produces spaces in which fans can construct identities and relationships. In discussing how football has created a sense of welcoming for players of different backgrounds in Chonburi, a player stated that:

> The fans are always hosting parties and events and the Club always asks us to join. It may be about image too but I think that football is more than just a weekly game for those in Chonburi province but it is part of their everyday life. I've recommended this destination [Thailand] to many football friends at home ... although it is definitely hard to imagine and explain what life will be like half way around the world in a non-Catholic country, but I tell them that life is good in Thailand. I show them it is good by what the opportunities it has brought to my family.[26]

Why it worked in Thailand

The migration of footballers from South America to Thailand can only be considered as a part of a multifaceted process that continues to expand.[27] Thailand has become a relatively successful destination for many international football talents, while promulgating a wider sense of interest in football among locals for several reasons. One of the most important factors was initial government support. The overall success of professional football in Thailand can be traced back to the continuous support provided by the Thai Government. In the past decade, government programmes and budget were proportionately allocated and designed to advance the domestic game of football. It raised the public's interest in the game. As provinces nationwide hopped on the bandwagon and formed their own Clubs, competition became fierce. From the beginning of the professional League, the government made it clear they were willing to invest in order to promote and enhance the game's popularity and professionalism. Continuous government support in the past decade is a direct reason why Thai people today, live and breathe football. With the absence of this strong support, it is questionable whether football would have become as influential and financially equipped as it is today.

Although the government primarily supported the establishment of the League as a whole, there has been little direct government intervention in the day-to-day affairs of the football clubs. Instead, various separate agencies associated with the League and the clubs themselves were able to attract and welcome overseas players. Furthermore, the clubs' legal statuses as private businesses, licensed and accredited by the Department of Business Promotion under the Ministry of Commerce, ensured that they were free from top-down government control. Free to manage their own affairs, the Thai clubs have grown commercial strength in line with the Asian Football Confederation's goal of improving the economic and financial capabilities and transparency of the Clubs. This financial stability separates the Thai clubs from those in other countries such as Indonesia, where there are two quarrelling Football Associations.

Furthermore, the environment surrounding the Thai Premier League is inviting to foreign nationals. There is no clear divide between the players who emigrated, (whether from South America or from Africa) and local Thai football players. The League and the clubs have facilitated positive relationships between the players – whom at the end of the day were football players, representing the same team. Local players knew very well that foreign players were entitled to a higher salary; however, this was never an issue. It is also inviting because the match-fixing scandals are not rampant in comparison to other countries, such as the highly modernized Singapore, a developed country with a professional football league plagued with match-fixing ordeals.

Aside from government support, business and environmental factors, an equally significant reason why the migration of South American footballers to Thailand has been so successful can be attributed to the League's greater access to the Champions League. The sound development of the TPL has resulted in a higher representation of Thai Clubs in the Asian Football Confederation's (AFC) Champions League. Serving as the equivalent to UEFA's Champions League, Clubs from Thailand stand a better chance in competing in the AFC Champions League, in turn increasing the migrant's chances to play against top Asian teams, particularly from Japan (J-League), South Korea (K-League) and China (Chinese Super League) or even from Australia (A-League). Champions of the AFC Champions League are entitled to play in the FIFA Club World Club, which is a dream for local and migrant players alike.

The sustainability of Thailand's football industry

The professional football industry in Thailand has potential to continue growing. Yet, to ensure that the different leagues, particularly the highest league (Thailand Premier League), are sustainable, various measures must be adopted in both the short and long term. Different stakeholders must know their responsibilities, rights and respect rules and regulations. One way to further build towards sustainability is through law.

As a result, Thailand's first-ever Professional Sport Act was enacted on the 14 February 2014.[28] It oversees and outlines the rights and mechanisms for professional athletes in Thailand. Included as one of the 12 categories of professional sports in Thailand, football received much attention. In the past few years, it has come to be accepted, by the general Thai population, as a professional career. With the Professional Sports Act, football among other sports has been recognized by law as a 'professional' career.

With the advent of the Professional Sport Act, professional football players, both men and women, are able to earn a living, and most importantly, they are able to receive government funding and financial assistance when in need. This applies to both Thai and non-Thai nationals, as they must be registered with the Sport Authority of Thailand. This Act is significant as it assures that as an accredited professional career, regardless of nationality, professional football players in Thailand are entitled to establish unions and to demand their rights as stipulated in the Act. If issues arise during official games, such as the unfair treatment or injustice is given to the professional athletes, they may appeal with the Appeal Committee for Professional Sport. From a legal perspective, this development in Thailand makes any individual's career in football much more sustainable, as it is implemented as a law. Furthermore, it provides a safety-net, attracting foreign players to Thailand. Being South-east Asia's first country to draft and implement a specific Act protecting the rights of professional athletes, Thailand has taken a substantial step forward in certifying the sustainability of Thailand's football industry.

Conclusion

Thailand may be known worldwide as a tourist destination. However, it has also gained increasing popularity and recognition as a destination for migrating football talents. Due to economic, social and political push and pull factors, South Americans have increasingly been choosing Thailand as a migration destination. The most important conclusion indicated by this research is that football is a global sport that can in fact serve as a feasible career. Although football migration is not a new phenomenon, just as with many other kinds of migration, football as a professional career allows people to move in search of better opportunities in countries outside their respective continents.[29] Football can be more than a game watched and enjoyed on a comfortable couch every weekend: it can be a spade, uprooting and replanting players in more fertile ground.

In Thailand's case, continuous government support in developing and educating clubs to function as companies has enabled them to pay for better players. The better players lead to more wins, which then attracts more fans. The new fans then pump more money back into the club, and the cycle starts all over again. Similarly, by providing the basic physical and legal infrastructure, through the newly enacted Professional Sport Act (2013), the Thai Government has proved that football is not merely just a passion, but also a stable career.

Disclosure statement

No potential conflict of interest was reported by the authors.

Notes

1. Manchester United, 'Manchester United Club History'.
2. Pattanamongkol, 'Thailand Premier League Insider'.
3. Ibid.
4. Matichon, 'Government Fuels an Additional 210 million Baht to Support Thai League'.
5. Royal Thai Senate, 'Professional Sport Act'.
6. The Nation, 'TrueVisions Retains Rights for Thai Premier League'.
7. Pattanamongkol, 'Thailand Premier League Insider'.
8. Ibid.
9. El Telégrafo Online, 'Los Sueldos Del Fútbol Local Son Atractivos Para Extranjeros'.
10. Riley, 'Study Note – Push and Pull Factors behind Migration'.
11. Ibid.
12. Player 1: Eduardo (player, Osotsapa FC), in discussion with the authors, February 2012.
13. Ibid.
14. Player 2: (Unattributed Interview) (player, Chonburi FC), in discussion with the authors, January 2012.
15. Arbena, 'Generals and Goles: Assessing the Connection between the Military and Soccer in Argentina'.
16. Arbena, 'Sport, Development, and Mexican Nationalism, 1920–1970'.
17. Kapuscinski, *The Soccer War*.
18. T. Bar-On, 'The Ambiguitites of Football, Politics, Culture, and Social Transformation in Latin America'.
19. Wilson Duarte et al., 'Football Violence: A View from around the World'.
20. World Bank, 'Migrants from Developing Countries to Send Home $414 Billion in Earnings in 2013'.
21. Player 3: (Luiz) (player, Ratchaburi FC), in discussion with the authors, January 2012.
22. Player 4: Cobo (player, former Chonburi FC and Trad FC player), in discussion with Chuenchanok Siriwat, January 2012.
23. Player 3: (Luiz) (player, Ratchaburi FC), in discussion with the authors, January 2012.
24. Player 5: Ferreira (player, TTM Chiang Mai FC), in discussion with Chuenchanok Siriwat, December 2011.
25. Player 2: (Unattributed Interview) (player, Chonburi FC), in discussion with the authors, January 2012.
26. Player 5: Ferreira (player, TTM Chiang Mai FC), in discussion with Chuenchanok Siriwat, December 2011.
27. Magee and Sugden, 'The World at Their Feet: Professional Football and International Labor Migration'.
28. Royal Thai Senate, 'Professional Sport Act'.
29. Taylor, 'Global Players?: Football Migration and Globalization, C. 1930–2000'.

References

Arbena, J. 'Generals and goles: assessing the connection between the military and soccer in Argentina'. *International Journal of the History of Sport* 7 (1990): 120–30.

Arbena, J. 'Sport, Development, and Mexican Nationalism, 1920–1970'. *Journal of Sport History* 18 (1991): 350–64.

Bar-On, T. 'The Ambiguitites of Football, Politics, Culture, and Social Transformation in Latin America'. *Sociological Research Online* 2, no. 4 (1997): 1–16.

Browning, W. 'World Cup Tournament Television Ratings'. *Yahoo Online*, 2010. http://voices.yahoo.com/world-cup-tournament-television-ratings-6138046.html?cat=2.

Duarte, Fernando, Jonathan Wilson, Shaun Walker, Paolo Bandini, and Paul Doyle. 'Football Violence: A View from around the World'. *The Guardian Online*, 2013. http://www.the guardian.com/football/2013/dec/19/football-violence-view-around-world.

El Telégrafo Online. 'Los Sueldos Del Fútbol Local Son Atractivos Para Extranjeros'. *El Telégrafo*, 2013. http://www.telegrafo.com.ec/deportes/item/los-sueldos-del-futbol-local-son-atractivos-para-extranjeros.html.

El Universal Online. 'El Salario Del Futbolista Colombiano Está En Promedio En $4 Millones'. *El Universal*, 2013. http://www.eluniversal.com.co/cartagena/deportes/el-sal ario-del-futbolista-colombiano-esta-en-promedio-en-4-millones-117930.

Houlihan, B. 'Sport, National Identity and Public Policy'. *Nations and Nationalism* 3 (1997): 113–37.

Jarvie, G. *Sport, Culture and Society: An Introduction*. London and New York: Routledge and Kegan Paul, 2006.

Kapuscinski, Ryszard. *The Soccer War*. London: Granta Books, 1990.

Lever, J. 'Soccer: Opium of the Brazilian People'. *Transactions* 7, no. 2 (1969): 36–43.

Magee, Johnathan, and John Sugden. "The World at their Feet': Professional Football and International Labor Migration'. *Journal of Sport and Social Issues* 26, no. 4 (2002): 421–37.

Manager Newspaper. 'Estimates of World Cup Viewers To Increase beyond 26%'. *Manager Newspaper*, 2007.

Manchester United. 'Manchester United Club History'. (2012). http://www.manutd.com/Home/Club/History By Decade.aspx.

Matichon Online. 'Government Fuels an Additional 210 Million Baht to Support Thai Lea- gue'. *Matichon Newspaper*, 2009. http://www.matichon.co.th/news_detail.php?newsid= 1254994636&grpid=03&catid=03.

The Nation Online. 'TrueVisions Retains Rights for Thai Premier League'. *The Nation Newspaper*, 2013. http://www.nationmultimedia.com/sports/TrueVisions-retains-rights-for-Thai-Premier-League-30213111.html.

Pattanamongkol, T. *Thai Premier League: TPL. Sarakadee Magazine*. Bangkok: Bangkok Printing Ltd, 2011.

Riley, C. 'Study Note – Push and Pull Factors behind Migration'. (2011). http://www.tutor2u. net/blog/index.php/geography/comments/study-note-push-and-pull-factors-behind-migration.

Royal Thai Senate. 'Professional Sport Act'. (2013). Bangkok.

Scambler, G. *Sport and Society: History, Power and Culture*. Berkshire: Open University Press, 2005.

Taylor, Matthew. 'Global Players?: Football Migration and Globalization, C. 1930–2000'. *Historical Social Research* 31, no. 1 (2006): 7–30.

Thailand Premier League. 'Players List 2012 Season'. (2012). http://thaipremierleague.co.th/ 2012/tplclubs.overview.php?clubID=10.

World Bank. 'Migrants from Developing Countries to Send Home $414 Billion in Earnings in 2013'. (2013). http://www.worldbank.org/en/news/feature/2013/10/02/Migrants-from-developing-countries-to-send-home-414-billion-in-earnings-in-2013.

Football clubs as symbols of regional identities

Adriano Gómez-Bantel

Looking at the terraces, into the pubs and the TV programme demonstrates how important football is for its followers – it is hard to believe that it is only a sport for them. In fact, a lot more is behind football than just an athletic competition. The core of the popularity of a football club is its identity. One possible model for understanding club identity analyses a club as a carrier of a group identity, in this case a regional one. Looking at the model more closely, a football club is not only a sports club – it is also seen as a symbol for a group or for a geographic entity in which it is located. Regional identity gives a football club a deeper meaning. And it is a sustainable philosophy for a club to focus on regional identity, as we see on traditional clubs like VfB Stuttgart in Germany or FC Barcelona and Athletic Bilbao in Spain. These clubs benefit in different ways from their local philosophy and furthermore these 'tradition keepers' have a charismatic aura, in comparison to clubs that focus on financial power and act as an economic unit.

Introduction

Evidence of the high profile of football in society today is all around us – in the stadiums, the bars, the daily TV schedules and the newspapers. There are many factors that make football clubs so important for us, but one of the principal reasons for the popularity of this sport is the identity of the respective clubs. It creates a feeling of belonging and helps to set them apart from other clubs and groups. In this way, clubs pass on their own identity to their supporters. It is the club identity as an individualizing feature that gives the football club its public profile.

To guarantee its individuality, the club has to be distinct from its rivals in the symbolism of its club identity. Club supporters need this symbolism when it comes to focusing their emotions and their identification on the club. The most strongly marked and robust identity feature of a football club is its role as cultural representative of a community.[1] But when clubs are perceived as no more than economic units the community does not feel warmly towards them. If a club is purely identified as a business enterprise, it is held in low regard among football fans and is treated as an artificial, commercial product. A club of this nature cannot serve as an identity-creating object. The clubs that incorporate identity and community are the ones which have, in many cases, a historical affinity with a region, milieu or city and which acknowledge and cultivate their identity as a cultural good.

An example of a club that defines itself through a social milieu is FC St. Pauli, based in Hamburg, which, remarkably, is one of Germany's 15 biggest sports clubs in terms of membership. The club is situated in a trendy district with a cosmopolitan air. The fan scene is openly political and strongly 'left wing'. Their piratical skull and crossbones symbol is a further expression of the club supporters' social nonconformity. Such is the authenticity of the club and its supporters that according to a study the club has around 11 million followers in Germany and has made a name for itself in other countries too. Another club that defines itself through its social milieu is Gelsenkirchen-based Schalke 04. Although the club has now developed into a commercially successful enterprise, its origins lie unmistakably within the ambit of the mining community. This is demonstrated, among other things, by the fact that even today the supporters describe themselves as *Knappen*.[2]

Alongside the social milieu a club's region of origin can also form part of its identity. Popular football clubs, which act as symbols of a region, have strong cultural appeal. The more effective the club's role as a symbol, the more the regional community is strengthened through it. The supporter feels part of a regional community that has a football club as a trademark of the region. The club represents its native region and that of its supporters, who are members and thus part of the club.[3] The principle that a football club is not only a sporting institution but at the same time a symbol of its region of origin may be applied to a large number of clubs in the world. But, whereas at the lower level, the clubs are undoubtedly representative of their region or locality, this is less true of the higher leagues. Here, the media and commercial interests exercise a more powerful influence – except where clubs have made a deliberate effort to work at their club philosophy and cultivate their public image.

In what follows, we propose to show, with reference to the example of VfB Stuttgart, exactly how football clubs acquire (or are given) a regional and cultural identity, and how they can thereby become emblematic of a region. In the same way, we shall demonstrate that conflict in regional politics adds to the importance of a football club as a symbol of regional identity. Sporting successes give an indication of the importance a club can have as a regional representative. We shall also take a brief look at the Spanish clubs FC Barcelona and Athletic Bilbao. All three clubs declare their allegiance to their home region and benefit from this in both sporting and economic respects. And even if these examples show that VfB Stuttgart, FC Barcelona and Athletic Bilbao are different in their traditions and history, there is a connecting element through which their roles were formed as carriers of a regional identity. The regional patriotic identities of these clubs have their origins in their territorial political conditions. This text will show that in all three examples a large part of the population was not satisfied with the geographic organization of their native regions.

Acquiring and communicating regional identities

VfB Stuttgart's coat of arms already points to the regional character of the club. The three black antlers on a gold field, which is the coat of arms of the House of Württemberg and is also a component of the coat of arms of VfB Stuttgart, are an indication of the club's traditional links with the region of Württemberg. To demonstrate its authentic regional identity, however, a club must meet further conditions. A regional pool of players, a board of directors with a public commitment to the home region of the club, politicians and officials who confer regional identity on the club and a body of supporters who establish a regional identity within the club – these are all factors that strengthen the club's regional identity.

A squad comprised of regional players is essential if a football club wishes to be seen by its supporters as representing a region. Conversely, where the majority of the players do not come from the region, the supporters of the club will feel alienated since in their view the players are no longer able to represent the region.[4] An important criterion for the identification of supporters with their football club is therefore to have common roots in the local town, city or region. As a consequence, it is necessary for the club management to build upon the willingness of its supporters (who are club members in many cases) to identify with the club due to its local ties. The integration of players from the club's home city or region into the football team authenticates its local or regional identity.[5] The squad of a club that is characterized by a strong regional identity, therefore, normally consists mainly of players who are known to have a connection with the region. In this way, not only the public but also the players themselves perceive the club to be a part of their home region. This has the effect of giving credibility to the city and regional identity.

The club leadership of VfB Stuttgart has explicitly emphasized that the club should assume the role of being a representative of the region of Württemberg. Eberhard Haaga, the match committee chairman of VfB Stuttgart, claimed that an important condition for fulfilling this role is that the main team is made up of Württemberg players. He attributed the VfB Stuttgart's success at the 1950 and 1952 championships to particular criteria which a team needed to fulfil. One criterion is 'Not too many foreign influences. The VfB-Team should represent the Swabian native region in the narrower sense'. This club leaders' understanding is that there is a direct connection between the playing success of team, the origins of the players and the regional identity of the club.[6]

In the 2013/2014 season, VfB Stuttgart has had a good half dozen players in the squad who have emerged from its own youth programme, and others who have come to be local crowd favourites, thanks to their long service to the club. This season the club has used a player, Timo Werner, who was born in Bad Cannstatt, the Stuttgart district which is home to the club itself. When only six years old, he was already playing in the club's youth team. He was the youngest player in the history of the Bundesliga to score two goals in one game and is accordingly something of a poster boy for the regional orientation of the club. A club that trains many players itself and then signs them up as professionals also gains prestige among everyone with an interest in football, provided always that the team enjoys success on the field. Although Timo Werner has not played as long for the club's professional team as many other players, and even though he has not shot as many goals for the team as his forward colleagues, it is his name that most VfB fans have had printed on their football shirts. Werner assumes that this is because he was born in Stuttgart and because he has played with VfB since his early youth.[7]

A further means of highlighting the regional affiliation of the club is for the club management to make public statements affirming their commitment to the local region.[8] Thus, again and again in the media we hear club officials stressing the role of the club as representing the region and occasionally the players also remind us that they have come through from the club's youth section. These public declarations can enhance the reputation of the club in the eyes of the fans.

Public figures representing local and state politics always make an effort to associate themselves with a club when it has achieved success. Success for a club, which arouses emotions of regional patriotism in the local population, is at the same time taken by political office-holders to be success for the region itself. It is therefore always important to politicians for a club to achieve success and to attract the attention of the public. Politicians then have the opportunity to express their closeness to the successful football club, the popular championship winners representing the city or region.

In order to highlight the connection between themselves and the successful club and to profit from its high media profile, they have to emphasize what it is that the politicians and the club have in common, which in the case of VfB Stuttgart is the Württemberg identity. To date, Stuttgart mayors have always hoped to increase their popularity by expressing their common identity with the club. Thus, politicians from city and state have used the club's influence, with its high media impact and its power to promote community and create identity, by making an appearance at major public events, such as victory celebrations or club matches. Thanks to the football club's regional links, political office-holders hoped that they would be associated with the club in the public mind and that this would be to their advantage. Through their professions of solidarity, politicians aimed to strengthen the club's regional identity while stressing their own closeness to the club in order to promote themselves alongside the club as symbols of regional identity. By associating themselves with VfB Stuttgart and publicly emphasizing their common regional identity, local and regional politicians have succeeded in reinforcing the significance of the club as an emblem of the region.

Once a club has achieved the status of representative of the region, the supporters give greater outward expression to this role. The huge crowds flocking to the stadium, the banners, the slogans, the singing and chanting of the supporters, the various noise-making instruments and the fireworks – all these are components of sporting events which should be seen against the background of affiliation and demarcation and which derive their sustenance, in part at least, from regional and cultural identification.[9] The emotional attachment of the club supporters to their home region is projected in an extrovert fashion on to the relevant football club as its representative. Since a football club functions as the representative of a region, its sporting successes mean heightened prestige for the club's supporters. The results of the matches – however achieved – are therefore of critical importance. The successes of the club are consequently relevant to the status of the region, as they result in an increase in the esteem in which it is held.[10]

In order to feel themselves represented through sport, the supporters recognized VfB Stuttgart as a representative of the region, as the club could only represent the cultural community in sporting competition with other regions if it played a representative role on behalf of Württemberg. As the most successful club in the region, VfB Stuttgart is best suited to enter into sporting competition with other regions as the representative of Württemberg. By recognizing the club as the representative of Württemberg, the supporters infuse the club with regional symbolic force, which the club then gives back to its supporters. Thus, we see a reciprocal relationship between club and supporters in the creation of identity. The idea that the club's games offer the supporters the opportunity to affirm their own regional and cultural identity through their support for VfB Stuttgart is borne out by the fact that the supporters rated wins by their own team against teams from other regions as a sign of regional superiority.

With the rise of 'ultra' groups, the fanatical behaviour of supporters has taken a new form, for which, on account of the multifaceted nature of the members' intentions and behaviour, the term 'club fanaticism' is no longer adequate. The 'ultra' groups relate this to their regional identity. These groups support their club vocally and visually during the games. As most of them are club members, they see themselves as an integral part of the club and regard themselves as defenders of tradition in football and not as mere consumers of the sport of football. With slogans that speak of friendship, loyalty, honesty and the like, they oppose club principles like profit maximization and efficiency and see themselves as opposed to the commodification of the football clubs.[11] These groups often complain about the commercial orientation of the sport of football and criticize the way in which the clubs' traditions are losing ground to the demands of marketing.

There are two contrasting views of the club. One sees the club as an ultramodern economic business, which is obliged to assert itself on the market and the other regards it as governed by sacrosanct traditions. The ultras favour the latter view.[12] The local and regional patriotic aspect is of particular significance for the 'ultra' groups. Their local and regional focus is implicit in their names, which, in the case of VfB Stuttgart, include 'Schwabensturm 02' and 'Commando Cannstatt'. The moderate supporters, members of the fan clubs, also show their allegiance through the names they choose, for example, 'Die WildenSchwaben', 'SiebenSchwaben' or 'Neckarsturm – Württemberg'. These names imply the desire for the club to have a role as representative of the region, so as to ensure that their own regional identity is given prominence.

The desire for dominance as a catalyst for the regional identity of football clubs

The competition for dominance between two different regions has moved to the football pitch. The club supporters project their regional identity on to their football club – it has become the symbol of a region. Clubs from the same region fight it out between them to decide which of them will exercise sovereignty within that region. Local derbies therefore hold a particular attraction for spectators. Football matches are thus settings for symbolic clashes that express regional rivalries. Such animosities in the stadium between different clubs and supporters are, however, also related to contentious issues in society.[13]

With regard to VfB Stuttgart, the founding of the federal state of Baden-Württemberg is of particular relevance. There was sporting rivalry between the football clubs of the states of Baden and Württemberg, which arose from the historical, cultural and religious differences between the two regions. The states of Württemberg-Baden, Württemberg-Hohenzollern and Baden (known as South Baden until the end of 1946), which were created after the Second World War, were considering a reorganization. The states were to be united to form a south-western state, although Catholic-dominated (South) Baden resisted this proposal on account of their antipathy towards Protestant Württemberg, with its supposedly restless work ethic and a fear of falling under its control. In the referendum (South) Baden voted against the creation of the south-western federal state, but the overall result of the referendum was in favour.

The dispute over the creation of the south-western state of Baden-Württemberg was an expression of antipathies that arose from a clash of political cultures and differing traditions and mentalities. The people of Württemberg, or 'Swabians', as they are often called, had developed an aversion to the people from Baden who kept coming to the surface.[14] This antipathy was very visible at the regional derby games between VfB Stuttgart and Karlsruher SC, which is a football club from Baden.

Accordingly, at every match between the two teams the political factor came into play. As a high proportion of the population of Baden had voted against the union of the states of Württemberg-Baden, Württemberg-Hohenzollern and Baden in the 1952 referendum, they were naturally unhappy at the outcome. The resentment caused by this issue in regional politics and the rivalry for leadership in the sporting arena in Baden-Württemberg was apparent in the behaviour of the crowd at the matches between VfB Stuttgart and Karlsruher SC (KSC).

Such football matches offer the opportunity to articulate latent aggression in the form of verbal abuse in a way that is not possible when conforming to social norms. Aggression and abuse reveal structures of thought that provide an insight into social attitudes.[15] It is evident that the mutual disaffection between these clubs is related to the respective native regions, as can be seen in this football chant of the VfB-Ultras: 'Oh VfB Stuttgart/Oh VfB Stuttgart/You are our life/For our colours/we will give everything/We hate Baden/and the KSC/because we are the Reds/from VfB'.[16]

In the final season of the *OberligaSüd*, five clubs from Baden-Württemberg were represented. In 1963 the Bundesliga was created. For VfB Stuttgart, this meant they were no longer restricted to playing against clubs from Hesse, Bavaria, Baden and Württemberg, as was the case in the *OberligaSüd*, but would now come up against opponents from the remainder of the Federal Republic as well. Among the 16 teams in the newly created Bundesliga were five teams from the *OberligaSüd*. Apart from VfB Stuttgart, however, Karlsruher SC was the only other team based in Baden-Württemberg. There was no other Württemberg team to compete with it in the Bundesliga, so VfB Stuttgart was the sole representative of Württemberg in the nationwide competition for the highest sporting honour in football. The same thing was true of Karlsruher SC and the Baden region. The matches between the Württemberg club (VfB Stuttgart) and the Baden club (Karlsruher SC) were therefore particularly highly charged, as both clubs carried the weight of their regional identity on their shoulders. For these two founding members of the Bundesliga, who were also the sole representatives of the federal state of Baden-Württemberg, their meetings were the only chance to engage in the regional conflict for dominance in the state at the highest level of the game. Furthermore, the political element previously mentioned occasioned additional rivalry.

Two matches stand out as typical examples of the desire for regional dominance as a catalyst for the regional identity of the two football clubs. On the 15th match day of the 1967/1968 season, VfB Stuttgart beat Karlsruher SC in an away match by four goals to one. By half-time, some of the spectators were already burning KSC banners on the terraces.[17] This was an evidence of the importance of these games, which was felt by supporters to be representative of regional conflicts.

The second example is the meeting of the two clubs at the Baden-Württemberg local derby on 21 September 2008. Shortly before kick-off, VfB Stuttgart's 'ultra' groups staged a tifo display that illustrated the supporters' regional patriotism. It was a clear declaration of commitment to Württemberg and expressed the rivalry between Baden and Württemberg. A 13-metre high image of a knight with three antlers on a gold field on his shield (the coat of arms of Württemberg) was displayed in the Stuttgart stadium, in the home fans' section of the terraces. Underneath, in Gothic script, was the motto of King William I of Württemberg: 'Furchtlos und treu' [Fearless and Loyal]. The old state flag of Württemberg appeared on the display panel. To the left and right of the knight, at the edge of the home supporters' section of the terraces, a lion and a stag were being held aloft – symbols of Württemberg.

The stadium was awash with black and red banners, the colours of the Kingdom of Württemberg. Banners bearing slogans in the Swabian dialect were raised up.

This sporting encounter made it plain that the supporters of VfB Stuttgart were trying to distance themselves as far as possible from their Baden rivals in the Bundesliga, Karlsruher SC and their supporters, by parading the Württemberg symbols to declare their commitment to their own region. It was also clear from the evidence of this local derby that the bond that so many supporters had with VfB Stuttgart was far more than simply a sense of belonging to their own club. Rather, in this particular encounter, it was about regional patriotism, represented by the team on the field of play. Furthermore, it was about the deeply ingrained rivalry between the two regions that make up Baden-Württemberg and about sporting supremacy in that state.

Sporting successes as indicators of regional identity

Championships won and victories in the cup are always successes for the region. This is demonstrated not only by the celebrations of the supporters but also by the presence of the political factor. In 1950, VfB Stuttgart won the German football championship for the first time, beating Kickers Offenbach in the final. The appeal of VfB Stuttgart as an object of identification for Württemberg was proved beyond doubt when 300,000 people turned out to greet the victorious team on their return, lining the streets to applaud the players and their manager. On 26 June, the champions returned to Stuttgart from Berlin, where the final had been played and celebrated with a victory parade through the city. Not only footballers, club supporters and followers of VfB Stuttgart, but also people who were not normally interested in football or even disliked it came out to welcome the club on their return.[18]

The winning of the German championship was undoubtedly a sporting success that brought joy to many. The extent of the celebrations was an expression of the importance for the city and the region of success in sporting contests, for winning the championship meant that the cultural area of Württemberg had achieved sporting supremacy in the Federal Republic. Consequently, the win not only filled VfB Stuttgart with pride, but also activated local and regional patriotic sentiments among the people of the city and the region who were normally indifferent to football or would even have said that they hated it. This was only possible because the club occupied an overriding role as a representative of the region – a role which, at the moment of winning the championship, was unconnected with sport.

Reporting on the final game of the German Championship in 1952, the *Stuttgarter Zeitung* wrote that the fans of VfB Stuttgart had travelled from the entire region of Württemberg in order to see the VfB play. One correspondent of this newspaper who was in the Black Forest at the time (which is also part of Baden-Württemberg) reported that even in the smallest villages the people crowded around speakers set up in windows in order to follow the game.[19] After the championship victory, the team returned home to Stuttgart on the train. Fans were cheering for them at train stations along the way. The team made a stopover in Asperg, where they were greeted with music and ladies of honour.[20] The fact that the team took this trip home in a transparent passenger compartment covered with glass (the 'train of glass') so that it could be cheered on at train stations between Ludwigshafen and Asperg (in the middle of Baden-Württemberg), shows how far-reaching the fan-base of VfB

Stuttgart is. This fan-base is not only limited to the city limits or the city's outskirts, but stretches across large parts of Württemberg.

In the football club magazine *Sports*, the Württemberg regional sports association called the championship victory of the VfB Stuttgart a 'day of fame' which would be commemorated in the 'annals of Württemberg football.'[21] Similar events unfolded in the club's later championship victories in the years 1984 and 1992. Judging by the celebrations accompanying their victory in the German championship in 2007, it is true to say that VfB Stuttgart continues to be regarded as an identity-creating factor for the region of Württemberg despite the increasing commercialization of the sport. The state flag was hoisted alongside the club flag in front of the *Neues Schloss* in Stuttgart, showing the importance of the club's success for the state of Baden-Württemberg. Baden-Württemberg's Premier Günther Oettinger stated that the German championship victory not only benefitted the club, but also the city and the entire state. At a public speech, the former Premier of Baden-Württemberg Lothar Späth, as well as the former politician RezzoSchlauch attributed this championship victory to Swabianvirtues.[22] Additionally, Premier Günther Oettinger underlined the importance of the club for the entire region when he expressed his congratulations and stated that thanks to the club Baden-Württemberg 'was now the number one state in sport'.[23] Some 250,000 people celebrated the winning of the championship in Stuttgart.

Further examples of regional representation roles

FC Barcelona is another football club that is fiercely proud of its regional identity. Its role as a symbol of Catalonia is political in character, as the club is not only an object of identification but at the same time also the voice of a separatist tradition. Hans Gamper, the founder of FC Barcelona, was himself a supporter of Catalanism, which is a cultural and political movement that desires independence from the Kingdom of Spain for Catalonia and attempts to bring this about. Especially in the years of Franco's dictatorship between 1930 and 1975, the club was seen as a symbol of Catalonian cultural identity and of Catalanism, as Franco suppressedany Catalan tendency in society. The intense rivalry between FC Barcelona and the capital city club Real Madrid, which favours the central state, is symbolic of the struggle between separatists and advocates of the central state.

An example of how the political conflict has found its way into the football stadiums is the encounter between the two teams on 2 October 2012. Precisely 17 min and 14 s into the game, the Barcelona supporters shouted out: 'Independencia! Independencia!' This action by the supporters harks back to the defeat of the Catalan troops by the army of the King of Spain in 1714. The defeat meant the end of Catalan autonomy and the integration of Catalonia into the Spanish Kingdom.

As in cases of VfB Stuttgart and FC Barcelona, the regional identity of the club Athletic Bilbao is catalyzed by the dissatisfaction among the population concerning their geopolitical situation. In the end, also this population is not satisfied that it is a part of Spain.And as already stated, regional identity is also engendered by the self-image of the club officials. When a team and the directors of the club are almost entirely recruited from the region, it is quite natural for the club to regard itself as an ambassador for this region. This is true not only of VfB Stuttgart and FC Barcelona, but also, to a particular degree, of Athletic Club Bilbao. Because of the value placed on regional patriotism, the team representing this Basque club consists chiefly of Basques. The principle by which the club operates is to integrate into the team mainly players who come from Basque provinces or who were trained in the youth section of one of these provincial clubs. Bilbao's players are extremely loyal to the club – many of them play for the club throughout their footballing career. Similarly, almost all the club's supporters are from the Basque country. Yet, despite this, somewhat restrictive club philosophy with regard to the regional focus of the club, Bilbao has never yet been relegated from the top Spanish division. The club has 24 cup victories and eight championships to its name.

Conclusion

More than 50 years after the founding of the Bundesliga, VfB Stuttgart is a business enterprise run on modern lines. The perception of the club as a representative of the region, however, has remained constant. Today VfB Stuttgart's management, under their president Bernd Wahler, continues to regard the club as a focus of identity for Württemberg and as a regional representative with a real commitment to the region. Many members of both management and squad have a long-standing connection with the club. The regional orientation of the club also finds expression in the promotion of its own youth section, with the aim of bringing on some promising youngsters to later become part of VfB Stuttgart's senior team. To this end, for example, in the 2013/2014 season, experienced players from the club's A youth team were allowed to train alongside the professional team and even to travel with them to their training camp in the close season.

In the final analysis, it is its local and regional identity that gives a club its unique selling point – one that will attract supporters and give them the opportunity to identify with the club. Regional identity gives a football club a deeper significance. Something that all the three clubs under consideration have in common is that they preserve their traditions. And thanks to the role that they take on they have a charismatic attraction for their supporters. The clubs derive lasting profit from their role as representatives of their home region, something which both the clubs themselves and their supporters communicate to the wider world. One benefit is the greater media interest and the sales opportunities provided by merchandising. Even if Bundesliga football is totally commercialized these days, clubs still need to maintain their regional representative role, because the club recruits its supporters chiefly through its regional character. And it is its regional character that gives it a great deal of its commercial value. To ensure a sustainable future, the club must cultivate its regional identity and publicly declare a commitment to it, as this represents a large part of its marketing potential.

A further benefit is a loyal body of supporters, whose passion for the club is not dependent on sporting success. After all, through its symbolic significance for the region, the club is also a symbolic representative of the identity of its regional supporters. The clubs are also responsible for much outstanding youth work. On average, over the years, all three clubs have had more of their own former youth players in the squad than the majority of their competitors in La Liga. For example, in the year 2009/2010, Barcelona won the Spanish championship with 10 players from their youth section. Finally, the clubs have a superb communications basis from which to address their supporters, who accept club, team and management as their own representatives.

For the football clubs it therefore makes sense, through things like club museums and targeted publicity work, to promote their own regional identity and to make it clear that as long as the club has been in existence this has always been a fundamental, defining component of the life of the club and has remained so despite necessary commercialization. It is, however, vital that more than mere lip service is paid to the need for communication and that the regional identity of the club truly is an integral part of the club's philosophy. In conclusion, it is important to stress that national sides also benefit from clubs that are committed to their own regional identity, not least because these clubs select many of their team members from players that they themselves have trained. The youth area is correspondingly strong and as a result there is a correspondingly large pool from which players for the national team can be recruited.

Disclosure statement

No potential conflict of interest was reported by the author.

Notes

1. Väth, *Profifußball: Zur Soziologie der Bundesliga*, 108.
2. *Knappe* is the term for someone who has successfully completed his apprenticeship as a miner.
3. Schütz, *Ausländische Spieler in der Fußball-Bundesliga: Die Auswirkungen des Bosman-Urteils auf die Identifikation mit den Vereinen*, 77.
4. Ibid., 82.
5. Väth, *Profifußball: Zur Soziologie der Bundesliga*, 108.
6. Jordan and Becker, *VfB Stuttgart 1893 e.V. Tradition, Leistung, Erfolg*, 83.
7. Vielberg and Nagler, 'Werner hängt die Alten ab!', *Bild*, August 22, 2015.
8. Väth, *Profifußball: Zur Soziologie der Bundesliga*, 168.
9. Lindner, 'Die Sportbegeisterung', in *Volkskultur in der Moderne: Probleme und Perspektiven empirischer Kulturforschung*, ed. Jeggle, Korff, Scharfe, and Wameken.
10. Väth, *Profifußball: Zur Soziologie der Bundesliga*, 168.
11. Sommerey, *Die Jugendkultur der Ultras: Zur Entstehung einer neuen Generation von Fußball fans*, 62.
12. Ibid., 75.
13. Schwenzer, 'Fußball als kulturelles Ereignis'.
14. Wehling, *Die deutschen Länder: Geschichte, Politik, Wirtschaft*, 20.
15. Schwenzer, 'Fußball als kulturelles Ereignis'.
16. Reustle, 'Oh VfB Stuttgart', *Stuttgart Supporter*, October 7, 2014.
17. 'In Karlsruhe brennen wieder Fahnen', *Schwäbisches Tagblatt*, November 27, 1967.
18. 'Nachklänge zum triumphalen VfB-Empfang: Elf Spieler in 24 wandelnden Blumengärten', *Sportmagazin* 27 (1950): 14.
19. 'Württembergisch-badische Invasion in die Pfalz', *Stuttgarter Zeitung*, June 23, 1952, Sports section, Main edition.
20. Krämer, 'Zum zweiten Mal tut sich der Himmel auf', in *100 Jahre VfB Stuttgart 1893 e.V.*, ed. Blickensdörfer.
21. 'Zwei deutsche Fußballmeister für Württemberg', *Der Sport: Organ des Württembergischen Landessportbundes* 26 (1952): 1.
22. 'Deutscher Meister VfB: die Region gratuliert von ganzem Herzen', *Stuttgarter Zeitung*, May 21, 2007, Sports section, Main edition.
23. 'Als Erster hüpft Timo Hildebrand auf die Bühne', *Stuttgarter Zeitung*, May 21, 2007, Sports section, Main edition.

References

'AlsErsterhüpftTimo Hildebrand auf die Bühne.' [Timo Hildebrand was the first to hop on to the stage.]. *Stuttgarter Zeitung*, May 21, 2007, Sports section, Main edition.

'Deutscher Meister VfB: die Region gratuliert von ganzem Herzen.' [German champion VfB: the region congratulates dearly.] *Stuttgarter Zeitung*, May 21, 2007, Sports section, Main edition.

'In Karlsruhe brennen wieder Fahnen.' [In Karlsruhe the banners are on fire.] *Schwäbisches Tagblatt*, November 27, 1967, Sports section, Tübingen edition.

Jordan, Harald, and Frank Becker. *VfB Stuttgart 1893 e.V. Tradition, Leistung, Erfolg* [VfB Stuttgart 1893 e.V. tradition, performance, success]. Stuttgart: Stuttgart VfB Sport-Shop, 1983.

Krämer, Gerd. 'Zum zweiten Mal tut sich der Himmel auf.' [The sky is clearing for the second time.] In *100 Jahre VfB Stuttgart 1893 e.V.* [100 years VfB Stuttgart 1893 e.V.], ed. Hans Blickensdörfer, 115–9. Stuttgart: VfB Stuttgart 1893 e.V., 1992.

Lindner, Rolf. 'Die Sportbegeisterung.' [Passion for sport.] In *Volkskultur in der Moderne: Probleme und Perspektiven empirischer Kulturforschung* [Popular culture in the modern era: problems and perspectives of empirical cultural research], eds. Utz Jeggle, Gottfried Korff, Martin Scharfe, and Bernd Jürgen Warneken, 249–59. Reinbek bei Hamburg: Rowohlt-Taschenbuch Verlag, 1986.

'Nachklänge zum triumphalen VfB-Empfang: Elf Spieler in 24 wandelnden Blumengärten.' [Reflections on the triumphal reception: eleven players in 24 walking flower gardens.] *Sportmagazin* 27 (1950): 14.

Schütz, Volker. *Ausländische Spieler in der Fußball-Bundesliga: Die Auswirkungen des Bosman-Urteils auf die Identifikation mit den Vereinen* [Foreign players in the Bundesliga: the effects of the Bosman ruling on identification with clubs]. Saarbrücken: VDM Verlag Dr. Müller, 2007.

Schwenzer, Victoria. 'Fußball als kulturelles Ereignis: Eine ethnologische Untersuchung am Beispiel des 1.FC Union Berlin.' [Football as a cultural event: an ethnological investigation with particular reference to 1.FC Union Berlin.] In *Fußballwelten: Zum Verhältnis von Sport, Politik, Ökonomie und Gesellschaft* [Football worlds: the relationship between sport, politics, economy and society], ed. Zentrum für Europa- und Nordamerika-Studien, 87–115. Opladen: Leske + Budrich Verlag, 2002.

Sommerey, Marcus. *Die Jugendkultur der Ultras: Zur Entstehung einer neuen Generation von Fußballfans* [The ultras' youth culture: the rise of a new generation of football fans]. Stuttgart: ibidem-Verlag, 2010.

Stuttgart Supporter. 'Oh VfB Stuttgart'. Markus Reustle. http://www.stuttgartsupporter.de/index.php?article_id=46.

Väth, Heinrich. *Profifußball: Zur Soziologie der Bundesliga* [Professional football: the sociology of the Bundesliga]. Frankfurt am Main: Campus Verlag GmbH, 1994.

Vielberg, U., and J. Nagler. 'Werner hängt die Alten ab!' [Werner outpaces the old.] *Bild*. http://www.bild.de/sport/fussball/timo-werner/haengt-die-alten-ab-37345970.bild.html.

Wehling, Hans-Georg. *Die deutschen Länder: Geschichte, Politik, Wirtschaft* [The German Länder: history, politics, economy]. Wiesbaden: VS Verlag für Sozialwissenschaften, 2004.

'Württembergisch-badische Invasion in die Pfalz.' [Württembergian-baden invasion to Palatinate.] *Stuttgarter Zeitung*, June 23, 1952, Sports section, Main edition.

'Zwei deutsche Fußballmeister für Württemberg.' [Two German champions for Württemberg.] *Der Sport: Organ des Württembergischen Landessportbundes* no. 26 (1952): 1.

Football and community empowerment: how FC Sankt Pauli fans organize to influence

Mick Totten

In an era when many traditional football fans feel increasingly alienated from corporate ownership and commercial imperatives, sites of resistance are emerging whereby football fans seek to empower themselves and increase their influence. Few fans rival those of FC Sankt Pauli for autonomous organization which has empowered them to create an authentic vibrant democratic culture which holds great influence over their club. But this empowerment has also led them to extend their influence beyond their own club and beyond football itself. This article based on years of research with Sankt Pauli fan activists reveals how the fans are cohesively organized, autonomously, bottom-up and non-hierarchically, how that gives rise to prolific community action, and how that in turn empowers the community in a transformational and sustainable way.

Introduction

The intensifying hyper-commercialization of football and corporate models of ownership are leading many football clubs to increasing commodify the football spectacle. This mission creep has alienated many traditional supporters as the sense of community previously experienced by fans is increasingly being replaced by a passive consumer experience. And community outreach work by clubs is often stealthily focused on product placement, good public relations and market development rather than community empowerment.[1] Such commercial imperatives and top-down corporate governance mean commercial and statutory agencies can seldom be trusted to empower football fans or be relied upon to deliver genuine community empowerment.

But community empowerment is not solely the domain of professional interventions as 'there are active citizens who use community development techniques on a voluntary basis'.[2] Many fans are expressing dissent towards their club ownership, sometimes organizing protests in an effort to gain more influence, and some are looking at new ways to organize themselves self-determinedly at arm's-length from the clubs. Autonomous fan organization can cultivate empowerment informally and engender it implicitly through community consultation and involvement in action for change.[3] And democratic processes can embed autonomous community control by enabling fans to participate in decision-making and gain greater long-term control over their circumstances.[4] It is the manifestation of fan organization which is entirely self-directed that is the focus of this paper. And FC Sankt Pauli fans have a prodigious reputation in this regard. Whilst previous articles published on Sankt Pauli have buoyed this reputation and offered interesting insights (Griggs on reportage, Merkel on fan struggles, McDougall on relationships with Celtic, and Daniel and Kassimeris on political culture), they have also tended to be composed from relatively remote observation without empirical fan perspective.[5] This paper offers findings from fieldwork with the fans themselves, and allows their voices and views to be heard loud and clear.

FC Sankt Pauli are a professional club from Hamburg, Germany, whose image as a left-wing, punk, fan-led club has attracted a significant global following.[6] For many, their fans offer a beacon of hope as leading lights exemplifying a never surrender attitude to the inducements of the neo-liberal commodification of football.[7] They have a colourful and radical history campaigning for fan power amidst a plethora of other left-wing causes.[8] But even at FC Sankt Pauli, autonomous fan organization needs to be distinguished from the relationship to the football club, which is quite ambiguous and often antagonistic. Despite strong fan representation at the football club their shared history is littered with conflict and acrimony. Many fans perceive the club as a 'parasite which feeds on the host of its iconic fans for commercial gains'.[9] The influence of the fans over the club and its commercializing tendencies has been fought hard for and that struggle continues.

Another important distinction has to be made with autonomous fan organization in relation to the Fanladen (fan social project) which is in part funded by the football authorities as well as other statutory organizations. The Fanladen is a significant social and cultural hub which engages fans in social and community projects and, unlike the club, is highly regarded as a significant contributor to fan culture. Project workers are drawn from the fan scene and so there is not the same distinction in identity compared to the club. But although the fans' relationship with the Fanladen is fascinating and worthy of further study elsewhere, it is not the object of this paper to explore that in any detail. This paper is firmly focused on fan organization that is entirely autonomous and the contribution of that to fan and community empowerment.

This paper considers the potential of football for community empowerment and how that has occurred at Sankt Pauli. It examines the autonomous Sankt Pauli fan network and its different constituents. It shows how these fans (perceived by some as seemingly anarchic) are actually highly organized. It explores how fan power is fostered and how democratic community leadership has been utilized to resist and fight football's commercial juggernaut. It analyses how football is used as a mechanism to develop and empower communities, bottom up. It will uncover how involvement in local community action is promoted and how this has extended outwards to the creation of international support networks. It will reveal how fan culture has cultivated the empowerment of individuals, the fan body itself, and broader communities too. It will shine a light behind the scenes on these iconic fans and illuminate how they actively manage to be who they are and how they keep on doing what they do. It tells a story of how fans are empowered through football.

Football and community empowerment

Sport has ambiguous credentials when it comes to community empowerment and is often perceived as quite a conservative rather than transformative phenomenon. It has been long observed that sport represents a dichotomy whereby it can act simultaneously as a tool for community development and also as an opiate which nullifies political consciousness.[10] And Dart observes a polarization amongst leftists between those who reject sport as being a cynical form of manipulation or distraction and those who seek to reclaim it believing it ripe with possibilities to reawaken consciousness and empower.[11] Football is particularly conspicuous for its rapacious commercialism and Kennedy describes how fans are co-opted and commodified as part of the spectacle.[12] But he also acknowledges that football only exerts relative commercial power and that there is also a capacity for resistance not least around the strong sense of community it can foster. Blackshaw and Long, and Coalter too, propose that sport can often be the starting point for the development of social capital that can result in the formation of networks that challenge oppressions.[13] And Hylton and Totten believe that community sport can aspire to citizen power when exercised bottom up in genuine partnerships with communities in control.[14]

In this sense, football inhabits a hegemonic context which includes incomplete attempts by dominant cultural groups to control opposition as well as resistance by that opposition.[15] Dominant institutions like football authorities and clubs attempt to exercise control and fans have the potential to offer resistance. But clubs also have the power to incorporate and disarm potentially radical opposition from fans. Popular cultural expressions, alternative to dominant hegemonies, can be incorporated through market forces like commercialization. This hegemonic process reflects an ongoing struggle; top-down control by football institutions and bottom-up resistance by many fans. These hegemonic dynamics are perpetual, all-encompassing, never completed and continually assembled and re-assembled, reproduced and secured (and setback!).[16] And Sankt Pauli fans have a long history of offering resistance in this hegemonic struggle with the club and football authorities.[17]

Many fans who feel alienated by corporate ownership and the passive consumer spectacle seek a more authentic and democratic grassroots culture. Disenchantment may signal the beginning of wakefulness[18] as some discontented fans believe silence is no longer an option, and are taking action to organize themselves. Increasingly fans are expressing dissent towards commercial orthodoxy, participating in protests, and pursuing more fan-centred ownership models. And just as Giroux contends that if society cannot question itself or imagine alternatives it becomes complicit with the existing order,[19] so resistance is as much a part of hegemony as control. As some fans fight back, Kaufman and Wolff observe that sport activism, when driven by social consciousness, has a potential for liberation and transformation.[20] Sankt Pauli fans are recognized for their political credentials, fostering a coalition of leftist and libertarian thought, and expressing support for a plethora of libertarian causes through a combination of campaigning, direct action and street protest.[21] This prolific sport activism and praxis (putting radical ideas into action) has given birth to community organization, networks of resistance, community action and empowerment.[22]

Empowerment is a process which can transform the relationship between the powerful and powerless and Baltiwala believes that empowerment begins when people recognize their oppressions and act to change the power relationship.[23] So, for football fans the very act of resistance can be empowering in its own right. Empowerment is an ongoing struggle which involves some shift in power from dominant groups to communities enabling them to influence decisions and services that affect them.[24] But whilst some imagine that empowerment can transcend social divisions and be mutually beneficial to all,[25] Schuftan counters that; 'empowerment of some, most of the time, entails the disempowerment of others – usually the current holders of power … it expands the political space'.[26] So, the empowerment of football fans and their communities is likely to necessitate the concession or seizure of power from established football institutions in order to establish influence.

Empowerment can be significantly facilitated though a process of community development which 'challenges passive consumer culture ... (and) necessitates social transformation and anti-discriminatory action against broader social inequality'.[27] Such clarity of purpose has not always been effective using sport which has often groped fuzzily towards community empowerment in a mechanistic way, critically unchallenging, lacking an engagement on socio-political level; so accommodating, and even perpetuating, sloppy practice and tokenism.[28] But effective community development can be driven by football fans allied to a heightened sense of critical consciousness and praxis; 'the action and reflection of women and men upon their world in order to transform it'.[29]

Community empowerment can act against injustice, enhance democracy, develop cooperative local economies and healthy communities. However, Ledwith declares 'this is not enough', that there is a difference between good work, (which may improve the quality of life in communities) and transformative work (that aims to tackle the unequal power relations that result in social inequality).[30] She bemoans 'action-less thought' founded on rhetoric not reality, and 'thoughtless action' without reflection; doing, at the expense of thinking, lacking critical analysis and preoccupied with skills rather than theory. 'Thoughtful action' necessitates critical consciousness based on social and environmental justice to challenge 'accepted' practice and dominant power relations, changing power structures that affect lives.[31] It is a synthesis of theory and practice. So the empowerment of football fans is more likely to be transformative if it is allied to this sense of critical consciousness and driven bottom up by the fans themselves.

Critical consciousness can be built through informal critical education which questions conventions and builds resistance to dominant hegemony through grassroots activism. And transformative potential is contingent on movements for change to empower communities to generate resistance and challenge dominant structures of power. For football fans this might involve vibrant local activism but linked, beyond purely local issues, to seek strategic networks and alliances between different fan groups. And Sankt Pauli fans have been proactive in establishing politicized national and international networks in pursuit of fan power.[32] This research sought to illuminate how autonomous community organization empowered fans to develop critical consciousness and act to further extend their influence.

Research and participants

The findings considered in this article were originally part of a broader piece of research conducted amongst Sankt Pauli fans on 'fan power'; which were initially disseminated in an accessible web format for public use in 2012.[33] The abundance of findings allowed two related themes to distinctly emerge for analysis and separate subsequent publication. Findings more specific to 'Sport Activism' were harvested and fashioned into a separate journal publication.[34] And the findings presented here are the result of a separate wave of analysis from other original source material more specifically related to community organization and empowerment.

The research was a combination of more than ten years of informal ethnography culminating in summative questionnaires and interviews with six key fan activists. All participants are prominent members of the fan community, were of mixed age and gender, regular supporters for many years, and closely involved in other forms of activism too as key contributors to different fan projects, activities, and cultural events. Their contributions were all in English, as a second language, so their words (hereafter in italics) sometimes reflect that challenge.

Participants neatly divided between those who began their support for Sankt Pauli in childhood and adulthood. Those whose support started in childhood described uncomfortable experiences watching other teams in atmospheres which were either intimidating or simply boring. But each felt a revelation upon encountering a special atmosphere at Sankt Pauli which (unlike other stadiums) was inclusive, and child and female-friendly. Those whose initial support began in adulthood described being attracted by the leftist libertarian politics of the fan scene. All experienced a strong and immediate sense of community; *'like in a big family ... something you felt that connected the people'*.

Autonomous fan organization

Fans felt that a sense of community was fostered in diverse overlapping ways and that they inhabited multiple communities of place, identity, experience, imagination and through shared processes of activity.[35] A strong sense of community is reflected in fan organization which acts as a springboard for community action, and subsequently to community empowerment. The composition and organization of the fan network has to be understood as a complicated and unruly organism and cannot be thought of as a highly ordered piece of machinery; *'it is very important to have different groups who are doing different things ... and organise it to make it friendly'*.

Organization encompasses both structure and processes with distinct component parts but also cross-fertilization between those parts which both enhance cohesion and buoy distinctions; *'everybody is united but divided also'*. So community organization takes place within and between different groupings with a sense of mutuality, tolerance and respect; *'All the groups want to satisfy the other groups and individuals'*. Organization also operates at different levels, locally around the Sankt Pauli district and other neighbourhoods, and regionally across the whole city of Hamburg and beyond. Nationally there are relationships with other teams' fan organizations and with Sankt Pauli fans across Germany. Internationally fans operate in conjunction with other fan groups across Europe and further afield. And allegiances are forged with a Sankt Pauli support drawn worldwide in a spirit of *'internationalism'*.

There are about 350 Sankt Pauli supporter clubs registered with the Fanclubsprecherrat (the body elected by the fan clubs to speak on their behalf). These include clubs whose members are season ticket holders as well as others more remotely affiliated elsewhere in Germany and around the world. The Fanclubsprecherrat incorporates delegates from the individual fan clubs who discuss issues democratically and vote on positions to be taken; for example to support initiatives, plan campaigns or declare a boycott; *'like a loud voice for the fans of Sankt Pauli'*. It makes public statements, represents the views of the fan clubs to others, and is bound by a constitution which declares 'Fanclubs act against every form of discrimination'.[36]

The largest fan club are the Ultras who number thousands on match days with a core of about eighty who are perceived as key organizers. For some it is a full-time vocation and the Ultras are by far the most active fans in the stadium and pride themselves on their inventiveness, political activity and frenetic endurance on the terraces. They have different working groups; some choreograph the stadium banners and chants, one group designs and makes merchandise to raise funds, and another works with refugees and brings them to matches. Another large and significant group are the Sankt Pauli Skinheads. Founded in 1996, they are one of the oldest and biggest supporter groups; a mixture of football and skinhead subculture. They are broadly left wing and (in contrast with the prevalence of fascism in skinhead culture elsewhere) undeniably anti-Nazi; 'we are all anti-fascists and if we see them we beat them'. They root their anti-fascism in their subculture's origins in 'rude boy' imagery and reggae music, and see fascist skinheads as a corruption or distortion of skinhead culture. The skinheads are actively involved in many forms of fan activity and protest.

As Sankt Pauli fans could be described as being broadly feminist or pro-feminist[37] the women and girls football department of the club are a very significant group. They operate much more autonomously from the club than the men's section and celebrated their twentieth anniversary in 2010 having arisen from women who were mostly season ticket holders, but who wanted to play football themselves. They choose to play in 'hobby' leagues (unlike the professional men's team), are very much drawn from the fans, and participate actively in other subgroups and initiatives like the women and girls' football project they have supported in a Nairobi slum since 2006. Although some younger members are perhaps more interested in playing football, the women's section retains the importance of putting politics first; 'There has always been this connection of being an active player yourself and of being socially or politically active'.

Websites, blogs and fanzines are all media controlled and utilized by fans. The Ubersteiger is the second biggest fanzine in Germany. It runs a weekly blog and issues hard-copy editions four or five times a year. The Ubersteiger is an extremely important organ for fans communicating information and ideas about football and politics. Important themes covered by the fanzine include anti-racism, anti-homophobia and local issues like gentrification and increasing housing costs. Football is not the only sport played under the Sankt Pauli banner and others such as handball, rugby league and activities such as chess are played and supported as well. All these and other components of the fan organization interact with each other as part of the whole; more streamlined organizational structures with a narrower democratic mandate are avoided, and a sense of participatory democracy has animated fans and united fan groups across difference. This has become the basis for collective action, building capacity for social capital and sustainable change; 'Some of them are very different from each other but there is always respect and interest ... and you can learn from each other like diversity'.

Community leadership and democracy

A vibrant 'participatory democracy' has helped to build capacity for self-help which strengthens community empowerment. This has led to enduring non-hierarchical community control and self-determined goals. Fans embrace an extremely democratic culture and were eager to assert that there were no formal 'leaders' or 'leadership' amongst fans; 'there is no hierarchy. If somebody was to go on and think that he is the speaker for the whole group then nobody would accept it. ... There is no one who speaks for all the other groups'. This does not mean that leadership does not take place but it is a fluid process of temporal involvement rather than the creation of positions of power.[38] Fans are actively encouraged to participate in decision-making; '*You can really influence it a lot if you are willing and able to put time and energy into that ... People are always asked to be more active ... It's quite a democratic thing that is going on*'.

In terms of the scale of fan organization and activity leadership could be thought of as quite prolific. Examples include fans following their own initiative to organize political activity; directing fan chants and choreography at matches, organizing their own protests on the streets, and the Ubersteiger collating and coordinating media strategy and information because of its ability to do so. Fans describe a meritocracy whereby opinions are thoroughly debated and talented or committed groups or individuals are informally adopted from the grassroots communities into leadership roles; '*Other persons are interested in their opinions but they are not really leaders*'. Autonomous fan organization can be seen to be implicitly in keeping with a community development approach, albeit informally; 'knitting society together at the grass roots and deepening democracy ... Strengthening the ability of people to act on joint interests and in the common interest'.[39]

The fragmented nature of fan organization has led to an immersed open access 'all points' communication model which enhances democracy, keeping different parts of the network in touch with the others. This process utilizes a blend of conventional and digital communications, from a plethora of meetings to the use of digital media linked to other networks globally. Meetings and discussions are especially valued as an essential part of democratic process and there are large ones like the Fanclubsprecherat, smaller ones amongst subgroups like the weekly Ultras assembly, and subgroups often share issues and ideas. But online communication is increasingly influential such as those that gave birth to the 'Jolly Rouge' protests (aimed at resisting increasing commercialization at the football club) which quite suddenly grew into a massive campaign with fans wearing red and subverting traditional flags and banners with red ones featuring Che Guevarra. But there are also some reservations about the restrictions of online communications; '*You can't discuss on the internet ... You have to be on the streets to decide*'.

Consensus on issues is valued by fans but not at the expense of self-determination. A recent protest in support of away supporters who had been banned from the stadium illustrates a balance; '*Every group had to decide either I do my protest inside the stadium or I do my protest outside ... Everybody can just do what you think is right and not disturb others*'. From these organizational processes there is recognition that an inner circle of about 1000 key activists have emerged whose 'unity of purpose and sustained contribution over decades cannot be underestimated'.[40] But they do not control the fan body and only exercise influence in as much as they have earned respect. Overall fans were very satisfied with the democratic nature of their organizational processes, felt very little improvements could be made, and celebrated their underpinning philosophy; '*I am happy but for me it's anarchistic in a democratic way*'.

Community involvement and action

Community here has to be considered as the multiple fan subcommunities but also the broader Sankt Pauli district itself. As many fans also inhabit the district, the boundaries between are blurred. They share the same shops, bars, cafes and public services though a distinction exists because not all inhabitants of the district are Sankt Pauli fans. But in as much as sustainable change grows through participation in local issues and the connections made amongst individuals,[41] if there are concerns in the district these become the concerns of the fans;

> *If the community has any problems, the fans pick them out as a central theme in their fanzines or with help of banners. They do influence what the fans do because the fans identify with the club and the district of Sankt Pauli.*

In addition to broad issues like anti-racism, fans outlined a range of social and political issues that affect their communities from the world of football and beyond. But participants were mostly concerned about issues affecting the district of Sankt Pauli itself. Fans characterized many local problems common to other inner urban areas. These included poverty, unemployment, homelessness, low educational attainment particularly amongst a large migrant population, inter-generational issues between the young and old, and oppression by the state and police against alternative lifestyles, '*against people they don't like; squatters, people who live in vans, graffiti sprayers, left radical youth*'. And fans unanimously emphasized these social problems were accentuated against a backdrop of creeping '*gentrification*'. Fans felt locals were being marginalized by state-led urban planning which favoured unwanted office blocks, colonization by mega-brand retail outlets and refurbishment of traditional housing in favour of more affluent house-buyers. This led to rising living and housing costs which are making life hard for locals and driving many away.

Fans have a long history of close relations to the squatting movement and have inherited traditions of agitprop tactics, street protest and direct action.[42] They are able to employ political imagination to connect community issues to broader structural, social and political causes. This, and unshakable conviction, lead to fearless confrontation of issues, and to social action. Fans sought to empower themselves and address those issues vigorously but were unequivocal that the broader community were ultimately in control. In terms of community involvement this relationship represents the apex of Arnstein's ladder of citizen participation, characterized as 'citizen control'; sustainable autonomous self-help.[43] This exceeds most community practice associated with sport which seldom grows beyond tokenistic consultation or aspirations for responsive partnerships.[44] These acts of allegiance between fans and community enhance community development and empowerment as they involve

> helping people find common cause on issues that affect them, helping people work together on such issues under their own control, building the strengths and independence of community groups, organisations and networks, building equity, inclusiveness, participation and cohesion amongst people and their groups and organisations, empowering people, and their organisations where appropriate.[45]

Fans were able to cite social, community and political project work and fundraising for a variety of causes, to recount demonstrations and clashes with the authorities. These and other alternative events (like the annual Anti-Ra anti-racist tournament) have features in common with the Mondiali Antirazzisti considered by Sterchele and Saint-Blancat who outline how the liminality of the alternative festival de-structures 'normality' and offers a creative potential to explore anti-discrimination in a more liberated way.[46] So much may be true of similar events in Sankt Pauli and even the match-day atmosphere, but the Sankt Pauli quarter itself is hardly a liminal phenomenon for its permanent inhabitants. The influence of the district on fans and vice versa is symbiotic; the community influences the fans and the fans the community. Fans were able to realize the transformative potential of all of this; '*Fans bring a lot of manpower and public attention. They put up new things in political action and attract young people for political causes'.*

Fan networks

Fan networks operate quite autonomously and are less like formal partnerships and more like a series of associations. And although many may enhance fan activity none engender a dependency. This collective power can be harnessed as strength for change as social capital 'comprises both the network and the assets that may be mobilized through that network'.[47] Networks have been cultivated within Sankt Pauli, but participatory democracy can cultivate links between grassroots and wider movements for change, beyond neighbourhoods to national and global levels, 'turning issues into causes, causes into movements and building in the process a new political culture, new communities of resistance that will take on power and capital and class'.[48]

Sankt Pauli fans play active and leading roles in an emerging wave of radical football fans worldwide[49]; *'where active football supporters want to change the world of football'*. Important relationships have been formed with other supporter groups across Germany with whom there is collaborative work addressing issues common to them all; a 'web of cooperative relationships between citizens that facilitate resolution of collective action problems'.[50] There is a strong relationship with Fare (Football against Racism in Europe) and with other fan groups in different countries too; *'International solidarity is an important thing'*. And the Alerta network was founded in 2007 to bring together football supporters from around the world with a perspective of active fan participation rather than passive consumerism;

> We are awake: We fight against the repression that tries to destroy our culture. We see the Xenophobia on the terraces and the whole situation wrong in the surroundings of football.. See you on the barricades or on the terraces.[51]

Political allegiances have forged strong relationships with supporters from other clubs, notably Glasgow Celtic, but subgroups have also forged individual alliances with others including 'rude boys bohemians' from Prague, Ultras from Bergamo, and Ultras and 'rude boys and girls' from Genoa. These alliances enhance social capital through 'social networks and the norms of reciprocity and trustworthiness that arise from them'.[52] Sankt Pauli may play a lead role organizing these activities and setting an example through taking action, but they are also influenced by those other groups; *'We are not living in our own island we have to learn from other groups as well and they can learn from us'*. Fans have built capacity by creating a durable network of alliances and by travelling and seeing other types of structure and organization, other reactions to issues and ways of handling them. Through these networks, meetings and exchanges take place where fans attempt to learn from each other and act collectively which 'grows in strength as individuals form groups, groups identify issues and develop projects, and projects form alliances that have the potential to become movements'.[53]

Community empowerment

Bedford determines that community empowerment includes five dimensions; organization, cooperation, confidence, inclusivity and influence,[54] which are all evident in fan activity. Strong organization is apparent through the coordinated range of groups engaged in prolific creative activity including community work, the protests, football matches, other tournaments, events, trips away and tours. And cooperation is central in the way fans foster democratic collaboration between different groups who work together and offer practical help and support; *'people who support an issue that you might have brought up. You experience that you can change things'*. These processes en-skill and build capacity, and that alongside participation in a rewarding social life increases confidence and self-esteem; *'It feels good when you know that you are not alone, to know that you are part of something bigger. You can experience solidarity'*.

Inclusivity is enhanced by cultivating awareness of discrimination and taking positive action. Fans expressed a special sense of responsibility, as Sankt Pauli, to be sensitized to issues like inequality, to counter prejudice, and educate others; *'You are somehow dealing with more issues than just the football'*. Immersion in fan culture offered opportunities to develop social and political awareness. And influence was experienced by involvement in decision-making, and through protest activities in the stadium, on the streets and throughout the district; a platform for political statements, which are amplified through the fanzines, internet and other media. Fans valued the chance to realize ambitions in alternative ways which in themselves felt empowering;

In a capitalist world where it just counts if you have material abundance it shows the possibility of an alternative life style, different values and solidarity in many ways. You are part of something big ... You can be huge in the things you do into the fan scene.

Empowering individuals

Fans felt that the cultivation of their own awareness was empowering and that it increased through insight, experience and exposure to new ideas through fan culture. Critical inquiry and discussion caused individuals to question the conventions of football and society, to reflect on their opinions and often to change minds; *'They have got other goals than society sets ... They are more happier and self-confident and have a more complex way to watch their things or the world'*. And fan culture offers many opportunities for informal education through which individual can develop as well as exposure to other ways of doing and thinking.

Although some benefits relate to football, they are certainly not confined to that. Fans were able to recount stories of how their own personal lives were enhanced and also how they had changed. They bore witness to changes brought about in others; *'It changes them very much because nobody is born as political active or football active, man, and you have to be teached by someone or by the people around you'*. Fan culture is flexible in its capacity as an arena to offer different opportunities for friendship, supporting, playing, as well as other activities too including the political. The inclusiveness of Sankt Pauli culture attracts people of different ages, genders and sexualities, ethnicities, and social classes. It offers a sense of community amongst a network of like-minded individuals and through this communion a confidence and sense of purpose;

People are getting more self-assurance, because you see a lot of people coming into the Sankt Pauli scene and they are having nothing and they look like they are broken people ... and after 3 years they have something. They have something they believe in,

something they can work with, something they can share their feelings ... They are get-
ting stronger with it.

Fans felt their activities led people to increase their self-esteem, acquire status, be happier, more ambitious and improve the quality of their lives. Fan culture offers support, creativity and solutions to personal problems and could inspire individuals to take action for more control over their lives;

There are many, many people who try to help. They can find competencies which are
exactly right to help and talk about this problem ... You get so many ideas, to talk and
say what is your problem?

Empowering fans

Fans expressed aspirations within football to maintain a phenomenal atmosphere at matches, that the football club lost interest in making money and that the team has the most successful season ever. But, Community empowerment also entails 'building active and sustainable communities based on social justice and mutual respect' and 'changing power structures'.[55] And Sankt Pauli's radical history of sport acti- vism has sustained conscious acts of *'resistance'* against powerful institutions which sometimes leads to conflict with the police because *'they do what the government tells them to do more or less'*. Fans believed that people had to take more control over their own circumstances and circumvent the authorities. They believe fans potentially have the power to solve their own problems; *'Sankt Pauli supporters are giving the first step to change things'*. They utilized football as a springboard for other causes; *'grow your own creative work and again you have some kind of a plat- form and a speaking tube'*.

Sankt Pauli leftist Ultra culture has spread nationally to other clubs too and they have been at the leading edge of campaigns adopted more widely in football like those against racism and homophobia. They have also campaigned for more Fan-friendly arrangements at stadia. They were consulted by the German football authorities on fan arrangements and hospitality prior to the 2006 world cup. The current head of security at the Millerntor stadium has his roots as a fan activist, fanzine editor and campaigner. And fans have worked closely with the club to pursue a relaxing of stewarding and a sympathetic embrace of fan banners and other home-made paraphernalia. The impact of these precedents is felt well beyond their own district. And key to these reforms has been their emergence from the grassroots fan base.

Fans were quick to acknowledge the contributions of many fans of other foot- ball clubs and the trend to exchange and copy ideas amongst them, but also acknowledged they were pioneers in German and world football in combatting racism and fascism and taking on the football authorities to do likewise. And many of their ideas have now become mainstream; *'This happened at Sankt Pauli, they changed the team and the club, and the supporters as well; we changed because of social influence'*. Since then fans have continued to play a leading role, nationally and internationally, creating and sustaining fan networks campaigning for fan rights and the power to fight against prejudice as well as rampant commercialization.

Empowering communities

If community empowerment is in some part the development of individuals and groups within a community whose activity enhances and empowers the community as a whole, then Sankt Pauli can certainly claim to that. Fans have been empowered to engage in collective action for justice and democracy as well as increasing the strength of community life and improving local conditions, especially for the disadvantaged.[56] Whether by accident or design, through this community development process Sankt Pauli fans have created a vibrant healthy community quite in line with Barr and Hashagen's ABCD model (Achieving Better Community Development).[57] This involves enhancing community empowerment dimensions with quality of life ones leading to a liveable, equitable, sustainable, strengthened healthy community.

Fans have built bedrock for community empowerment through the personal empowerment of fans, an infrastructure of community organization, democratic participation and involvement, leading to positive social and political action. Fans are involved in many community projects including youth work and computer literacy. Fans engage in community campaigns like resistance to gentrification through protests and demonstrations because of a *'great commitment from Sankt Pauli towards the community ... This quarter is a lot hipper because a lot of people there watch Sankt Pauli, a lot of left wing people'*. Fans have set up social housing projects. The proposed conversion of a massive shopping mall to an Ikea retail outlet was undermined by the squatted seizure of the building and its conversion to community use, including artists in residence and sometimes a night club. And many other squats have been utilized as nightclubs and fan group clubhouses through collective action; *'When there is a very big problem or occurrence many, many people (sometimes more than you believe) staying together and give the community a voice'*.

From this fans have enhanced the quality of life by cultivating a caring, safe and creative community with shared resources and active citizenship. By adopting a community-centred focus fans have placed their club at the heart of its local community, addressed community issues allied to social projects with community benefits, and created non-hierarchical participatory activity; *'When you do something together as a group you can experience solidarity and you can also change things'*. Fans were positive about the deep links between the fan scene and the district, and the economic and social benefits that cultivated; *'Sankt Pauli Fans bring life and a lot of money into the quarter ... They also care about social and political issues in the neighbourhood'*. Fan culture plays a central role in community identity and creating a sense of community pride. It offers camaraderie, a vibrant rallying point for many other causes, and tolerance of diversity and alternative lifestyles;

> *Because the district is very colourful and different ... and people livelier here. The football club is not only a topic in every bar or takeaway or on the street, It's even just a big part of the whole district and if you took that away it would be a little empty. It would be like a gap, which nobody could fill.*

Despite evidence in support of these significant accomplishments and their undisputed influence, fans were quite modest about the extent of community empowerment. This can perhaps be understood in relation to the scale of their social and political ambitions beyond their local communities and a perception of relative impotence in the face of some broader structural barriers. So, whilst undoubtedly impressive, the extent of any transformation is also viewed with a healthy scepticism by fans;

We haven't really changed the politics or the community fundamentally, but still it means that in this quarter, in this part of Hamburg there is a lot more social and political activity going on than in a lot of other parts of Hamburg, and this has to do with the Sankt Pauli fans.

Sustainability

Taylor states 'there will be no sustainable change unless communities themselves are given the power and responsibility to take action'.[58] Sankt Pauli Fans have certainly ensured that, and the fact that they have a consistently radical history dating back to the early 1980s is evidence of sustainability itself. There have been many struggles along that road and that sense of engaging in struggle is perceived as empowering in its own right. Fans are generally satisfied with current organization, but also express concerns about where future threats may lay, the need for vigilance, and are wary of resting on their laurels. There is an ingrained distrust of the German football authorities with their capacity to act against fan interests, the mainstream media and their tendency to distort images of fans, and of oppressive police practices at matches and protests treating all fans as troublemakers especially at away games; '*They try to stop us being united*'. But fans challenge the authorities and use their own media to offer alternative voices.

There were also some concerns related to the success of their campaigns. There was recognition that as mere football fans, and not a political party, that their impact was restricted. But equally the fan body is connected to many other social movements. Some felt if they were too successful and threatened to create major social change the authorities would try harder to stop them beforehand. Others were concerned that street protests sometimes attracted voyeurs and riot tourism whereby troublemakers with little interest in FC Sankt Pauli would attach themselves and agitate for a violent outcome, not entirely sharing the community values of the fans;

who are not interested in being a football fan or Sankt Pauli fan, who are only interested in these riots ... you only see them if something happens outside, It's difficult to talk to them because you don't see them very often.

Fans were also disdainful of the superficiality and passivity of some who maybe only supported Sankt Pauli because it was trendy and who only '*go to the ground and take their seat and leave after the game*'. They were concerned that their whole message should reach everyone and some feared that the degree of activism might diminish, that although the majority of fans were '*politically minded*' many were not '*politically active*'. They felt there should always be a balance between football support and political support and that there was an ongoing mission to be inclusive, to politicize and empower others. Some expressed concern that the radical culture maybe slowly diluted, that many of the original key activists were getting older, that the younger generation of new activists had yet to fully emerge, and a recent protest was cited to illustrate;

They now have family and kids and a good job, so now they have no time and they have another way of life today ... There were only about 1000 people who made demonstrations out of the ground and I think out of the people there were 600 or 700 Ultra and the rest were from the inner circle.

And yet many other protests and campaigns evidence the virility of the current culture and struggles. Some fans differentiated between the outlook and behaviour of younger and older generations. They described observing more young people in the stadium and their enthusiastic antics which carry on into the streets of the district, where banners are draped and walls painted with political campaign slogans. But they were also concerned about some hedonistic aspects of youth culture like anti-social behaviour and drunkenness. Fans described a process of informal education to raise awareness and also project work carried out with young people and the structure and knowledge that it offered. But they were also wary of indoctrination and not simply producing younger clones of themselves;

You are not making them brainwashed or something. With your work or your behaviour you start to set up thoughts which are developed in these young guys. And it's a very good thing for young guys to think in different ways.

Over a quarter century of radicalism, support has not really waned despite the club's travails up and down the top three divisions of German football. And although there was some concern about the impact on numbers if ever demoted as far down as the fifth division, there was more of a sense of potential threat from the commercializing tendency of the club to the do-it-yourself left-wing culture of the fans. So, the protection of political integrity is more important for fans than compromise in pursuit of playing success. Fans felt a need for eternal vigilance upon the football club itself; '*a big machine who sells marketing ideas, big numbers of merchandise, earn millions of euros, you must watch*'. Because Sankt Pauli fans embrace and address all these concerns, they continue to enjoy a uniquely vibrant and empowering culture which fosters democracy and community action, and which they work hard to ensure will prosper into the future.

Conclusions

Despite the tendency of football clubs to project neo-liberal ideology and conservative values, Sankt Pauli fans have shown unambiguously that professional football can be reclaimed as a site for resistance and for the propagation of leftist libertarian ideas and culture. Though not the only fans engaged in this struggle, Sankt Pauli fans have created their own radical oasis in a turbulent world. Sankt Pauli acts as a beacon for fellow travellers who share alternative ideals for football and politics. Other fans visit from across the world to witness this iconic phenomenon. And Sankt Pauli fans also reach out to others across different networks offering solidarity and messages of hope.

Fans have challenged the dominant hegemony of passive consumption, resisted commercialization, and created a radical do-it-yourself culture in its place. Fans are knowingly engaged in a political and cultural struggle and have fought long and hard to achieve their uniqueness and to hold onto it. Sankt Pauli fans illustrate the potential of sport for community empowerment and offer insights beyond mere sport of the transformative potential of community activity. As leading lights, many of their radical practices have been adopted elsewhere by others.

Sankt Pauli fans have proven themselves to be highly organized in self-determined imaginative and creative ways. Their cohesive autonomy has allowed them to be flexible and non-hierarchical with no formal leadership. By promoting community involvement from the bottom up, fans have fostered a participatory democracy. But they have also extended their reach and influence locally, nationally and internationally to rally others, forge alliances and create networks of mutual support. Fans have adopted a community-centred focus, embracing community issues, and engaged in prolific community activity, projects, and campaigns. And by informally following community development principles, fan culture has empowered individuals, the fan body itself, and broader communities in a transformative way.

Political conviction has led Sankt Pauli fans to embody sport activism and to utilize direct action methods to campaign and take community issues inside the stadium, onto the streets, online, and into mainstream media. These acts of resistance have proved empowering in their own right. Fans have challenged power and oppression, cultivated critical consciousness, promoted leftist libertarian thought, and politicized the fan base. Sankt Pauli has created thousands of activists who inhabit a richly saturated political theatre, a weekly carnival of football, politics, protest and fun. Fans have been vigilant and kept the commercializing tendencies of their own club in check and sustained an authentic grassroots fan culture in the process admired by many others. Through thoughtful action, fans have addressed underlying structural issues and sustainably demonstrated the potential of football for transformative community empowerment and radical community action. And fans have guarded against complacency by vigorously defending the idea that they are supporting a cause, not just a football club, and from that; they organize to influence.

Disclosure statement

No potential conflict of interest was reported by the author.

Notes

1. Hylton and Totten, 'Community Sport Development'.
2. Department for Communities and Local Government, 'The Community Development Challenge', 13.
3. Hylton and Totten, 'Community Sport Development'.
4. SCCD, *Strategic Framework for Community Development*.
5. See Griggs, 'Carlsberg don't Make Football Teams ... But If They did'; Merkel, 'Football Fans and Clubs in Germany: Conflicts, Crises and Compromises'; W. McDougall, 'Kicking from the Left: The Friendship of Celtic and FC St. Pauli Supporters'; and Daniel and Kassimeris, 'The Politics and Culture of FC St. Pauli: From Leftism, through Anti-establishment, to Commercialization'.
6. Montague, 'Punks, Prostitutes and St Pauli; Inside Soccer's Coolest Club'.
7. Davidson, *Pirates, Punks & Politics.*
8. Sanderson, 'Nie wieder Faschismus, Nie wieder Krieg, Nie wieder 3. Liga!'.
9. Totten, 'Sport Activism and Political Praxis within the FC Sankt Pauli Fan Subculture', 12.
10. Long, 'Leisure as a Tool for Community Development and the Opiate of the Masses'.
11. Dart, 'Representations of Sport in the Revolutionary Socialist Press in Britain, 1988–2012'.
12. Kennedy, 'Left Wing Supporter Movements and the Political Economy of Football'.
13. Blackshaw and Long, 'What's the Big Idea? A Critical Exploration of the Concept of Social Capital and its Incorporation into Leisure Policy Discourse'; and Coalter, *A Wider Role for Sport. Who's Keeping the Score?*
14. Hylton and Totten, 'Community Sport Development'.
15. Williams, *Marxism and Literature*.
16. Bennett, *Popular Culture: History and Theory, Popular Culture: Themes and Issues 2.*

17. See Sanderson, 'Nie wieder Faschismus, Nie wieder Krieg, Nie wieder 3. Liga!'; Totten, 'Freedom through Football; A Tale of Football, Community, Activism and Resistance'; and Merkel, 'Football Fans and Clubs in Germany: Conflicts, Crises and Compromises'.
18. Baird, 'The Beauty of Big Democracy'.
19. Giroux, *Youth in a Suspect Society; Democracy or Disposability.*
20. Kaufman and Wolff, 'Playing and Protesting: Sport as a Vehicle for Social Change'.
21. See Sanderson, 'Nie wieder Faschismus, Nie wieder Krieg, Nie wieder 3. Liga!'; Kuhn, *Soccer versus the State*; and Davidson, *Pirates, Punks & Politics.*
22. Totten, 'Sport Activism and Political Praxis within the FC Sankt Pauli Fan Subculture'.
23. Batliwala, 'The Meaning of Women's Empowerment: New Concepts from Action'.
24. Partington and Totten, 'Community Sports Projects and Effective Community Empowerment'.
25. See Bolton, Fleming, and Elias, 'The Experience of Community Sport Development'; and Sugden and Tomlinson, 'Theory and Method for a Critical Sociology of Sport'.
26. Schuftan, 'The Community Development Dilemma: What is Really Empowering?', 260.
27. Hylton and Totten, 'Community Sport Development', 86.
28. Hylton and Totten, 'Community Sport Development'.
29. Freire, 'Pedagogy of the Heart', 73.
30. Ledwith, *Community Development: A Critical Approach.*
31. SCCD, *Strategic Framework for Community Development.*
32. Totten, 'Sport Activism and Political Praxis within the FC Sankt Pauli Fan Subculture'.
33. Totten, 'Fan Power: Calling the Shots; Lessons from the Iconic Fans of Cult Club Sankt Pauli F.C.'.
34. Totten, 'Sport Activism and Political Praxis within the FC Sankt Pauli Fan Subculture'.
35. Totten, 'Freedom through Football; A Tale of Football, Community, Activism and Resistance'.
36. Fanclubsprecherrat, 'Fanclubs; Constitution'.
37. Davidson, *Pirates, Punks & Politics.*
38. Totten, 'Sport Activism and Political Praxis within the FC Sankt Pauli Fan Subculture'.
39. Department for Communities and Local Government, 'The Community Development Challenge', 13.
40. Totten, 'Sport Activism and Political Praxis within the FC Sankt Pauli Fan Subculture', 10.
41. J. Partington and M. Totten, 'Community Sports Projects and Effective Community Empowerment.
42. See Sanderson, 'Nie wieder Faschismus, Nie wieder Krieg, Nie wieder 3. Liga!'; and Totten, 'Sport Activism and Political Praxis within the FC Sankt Pauli Fan Subculture'.
43. Arnstein, 'A Ladder of Citizen Participation'.
44. Hylton and Totten, 'Community Sport Development'.
45. Department for Communities and Local Government, 'The Community Development Challenge', 39.
46. Sterchele and Saint-Blancat, 'Keeping It Liminal. The Mondiali Antirazzisti'.
47. Nahapiet and Ghoshal, 'Social Capital, Intellectual Capital, and the Organizational Advantage', 243.
48. Sivanandan, cited in Cooke, 'Whatever Happened to the Class of 68? – The Changing Context of Radical Community Work Practice', 22.
49. See Totten, 'Sport Activism and Political Praxis within the FC Sankt Pauli Fan Subculture'; and Kuhn, *Soccer versus the State.*
50. Brehm and Rahn, 'Individual-level Evidence for the Causes and Consequences of Social Capital', 999.
51. Alerta, 'About Alerta', 2012.
52. Putnam, *Bowling Alone. The Collapse and Revival of American Community*, 19.
53. Ledwith, *Community Development: A Critical Approach,* 3.
54. Bedford, 'Empowering Evaluation; Evaluating Empowerment'.
55. SCCD, *Strategic Framework for Community Development*, 4.
56. SCCD, *Strategic Framework for Community Development.*

57. Barr and Hashagan, *ABCD Handbook; A Framework for Evaluating Community Development*.
58. Taylor, 'Top Down Meets Bottom Up; Neighbourhood Management', 48.

References

Alerta. 'About Alerta'. *Alerta*, 2012. http://www.alerta-network.org/about.

Arnstein, S. 'A Ladder of Citizen Participation', *Journal of American Institute of Planning* 35, no. 4 (1969): 216-24, and reproduced in R. Gates and F. Stout. *The City Reader.* 2nd ed. RoutledgePress, 1996.

Baird, V. 'The Beauty of Big Democracy'. *New Internationalist*, no. 436 (2010): 15–9.

Barr, A., and S. Hashagan *ABCD Handbook; A Framework for Evaluating Community Development*. London: Community Development Foundation, 2000.

Batliwala, S. 'The Meaning of Women's Empowerment: New Concepts from Action'. In *Population Policies Reconsidered: Health, Empowerment and Rights*, ed. G. Sen. A. Germain, and L.C. Chen, 127–38. Boston, MA: Harvard University Press, 1994.

Bedford, J. *Empowering Evaluation; Evaluating Empowerment*. National Empowerment Partnership, 2014. http://www.cdf.org.uk/nep-microsite/files/resources/Guidance/Empowering%20evaluation-%20evaluating%20empowerment.pdf.

Bennett, T. *Popular Culture: History and Theory, Popular Culture: Themes and Issues 2*. Milton Keynes: Open University, 1981.

Blackshaw, T., and J. Long. 'What's the Big Idea? A Critical Exploration of the Concept of Social Capital and its Incorporation into Leisure Policy Discourse'. *Leisure Studies* 24, no. 3 (2005): 239–58.

Bolton, B., S. Fleming, and B. Elias. 'The Experience of Community Sport Development: A Case Study in Blaenau Gwent'. *Managing Leisure* 13 (2008): 92–103.

Bourdieu, P., and L. Wacquant *An Invitation to Reflexive Sociology*. Chicago: University of Chicago Press, 1992.

Brehm, J. and W. Rahn. 'Individual-level Evidence for the Causes and Consequences of Social Capital'. *American Journal of Political Science* 41, no. 3 (1997): 999–1023.

Coalter, F. *A Wider Role for Sport. Who's Keeping the Score?* Abingdon: Routledge, 2007.

Cooke, I. 'Whatever Happened to the Class of 68? – The Changing Context of Radical Community Work Practice'. In *Radical community work; Perspectives of practice from Scotland*, ed. I. Cooke and M. Shaw, 6–25. Edinburgh: Moray House, 1996.

Daniel, P., and C. Kassimeris. 'The Politics and Culture of FC St. Pauli: From Leftism, through Anti-establishment, to Commercialization'. *Soccer & Society* 14, no. 2 (2013): 167–182.. doi:10.1080/14660970.2013.776466.

Dart, J. 'Representations of sport in the revolutionary socialist press in Britain, 1988–2012'. *International Review for the Sociology of Sport* 49 no. 6 (2012): 645–668. doi:10.1177/1012690213497352.

Davidson, N. *Pirates, Punks & Politics*. York: Sportbooks, 2014.

Department for Communities and Local Government. 'The Community Development Challenge'. *CDF*, 2006/2011. http://www.cdf.org.uk/c/document_library/get_file?uuid=483850bf-ba92-46d0-9bc4-a35c635c5ae3&groupId=10128.

Fanclubsprecherrat. 'Fanclubs; Constitution'. *Fanclubsprecherrat*. (2012/2013). http://www.fanclubsprecherrat.de/site/?page_id=6.

Freire, P. 'Pedagogy of the heart'. In *The Paulo Friere Reader*, ed. A. Friere and D. Macedo (p. 73), New York: Continuum, 1998.

Giroux, H. *Youth in a suspect society; democracy or disposability*. New York: Palgrave MacMilan, 2009.

Griggs, G. '"Carlsberg don't Make Football Teams … But If They did": The Utopian Reporting of FC St Pauli in the British Media'. *Soccer & Society* 13, no. 1 (2012): 73–82.

Hylton, K., and M. Totten. 'Community Sport Development'. In *Sport Development; Policy, Process and Practice*, ed. K. Hylton, 80–126. Abingdon: Routledge, 2013.

Kaufman, P., and E. Wolff. "Playing and Protesting: Sport as a Vehicle for Social Change". *Journal of Sport and Social Issues* 34 no. 2 (2010): 154–75. doi:10.1177/0193723509360218.

Kennedy, P. 'Left Wing Supporter Movements and the Political Economy of Football'. *Soccer and Society* 14 no. 2 (2013): 277–90. doi:10.1080/14660970.2013.776462.

Kuhn, G. *Soccer versus the State*. Oakland, CA: PM Press, 2011.

Ledwith, M. *Community Development: A Critical Approach*. Bristol: The Polity Press, 2011.

Long, J. 'Leisure as a Tool for Community Development and the Opiate of the Masses'. In *Leisure and Social Control*, ed. A. Tomlinson, 161–165. Brighton: Leisure Studies Association, 1981.

McDougall, W. 'Kicking from the Left: The Friendship of Celtic and FC St. Pauli Supporters'. *Soccer & Society* 14 no. 2 (2013): 230–45. doi:10.1080/14660970.2013.776470.

Merkel, U. 'Football Fans and Clubs in Germany: Conflicts, Crises and Compromises'. *Soccer & Society* 13, no. 3 (2012): 359–76.

Montague, J. 'Punks, Prostitutes and St Pauli; Inside Soccer's Coolest Club'. *CNN*, 2012. http://edition.cnn.com/2010/SPORT/football/08/18/football.st.pauli.punks/index.html.

Nahapiet, J., and S. Ghoshal. 'Social Capital, Intellectual Capital, and the Organizational Advantage'. *The Academy of Management Review* 23, no. 2 (1998): 242–67.

Partington, J., and M. Totten. 'Community Sports Projects and Effective Community Empowerment: A Case Study in Rochdale'. *Managing Leisure* 17, no. 1 (2012): 29–46.

Putnam, R.D. *Bowling Alone. The Collapse and Revival of American Community*. New York, NY: Simon and Schuster, 2000.

Sanderson, C. '"Nie wieder Faschismus, Nie wieder Krieg, Nie wieder 3. Liga!"; A Social History of FC St. Pauli, 1986–1991'. *Playleftwing*, 2014. http://www.playleftwing.org.

SCCD. *Strategic Framework for Community Development*. Sheffield: Standing Conference for Community Development, 2001.

Schuftan, C. "The Community Development Dilemma: What is Really Empowering?". *Community Development Journal* 31, no. 3 (1996): 260–4.

Sterchele, D., and C. Saint-Blancat. 'Keeping It Liminal. The Mondiali Antirazzisti (Antiracist World Cup) as a Multifocal Interaction Ritual'. *Leisure Studies* 34 no. 2 (2013): 182–96. doi:10/1080/02614367.2013.855937.

Sugden, J., and A. Tomlinson. "Theory and Method for a Critical Sociology of Sport". In *Power Games; A critical Sociology of Sport*, ed. J. Sugden and A. Tomlinson, 3–22. London: Routledge, 2002.

Taylor, M. *Top Down Meets Bottom Up; Neighbourhood Management*. York: Joseph Rowntree Foundation, 2000.

Totten, M. '"Fan Power: Calling the Shots"; Lessons from the Iconic Fans of Cult Club Sankt Pauli F.C.'. 2014. http://www.playleftwing.org.

Totten, M. 'Freedom through Football; A Tale of Football, Community, Activism and Resistance'. In *Community and Inclusion in Leisure Research and Sport Development*, ed. A. Ratna and B. Lashua, . 155–68 Eastbourne: LSA, 2011.

Totten, M. 'Sport Activism and Political Praxis within the FC Sankt Pauli Fan Subculture'. *Soccer and Society* 16 no. 4 (2014): 453–68. doi:10.1080/14660970.2014.882828.

Williams, R. *Marxism and Literature*. Oxford: Oxford University Press, 1977.

Easton Cowboys and Cowgirls: anatomy of an alternative sports club

Will Simpson

This is a personal narrative account of the history and ideas of Easton Cowboys and Cowgirls. I'll firstly describe the achievements and history of the club. I'll look at what makes it different, even within the anarchist or activist 'scene', what its values are (and how these manifest themselves) and the way that the club organizes itself. I'll also discuss the club's future and whether its unique approach to sport and community organization can be sustained over a number of generations.

Put simply, the Easton Cowboys and Cowgirls is an amateur sports club based in inner city Bristol. We don't have our own ground and most people haven't heard of us. We play at the very bottom of the UK football pyramid – in the Sunday and Saturday leagues, on the muddy pitches and municipal sports grounds where week after week players run around for their own enjoyment, without the expectation of financial gain of any sort.

BUT there is something extraordinary about the Cowboys and Cowgirls. We have done some astonishing, amazing things, some of which reside beyond the imagination of most professional clubs. And it's only now, two decades after we first formed, that we can stand back and appreciate what we have achieved and the role we have played in developing a network of teams that stand at odds to the way society is organized and (to a certain extent) the mediated, moneyed world of professional sport.

What we have done

The club adopted the name 'Easton Cowboys' in May 1992, but its roots lie a little further back than that, at Baptist Mills primary school playing field in Easton. It was here, adjacent to the M32 motorway that, from the late '80s onwards, various punks, hippies and general ne'er do wells congregated for a regular Sunday afternoon kick around. These were generally a lighthearted way to sweat out the previous night's alcohol, but gradually over time they developed a more serious intent. After one session in May that year, one player suggested that we could join one of the local Sunday leagues for season 1992/1993. Our country music-obsessed secretary came up with the name. Geographically certain and pitched perfectly between self-deprecation and swagger, it wasn't a bad choice.

Our first season was fairly typical for many teams – we managed to achieve the minimum level of organization necessary for an amateur side to function at this level and ended up finishing in mid table. Then at the end of 1992/1993 came an event that changed the whole direction of the club, indeed many of our lives.

Two team members also played in a dimly remembered rock band called The Herb Garden (signed briefly to East West Records in the early 90s). They had performed at an event in Stuttgart in Germany the previous year to which the organizers invited the whole Cowboys team in May 1993.

What we found when we arrived there that weekend was something we had never encountered before – a 'festival' that included football, music, socializing between the teams and an easy going inclusive atmosphere. We discovered that the Stuttgart teams that had organized it – ASV Filderstadt and ICE Neckerstrasse – were very much like us. They were comprised of squatters and ex-squatters, both were broadly left wing, explicitly anti-racist and anti-fascist and, in no particular order, liked punk rock, beer and football.

We had not expected this. Most of the other teams in our division of the Bristol and Wessex League were normal pub teams who tended to regard us as weirdos and layabouts. 'A bunch of jitters' was the most commonly hurled insult – 'jitter' being a Bristolian expression denoting a student or alternative-looking person.

Going to Stuttgart opened our eyes – there were other people out there like us! And it fired us up with the idea that we could put on our own international football festival in Bristol. This would be difficult – 1994 was the year of the Criminal Justice Bill, a mean-spirited piece of legislation designed to crush the burgeoning rave scene. It seemed designed to stop gatherings like the one we had just witnessed.

But in October 1993, we sat down for a meeting, looked around and decided that we should at least give it a go. 'We started organising and pooled all our resources', remembers then-club secretary Paul Christie. 'It was incredible what people could pull out of the bag – their links through their work, their personal friendships'.[1]

The beer licence for the event was obtained through the landlord of our newly adopted pub The Plough, the entertainment was booked via friends. Our midfielder Dave 'Torpedo' Richards worked for the council which meant he could pull a few strings regarding getting a piece of land in one of the municipal parks in the Fishponds area of the city. Amazingly, they agreed. 'At the time I didn't have any fears about it', says Christie. 'I just thought it was going to be this great party'.

It was. Despite misgivings about the event's location in Fishponds (then an area known for its far right activity), everything went smoothly. The sun shone, even the locals seemed to enjoy it. The East German team Bad Muskau won it on penalties and we vowed to do the same next year, which we did at Shipham, a village 10 miles south of Bristol, and the year after that.

In 1994, '95 and '96 we were also invited back to Stuttgart. Gradually over this period friendships began to be formed, and a rapport started to build between all the teams. More clubs started to come to the tournaments and a network began to coalesce around these events, including clubs from Belgium, Poland, Norway and Lithuania as well as others from England and Germany.

These teams were not identical. Republica Internationale from Leeds defined themselves strictly as a socialist team, Wessex Allstars were a free-spirited occasional aggregation based around two well-known anarcho punk scene bands; 1 in 12 were the football team that represented the Bradford punk venue/ social centre of the same name; the Belgian team The Lunatics put more emphasis on partying and having a good time whereas Bad Muskau and Boys Leknica from Poland are both 'town' sides, for whom the politics was less of a concern. Each viewed the world through a slightly differently shaped lens.

'The best thing for me was meeting people you knew you were going to meet once a year,' says Paul Christie. 'It was just an unconditional friendship, a common bond that became really apparent very early on. It was really about people getting together, regardless of what their political and social ideologies were'.[2]

By 1998, our confidence had grown sufficiently that we felt that we could hold our biggest event yet. We devised a 20-team 'Alternative World Cup'. All the teams in the network were invited, but we also managed to recruit some new ones. A French team that works on the Le Havre ferry was recruited, an Irish team from Leeds, an Italian team was invited. Knowing that a lot of sides from outside Western Europe might not be able to afford to come, we fundraised separately and together with £10,000 of matched funding from UNISON we brought over a team of youngsters from Soweto in the newly free South Africa.

By now we truly had an event the size of a small festival. Word spread – the media started sniffing around and the event was filmed by Sky (who eventually featured it on their Futbol Mundial programme). Some members of the team panicked about this. Thinking ahead, we engaged with the locals and put leaflets through every door in the village of Thorncombe where it was being held, thinking that perhaps they might even enjoy it.

In the end we needn't have worried. The event went without a hitch, aside from a few minor complaints about the noise on Saturday night. On the pitch, the lads from Soweto ended up winners, beating Neckerstrasse 1–0 in the final. As the young South Africans were carried on shoulders to the big top where the prizes were awarded, we could see hundreds of people crammed into the tent, all ready to welcome the champions. One moment will stay with us forever, as the 77-year-old President of Thorncombe FC arrived at the mic to present the trophies, the assembled crowd struck up a song – 'Stand up for the president' (to the tune of 'Go West'). The man in question looked deeply moved and wiping back the tears he announced: 'I have never heard or seen anything like this in all my years at this club. This is extraordinary'.[3]

To the new world!

Even as we were basking in the light of our greatest triumph, something more remarkable was being planned. Lurking at Thorncombe that weekend were a pair of activists who had just come back from Chiapas, where they had been peace observers to a low level conflict that had been going on since 1994.

Few of us have heard of the Zapatistas prior to this, but when the couple put their idea to us – a solidarity football tour to the Zapatista-held village of Chiapas – we bit their hand off. Their hope was that this would raise morale in the rebel communities (who like all of Mexico were football crazy) and garner some publicity to the cause. By this point, the club as a whole was brimming with confidence, and although only a proportion of the Cowboys (which by this point consisted of three football teams and three cricket teams) were interested – there were enough, including members of Republica and the 1 in 12 clubs – to make the trip viable. Football in a jungle war zone – bring it on!

And so on the 30 April 1999 we flew out to Cancun, Mexico to become the first sports team to tour the Zapatista communities. It felt risky – there was a chance that we would be deported and would be unable to reach our destination. There were other worries – extreme heat, altitude, bugs, illness – that some team members were apprehensive about.

Then there were the logistics. 'We literally had to sneak around the communities', remembers right back Paul Moylan. 'The army would get on the coach and we had to pretend we didn't speak Spanish and were just tourists. It was clandestine and unknown. But it worked'.

In the event, it all ran remarkably smoothly. We were safely smuggled into the village of Diez D'Abril under cover of darkness in a battered old bus, which set the pattern of the next 10 days – lots of football, no alcohol (the Zapatista communities are dry) and much falling out of hammocks. We also brought gifts for our hosts – a consignment of T-shirts bearing the slogan *Freedom Through Football*.

The trip was a hugely educational experience. For many of us hearing how the Zapatistas companeros viewed their place in the world, how they had changed their situation for the better and how they were defending and building their revolution in the face of constant government harassment and army surveillance was deeply moving.

'Going in there my main thing was the level of the war and how much they were being oppressed and dangerous it was for them', Moylan explains:

> Just the fact that they had kicked the landlords off the land. I was intrigued about how dangerous their lives were. There was one particular place where there was an army base right next to it. Then you actually saw the army and the spotter planes flying over regularly. There was no confrontation while we were there, but we heard a lot about it.[4]

We also learned that there were enormous problems that the communities faced on a daily basis – a lack of clean running water and a decent health care system. It didn't take us long to realize that these were things we could actually do something about.

On their return, the Cowboys set up a succession of public meetings and events about the trip. We also started fundraising for a water project by selling T shirts (designed by an up and coming Easton street artist called Banksy) and club nights. A separate entity – Kiptik ('inner strength' in the indigenous language Tzetzal) – was created for the purposes of the project. In the last 10 years, it has raised over £100,000 and supplied fresh clean water to thousands of people. Some Cowfolk have even got their hands dirty and returned to work on water projects themselves. And the sports tours continued. We encouraged other teams in the European network and so Chiapas was visited by The Lunatics (Nov '99), the Cowboys again (Jan 01), Republica Internationale (Spring 03) and by a Cowgirls/boys basketball team (April 06).

'To me it's a really concrete achievement', says Roger Wilson, the centre back who was a pivotal figure in both Kiptik and the organization of the tour. 'We've supplied fresh water for thousands of people. And that has inspired people in the club to do other interesting things'.[5]

Indeed the cricket team was inspired to turn a crazy idea of its own into reality. In September 2000, they travelled to California for a tour that included a series of games against the Compton Homies and Popz, a community project that attempts to steer young kids away from that community's gang culture via the medium of cricket. Well, if the football team had played in the jungles of Chiapas, why not cricket in the urban jungle of South Central LA?

A BBC film crew followed the team to California and a documentary, imaginatively titled 'Easton Cowboys' was screened on BBC1 in the West that October. And the relationship with the Compton Homies continued. When the young side toured the UK in 2001, they ensured that in addition to games in Hambledon and at Windsor Castle, a date in Bristol with the Cowboys was pencilled into their schedule.

In the years that followed, the club expanded still further. A Cowgirls side emerged in 2002 when a group of women in the organization decided it was high time they formed a women's football team. A couple of years later another group of women – a netball team named Easton Crack Whores – approached the club. With that name they had (not surprisingly) been given the cold shoulder by local leagues, so they asked whether they could become the Cowgirls netball team. 'Of course', we replied. A basketball team developed out of the tour to Chiapas in 2006 that played mixed gender games for a number of years. A children's section CACKK (Cowboys and Cowgirls Kids Klub) formed in the middle of the decade, and the existing sports kept on attracting new members – the cricket team expanded to three teams in 2006 and four by 2012. And the men's football side of the club continues to expand exponentially. By the end of the decade, we encompassed four senior teams and three veterans' sides. We had even won our first major trophy – the GFA Sunday Cup in 2011, the premier amateur Cup competition at local level.

Around the world

Inspired by the success of our tours to Mexico and California, we cast our net ever further. In 2003, we ventured to Morocco on a tour set up via a local Arabic cafe owner in Easton. In 2009 we flew to Brazil, to play a like-minded anarcho team from Sao Paulo called Los Autonomos. In 2012, we went to Argentina to play in the first South American version of the network tournaments. We have now played football on five continents. Not bad for a bunch of cash-strapped punks.

We have also applied the *Freedom Through Football* principle beyond Chiapas. In 2007, we became the first UK football team to tour the West Bank. This was an even riskier venture than Mexico, with more at stake and a higher level of danger. But the club pulled it off with aplomb. None of the 14 players who made it over there will forget the tour, what they learned or the friends they made there.

'It was an incredible experience', remembers midfielder Kev Davis.

> We'd been on a lot of foreign tours by this point but this one felt like it was pushing the boundaries. There were nerves within the group. We didn't really know the people we were going to see or how they would think about us culturally… but the people we met were amazing. It was pretty humbling – these people have often really put themselves on the line for their cause – sometimes with their lives. But they treated us beautifully and were so welcoming.[6]

Back to Easton

All this globe-trotting led some critics within the club (and some outside) to complain that the Cowboys were only interested in getting involved in exotic struggles on the other side of the world. But in 2005, the club did get involved in local politics when it played a role in the campaign to save a local sports field. Generations of local people had played on Packer's Field in East Bristol; so when it as announced that a local Academy school wanted to enclose it and build an athletics stadium on the site, we joined forces with a group of local people in an attempt to stop the development.

This was grass roots politics at its most unglamorous. A group of Cowfolk got stuck in to all the petitioning, turning up at council meetings and lobbying that such a campaign entails. We also organized a series of 'Community Fun Days' that featured men's and women's football, netball, as well as kids' activities, music and stalls that encouraged local people to make the most of the field. Two club members also made a film about the fight to keep the field open, which we hoped would generate some positive publicity.

Building our community

But perhaps our greatest achievement hasn't been all the exotic tours, politics or tournaments; it's been the creation of a community. In Britain, at least, it's a word that has been much used (and misused) in recent years. Since the start of the economic crisis in 2008, there has been a general yearning in the air for a simpler time when you knew your neighbours and there was unified spirit in local areas (something the Coalition government's 'Big Society' wheeze attempted to piggyback on).

In this the Cowboys have been ahead of the curve. The community we have created, based around our local pub The Plough, is self supportive and essentially beneficent. This has been expressed by both the way it supports struggles abroad and also the way it looks after its own.

This can be demonstrated by two examples. Back in the 1990s we sheltered two asylum seekers from Mozambique who had run away from their country's civil war. We befriended Freddie and Jeraldo after they came training with us one time and over the course of two years we provided them with a safe house – they were in imminent danger of being deported – and supported them financially. Eventually, we managed to supply them with work in London where the pair of them moved to in 1998.

More recently, the Cowgirls netball team was hit by some devastating news when a team member's teenage daughter was diagnosed with terminal cancer. The club had recently organized another European network tournament and had quite a bit of money in the bank. £1000 was diverted from the profits from the tournament and given to the team member so she could take some time off work and enjoy the last months of her daughter's life without worrying about having to make ends meet. Since the team member's daughter's death in Spring 2013, the club has continued to raise money for the Teenage Cancer Trust by taking part in a number of sponsored events.

Many club members see this sort of thing as crucial. 'It's vital to the essence of the club', says Kev Davis.

> It's what we state that we do. And the only way that the club can continue to prosper and be looked upon well is that if it looks after its own. Before we go off abroad and have all these adventures you have to put your money where your mouth is in your own community. A lot of professional clubs go on about 'community' but it doesn't translate to anything in reality.[7]

How do we do it?

Like most voluntary organizations, the Cowboys and Cowgirls is entirely dependent on the ideas and energy of its members. There is no great secret that explains the success of the club. Much of it is nothing more elaborate than being organized and having a group of committed people prepared to follow through and turn idealistic pub talk into reality. The fact that we have occasional mass assemblies (bi-annual general meetings) where ideas, be it touring Palestine, raising money for cancer charities or forming a new team are discussed, is useful. Usually, it is down to the club member who has had the idea to energize his or her fellow Cowfolk into supporting them and then turn dreams into action.

Why do all this?

Here we stumble across a very common misconception about the Cowboys and Cowgirls – the notion that we are specifically a 'political' sports club where all the members are activists plotting some sort of revolution via the medium of football (or cricket or netball). Outsiders, meeting us for the first time, have sometimes expressed disappointment at this. Usually, it is then gently explained to them that the *raison d'être* of the club had always first and foremost to facilitate the playing of sport and (most importantly) to have fun. We are a sports and social club, NOT a political party or pressure group. But of course, if, on some occasions, the two can be combined then, well ... fantastic.

The reality is that only a fraction of the people playing sport under the Cowfolk banner are 'active' in any meaningful way. Of the 150 or so people who are on the club mailing list, whilst most would probably espouse left wing views of some description, a fair proportion would probably describe themselves as 'apolitical'. And what's wrong with that?

So what does the club stand for? Well, in an article that he wrote for Gabriel Kuhn's 2011 book Soccer Against The State,[8] team member Roger Wilson picked out four elements that have made the Easton Cowboys and Cowgirls the club it is today. I'd agree with this, that if you were to boil down what 'it' is all about, it revolves around …

1. Internationalism

In the twenty-first century, many fans pretend to be (or even are) experts about European club football. But in the early 90s when we started it was very different. Little Englander attitudes prevailed in grass roots football, meaning that anyone who stood out was a target for abuse by opposition players. From the start, we were a multiracial team with Kurds and Asian kids in our early line ups and this had an effect on us. We knew we stood out. 'Most of the teams were ok – indeed the first few seasons were surprisingly trouble free', remembers Roger. 'But if there was any trouble we'd be on it. We didn't back down'.[9]

Our anti-racist stance extended to our tours abroad. The trips to Germany and beyond were conducted on a non-mediated one-to-one level. When we travelled to Chiapas we weren't an official delegation, like the trade unionists on a 'fact finding mission'. We went in at grass roots level and mixed with the other teams. Many have become our friends and lifelong relationships have blossomed out of these links.

67

2. Democracy

As previously noted, we have regular assemblies of the club where anybody is allowed to speak and people are encouraged to express their views. Positions of responsibility are rotated – managers and secretaries are moved on every few years to stop private fiefdoms being built up and new people are encouraged to take on these positions. It's been the making of many players who perhaps didn't believe that they could do such things, but have learned loads by being manager or treasurer. Unlike other clubs, the Cowboys has never been run by a cabal of the same few blokes.

3. DIY

It's no secret that the club's roots lie in punk rock and the squatting/activist scene of the 1980s. In Bristol, punk peaked a little later than in many other British cities and the city still retained a healthy scene long after it had died away in London. This meant that the teenage boys and girls who would go onto become Cowfolk drank deep from its ethics. Most influential was the idea that you shouldn't wait to form a band/start a team, you should just go on and do it. And don't expect anyone to give you the money – raise it yourselves and retain autonomy. Over the years, the Cowboys have followed this to the letter. With just a couple of exceptions, we have never gone cap in hand to outside funding bodies and have raised all our funds off our own backs. 'The Cowboys have over the years just been a fundraising machine', notes Cowgirls co-founder Sue Mennear. 'I've been amazed at how much we've raised, for good causes, for tournaments, to get other teams over to the UK'.[10] Our greatest resources have always been ourselves and the friendships we've nurtured, both inside and outside the club.

4. Inclusivity

This doesn't just mean fostering an inclusive atmosphere within the club that doesn't exclude people because of race, gender, sexuality or background. It encompasses including people *whether or not* they play a sport. Friends, relatives, partners, children and supporters can all be Cowboys or Cowgirls. There is no fixed membership – no form you have you fill in to join, no fee, no constitution you have to abide by. Participation in any aspect of the club's activities is enough to make you a Cowboy or Cowgirl.

Of course sport by its very nature is exclusive – after all, teams are usually selected on the basis of ability, meaning that those with a perceived 'lesser' ability are left out in the cold. But the club has balanced its determination to improve at its chosen sports with a commitment to inclusivity. This has been achieved by opening up new teams when there is a clear demand. This has meant the club has grown to now having six men's teams, two women's teams, two netball teams and four cricket teams. Everybody who wants to play sport can find their own level and no one gets left out.

In addition to this, I'd argue that there is something that is perhaps harder to pin down – a streak of irreverence, a dash of free-spirited absurdism. The story of the Cowboys and Cowgirls is as much about the naked penalty shoot outs and fundraising fancy dress parties as it is about grinding out results on a Sunday morning. The club has always provided a welcome home for unusual ideas, from buying a boat and sailing it to Jamaica to play football and cricket (this was seriously discussed at one club meeting in the '90s), to the Mexico tour. The latter, after all, was initially sold to the club not as some dull n' worthy exercise in solidarity but because playing football in the jungles of Chiapas sounded like a right laugh. Rather than get hung up on points of principle, we have always taken things as they come. Rather than get hung up on points of principle, we perfer to take things as they come.

Where does this come from? Certain individuals, perhaps. The Cowboys and Cowgirls have always provided a haven for a great number of creative types over the years – artists (yes, Banksy was briefly a Cowboy) musicians, writers, photographers, even actors have all played for us over the years. We've also sheltered a great number of unusual, quirky individuals who might have been spurned by other, straighter, clubs. It's not that much of a stretch to argue that it is they that have located the club within an unusual, alternative postcode, somewhere between the left wing and the left field.

This vagueness, this standing for something even if it is impossible to pin down has been a source of great strength down the years. We know of some teams that have identified themselves specifically as 'socialist' or 'anarchist'. The Cowboys and Cowgirls have never had a set agenda or manifesto that you have to sign up to when you join. Doing such a thing would be so prescriptive, so deathly and so, well, un-Cowboyish.

Of course that's not to say that we don't have principles that are non-negotiable. Essentially, these can really be condensed down to the commitment to a strong anti-racist, anti-prejudicial stance. Other than that, everything else is up for discussion. In some ways, it is better to see the club as a medium through which things (some of which are explicitly political) can be achieved. The actual number of Cowboys or Cowgirls that were involved in the Mexico or Palestine tours was actually small compared to the total number of members, but that matters not. The club was the instrument through which these were achieved.

It's fair to say that being a Cowboy has led some of us down a few unexpected paths. When we first formed in the early '90s there was no intention to form a 'sports team with a political dimension'. Indeed for a lot of the early team, football was a welcome distraction to the self-imposed strictures of being an activist. What has happened is in many ways an example of the Marxist concept of praxis – the idea that you learn why and how to do something by getting on and doing it. When we first started, none of us would have had a clue how to organize a tour to Mexico or Palestine or to make links with like-minded teams around the world. But we've achieved all these things through a combination of common sense, trusting in each other (and third parties) and learning on the job.

That's one way of looking at it. It's also a valid argument that somehow the Cowboys and politics would have collided at some point. Many of the original team had been active politically in the 1980s, from anti-fascist work to the Anti Poll Tax movement, to more obscure local campaigns. Some were getting exhausted and thus playing football provided relief from the self-imposed burdens of the activist lifestyle. But the mere fact that many of us had been activists in some shape or form meant that at some point the ideas that the Cowboys had incubated from day one were going to bloom.

At first, this found expression in simple internationalism. Inviting a bunch of teams from around the world to our tournaments may not seem a terribly daring left-field thing to do now, but in the context of the late '80s and early '90s, an era when Little Englander attitudes were still prevalent, it very much seemed so. Bringing together a team of South African kids from Soweto and a load of German and Belgian punks to a tiny village in Dorset was a statement in itself. Later of course we (or to be more accurate some people within the club) became more involved in specific political causes.

Over the years, we've developed a fine intuition about what suits us. A year or two back, a local Oxfam representative tried to interest us in their 'Don't Drop The Ball On Aid' campaign whereby football stars performed keepy uppies in support of writing off Third World debt. We decided to turn that one down. Getting involved with large NGOs has never felt right to us. Neither has getting involved with big business of any description. On the 2007 Palestine tour, we were offered the chance to play a televised game against a side from Hebron in the city's new football stadium. When we found out the game would be sponsored by a major telecoms firm, the team decided to turn it down, albeit after a long and meticulous debate.

Not a smooth ride

There have been times, of course, when the club's impulses have collided with one another. The most notorious of these came at the club's End Of Season Awards ceremony in June 2009. Matters came to a head when it was heard that some members from the Sunday football team had been making homophobic comments about some of the Cowgirl footballers. One Cowgirl challenged this and there was a scuffle that led to insults being exchanged and bad feeling all round. The following day the dispute escalated onto the club's message board and things deteriorated further. It appeared that the club's quest to create an anti-prejudicial atmosphere had run slap bang up against its equally valid desire to be inclusive.

'It was a horrendous time', recalls Kev Davis,

> but in some ways really interesting. I mean, these things happen. The reality is in any organisation has to be challenged by these issues and I think we should talk about it as a club. These things are challenges and we shouldn't be embarrassed about it.[11]

In the end, the club resolved the dispute by a mass meeting where these issues were brought out into the open. It was agreed that an introductory leaflet should be distributed to new players so they would be aware of the club's values. And with the air having been cleared, relations between the constituent parts of the club settled down once more. 'The club came out of that stronger', says Davis.

> To have a negative situation like that was difficult at the time. But we don't have schisms in the club based on that, and we know a little more about ourselves as a result of it. If it came up again we'd be able to deal it more easily.[12]

What now?

Every sportsperson or sports fan believes that their club is 'different', but from my own personal experience I have yet to encounter another sports club quite like the Cowboys and Cowgirls. Many older Cowpeople wonder about what the future holds for the club. Perhaps the biggest challenge it faces – tougher than organizing any tour or political campaign – is achieving its own sustainability over the long term – i.e. another 20, 30 years. Can that difficult-to-define club 'spirit' be preserved and passed on to a new generation? This generational shift is a problem that many amateur sports teams face, but in an organization such as the Cowboys with a deeply felt sense of its own difference and a unique ethos, it's a matter of special concern. Much will depend on whether Cowboys and Cowgirls that are now in their late teens and early 20s feel able to take 'possession' of the club, claim it as their own, adapt and build on what the original members have created. Will youngsters, now in CACKK, even want to follow their mums and dads into the main club?

Some club members view even talking about this notion of passing on the Cowboys 'flame' as being too heavy handed. 'It's not something you can pass on', contends Casuals centre back Jack Daniells.

> Not consciously, anyway. You can't enforce something like that. If the question is 'how can we do it?' Then I'd say we never will. People will either want to pick up the baton from their own volition or they won't.[13]

Kev Davis, though, is confident of the club's future.

> Every time I go to the Plough and I spend time with different club members I continue to be amazed at how much stuff goes on and how well people get on with one another. If you ask will we still be like that in ten years' time? Then I'd say definitely. I can't see it falling apart. There are too many people that do so much. There is collective strength there in our sheer numbers. I hope that the club will outlive me.[14]

Ultimately, like any voluntary organization, the Cowboys and Girls will stand or fall on the ideas and energy of its members. None of us know for certain if the club will be sustainable for another 20 years, but any organization that manages to still maintain a sense of purpose, its spirit and ethics for over two decades is doing something right. Year after year, life in the Cowboys never gets any less exciting, any less interesting. I sincerely hope that continues.

Disclosure statement

No potential conflict of interest was reported by the author.

Notes

1. Interview with author, March 2011.
2. Ibid.
3. Simpson and McMahon, *Freedom Through Football*, 85.
4. Interview with author, September 2010.
5. Interview with author, December 2010.
6. Interview with author, March 2011.
7. Ibid.
8. See Roger Wilson, 'The Easton Cowboys and Girls'.
9. Interview with author, December 2010.
10. Interview with author, October 2010
11. Interview with author, March 2011.
12. Ibid.
13. Interview with author, July 2010.
14. Interview with author, March 2011.

References

Simpson, W., and M. McMahon. *Freedom Through Football*. Bristol: Tangent Books, 2012.
Wilson, R. 'The Easton Cowboys and Girls'. In *Soccer Vs. The State: Tackling Football and Radical Politics*, ed. G. Kuhn, 124–30. Oakland, CA: PM Press, 2011.

Ten years of Supporters Trust ownership at Exeter City AFC: an overview

David Treharne

Fan ownership has long been predicated as a possible route by which struggling Football Clubs may survive. After a long period of financial turbulence and using the Supporters Direct ownership model, Exeter City Supporters took majority control of the Club in 2003. The paper charts the progress and changes in that the model of supporter control in the 10 years from 2003, and attempts an overview and critique of the situation in 2013.

Reflecting on all the changes that have taken place at Exeter City Football Club since the Trust assumed majority ownership in 2003 is virtually impossible, but there are a series of key moments that have shaped the way in which the Trust helps run the Club in 2014. This paper aims to highlight some of those that, in the view of the author, have been key moments and issues that now drive the way in which the Club and the Trust are run. It is a personal viewpoint that in no way represents any 'official' view that the Trust might to put forward. Indeed some conclusions may be regarded as contentious, but they are based on the views of someone who was a founder member of the Trust, sometime Chair of the Club, long-term Trustee and for the last two years an interested observer and season ticket holder.

Exeter City Supporters Trust was set up in 2000 with the avowed aim of 'supporting the football club'.[1] At the outset, with help from Supporters Direct, and more specifically Dave Boyle the then Chair, it adopted the then standard constitution suggested by the organization and set about putting in place a workable version of its suggested management structure. Support grew very slowly in terms of membership, though unbeknownst to the embryonic organization the Club was moving inexorably towards yet another of the crises that had marked its recent history. As ever the causes were deeply seated financial problems caused by the mismanagement of the structure that was in place to run the Club. These problems not only extended to the expense of the playing side, but also the failure of the Board to project manage the redevelopment of the ground, which was in part financed by the Football Ground development fund. A report by the Football Compliance Unit during 2003 was to point out that the Club was trading insolvently,[2] but not before the despairing owner had imported two 'businessmen' John Russell and Mike Lewis to run the Club with an arrangement that has never been fully made public (if indeed there was ever a fully explicit or understood template for what was being done) leading to off and on the field problems that were not to be resolved by the three managers employed during the 2002–2003 season.

In February 2003, The Trust held one of its monthly open meetings and invited John Russell to attend and to answer some issues of concern to the members. There followed an unedifying and painful exchange in which Russell opined that he and his partner were working hard to bring success to the Club though it was being undermined 'by a sniping press and internet campaign' before leaving without giving any answers to questions posed by the assembled members.[3] The outcome was that the Trust and its 211 members took the decision to alter the aims to 'ownership of the Club'[4] a somewhat ambitious aim given the size of the membership and the £11,044 in the bank account. This meeting almost coincided with the arrival of the financial report, and the resignation of all but three members of the then Board.

Retrospectively, it is possible to say that the Trust ought to have concentrated on putting together a potential management plan, including the foundation of a community fundraising arm and executive to deal with the impending implosion that was a constant rumour during March and April 2003. However, it was decided to concentrate on growing membership so that in the event of a crisis the Trust would be better able to claim to represent a sizeable proportion of fans. Indeed it was during this period that several of those who were to play a prominent part in the immediate rescue of the Club during summer 2003 were recruited.

When the final crisis occurred, it coincided with Exeter City's relegation from the Football League in the season before its centenary as a Club. Thereafter in rapid succession came the arrest of Russell and Lewis and a request from the owner for the Trust to take over the day-to-day management of the Club. Consequently, any rational or sane implementation of Trust management was put on hold, as creditors started to appear claiming money and in many cases also seeking to seize goods. Perhaps fortuitously, the Club did not own its ground, its training pitch, or indeed the offices from which it operated on a day-to-day basis. It was a depressing and gloomy period during which ordinary Trust business was almost entirely suspended as members sought to find answers to five pressing questions;

(1) Would Exeter City be able to continue to trade as Exeter City or would there need to be the formation of a 'newco?' (And all that that entailed in terms of league status).
(2) What was the true extent of the Club's indebtedness?
(3) If the Club survived, what was to be the relationship with the new League and how would it be managed?
(4) Would the Club be able to find someone willing to manage the footballing side given the volatile nature of the finances and the relationship that the previous regime had had with the three managers used during 2002–2003?
(5) How would the Club survive from May to July without income of any kind?

It is not the remit of this paper to give answers to those questions, though they were all managed to the extent of allowing the Club to plan for life outside the Football League, but it dissipated the efforts of the Trust to put in place a management structure that would allow it to function independently of the Club Board, since in the main those running the Club at the time were those running the Trust. Possibly the only joint Trust/Club Board decisions that were agreed were that it was a hopeless proposition to run the Club on behalf of a third party, and that however horrendous the debts (and during summer 2003 the extent became clearer – though not transparent) the decision had to be taken, that whatever the eventual outcome, the Trust needed to own a majority shareholding. The Trust secretary was empowered to negotiate with the owner, and a deal was concluded in early September 2003, by which time the season was underway and the financial realities of the Club were becoming apparent, and the decision taken to enter (if possible) a Company Voluntary Arrangement (CVA), though even at this stage it was evident that expertise was needed that no-one on the Board had, and the Board resorted once again to experts to bring this into place. Even this issue left unresolved several potentially divisive matters, amongst which were:

(1) What would the relationship be with the 220 other known shareholders, many of whom had extremely small holdings?
(2) Would it be possible to implement the avowed decision not to involve the Board in football matters?
(3) How would the club manage the day-to-day issues that arose with minimal clerical staff?

With the season 2003–2004 under way with a makeshift squad, but a determined manager, the period from September to November 2003 was turbulent, the more so as plans had to be made for the CVA and the reality of what was to be undertaken became more apparent, as the forensic work of the supervisor brought to light more and more areas of concern and anxiety. Often, significant parts of the necessary paperwork were unavailable as they were being held by the police. The Trust was left to undertake massive fundraising by means of a vast number of enterprises, the two most significant of which were 'The last grand stand appeal' (Local businesses to donate £1000 without any guarantee of repayment) and 'Red or Dead' (Trust members to individually raise at least £500 each). Whilst this was put in train, a number of difficult meetings were held at which the supervisor laid out what lay ahead. These were to effectively shape the subsequent relationship between the Trust and the Club Boards.

Of particular concern were three pressing and inter-related problems, summarized to the Board in a momentous meeting on 18 November 2004. These were:

(1) In the period from 17 October 2003 to 31 May 2004, the Club showed a loss of £104,586.04.
(2) The Club had a liability to football creditors in October 2004 that totalled £390,627.
(3) Although it was reducing the wages and the euphemistically labelled 'on-costs' for the team and management as contracts were due for renewal, the outgoings on the squad for 2004–2005 totalled £720,000 – a basic figure of £570,000 swollen by appearance costs, bonus costs and on-costs.[5]

In these circumstances, and driven by the imperatives imposed upon the Club by the administrator of the CVA to appoint 'a figurehead' as Chair of the Club Board, the Trust members who had guided the Club through a difficult summer were appointed almost en bloc to the Club Board, and though these people continued to attend Trust Board meetings, their major focus was firmly focused on the survival of the Club. The Trust was empowered to continue to raise cash and to carry out such ground works and maintenance as was possible and needed.

2004 was, to say the least, a year of tribulations, but it was a year in which the change of ownership meant that the Club and Trust were able for the first time to start to lay out for fans the catastrophic inheritance of a series of previous regimes, the parlous hold on even Conference status, and probably most important of all to help persuade supporters that there was no question of spending its way to promotion. This meant living within the greatly reduced means available. However, as footballing budgets decreased to more manageable proportions, the manager was persuaded by Reading Football Club to manage their brand new Youth Academy and the club were left seeking a new incumbent for the job. The appointment of the new manager can be seen as the first evidence of the divergence of thought that has become a part of the current difficulty of sustaining a club under Trust ownership. The selection process was undertaken by those who had a perceived 'football' background, and though the Trust made an input through the presence of Trust representatives at the interviews, it was evidence that there was a divergence of opinion between the Trust and the football management about what specific functions they should be asked to fulfil.

The appointment of Alex Inglethorpe (previously Manager at non-league Leatherhead, and currently Youth Coach at Liverpool FC), was to prove even more divisive for the Trust, though ultimately not because of his ability or long-term achievements, but because he delivered the much needed financial impetus that would see the Club satisfy the aims of the supervisor of the CVA. It is well documented that wins against Grimsby and Doncaster Rovers in the FA Cup competition led to a tie with Manchester United and subsequent replay after a memorable 0–0 draw at Old Trafford. This virtually eliminated the rearranged indebtedness at a stroke (though it was to take a further 12 months for its eventual clearance – mainly due to claims on the income by some of the dissatisfied previous Board and shareholders). However, in the aftermath of these matches, the Trust relaxed its efforts in fund-raising at a time when it ought to have heeded the warning given in the summary report of the Deloitte/Birkbeck Football Governance Research Centre where they noted:

> … Supporters' Trusts themselves need to ensure that they have the appropriate mix of skills, along with the depth of skills in such key areas as fundraising, to enable them to rise to the challenge of taking and fully utilising ownership stakes in the clubs.[6]

So euphoric was the mood engendered by the relatively early payment of these debts that little attention was given to what the needs of the Trust Board would be in enabling the balanced management of all aspects of the Club. In retrospect, this was probably the period during which the divisions between the 'Footballing' and the 'Trust' management started to widen and diverge. The skills within the Trust Board had been securely focused on the need to fund raise and with the repayment clearly in sight the members started to concentrate on their own particular focus within the Club. Thus, there were those who prioritized ground redevelopment, others who were concerned with reorganizing the constitution of the Trust and another group who were anxious to reorganize 'the match-day experience'. This contrasted with the Club Board who were increasingly focused on footballing issues, and had the advantage of being able to make decisions much quicker than was possible with a Trust Board which contained 18 members and met once a month. This shift also started to divorce the Trust Board from several aspects of the Club and its funding, especially in matters concerned with Football in the Community, youth development schemes and the training ground where increasingly small group meetings were held and Club decisions made.

It is difficult to attempt to view these events without mentioning that during the period until February/March 2006 the author was both Chair of the Club Board and for some of the period Chair of the Trust as well. Another contributory factor to the schism that was developing between the two Boards was that a corporate Board decision was taken early in Trust ownership that there would be remuneration for some of those involved in the football side, whilst nobody else on either Board received any remuneration, with many members of both boards attempting to hold down full time, and often demanding day jobs. Indeed the original and well-qualified candidate as Company Secretary was living in Germany during the whole of this period.

The attentions of the non-'football' members of the Board were, in any case, fully involved in a series of events that occurred during the early part of 2005 which were causing particular problems. Most serious was the return of the FA Compliance Unit during the aftermath of the Manchester United games. It was a return visit of re-inspection. Their visits were a salutary reminder that though the immediate problems were about to be solved, the Club was far from being in good health.[7] In particular, it noted that if it were not for income from the Cup game, the Club would have been trading at a deficit only made up via the continuing income from the Supporters Trust. This income had also been the subject of a dispute by some creditors under the CVA who insisted that it should be dealt with as a 'windfall'. The unit was also critical of the way that match-day receipts were handled, of the unresolved nature of the 'loan' from the Supporters Trust, expenses paid to some players, payments to some persons (including one Director) and the relationship between one of the companies associated with Club. The directors responded on 15 May 2005, but spent much time and effort that summer trying to address the matters that were highlighted. The Club Board also continued to grapple with the difficulties of missing paperwork from the previous regime ca. season 2002–2003, pending the possibilities of much of it being used as evidence in any subsequent court hearings. Initially, there were difficulties over the compilation of accounts, but the problems later extended to issues such as contractual obligations with a whole slew of individuals and organizations. There were also resignations amongst both the Club and the Trust Directors which led to increased workloads for those still in post.

As the matters related to the completion and signing off of the CVA moved towards completion at the end of 2005, the Trust Board were approached by an individual Trust member who proposed a plan to move the Club forward when the debt was discharged. It became known as V10, and after discussion at Trust Board level, it was taken forward for scrutiny by the Club Board. Although in reality, it never existed in anything other than draft form, it was seen as a template to take the Club forward in the post-CVA era. It was decided to implement it in the early months of 2006. It entailed an addition to the Club Board and also the resignation of three other directors, with the newly elected Chair of the Trust taking over as Club Chair. This fundamentally shifted the power base away from those who had espoused the Trust 'ethos' to a group who were dominated by the 'footballing' interests, and were to be chaired by someone who was a relative newcomer to the Board of Society. From this point onward, the Trust would play a less determining role in developments that would take place at the Club. The plan was, according to the Exeter *Express and Echo*,[8] designed to give:

> ... a radical shake-up needed to enable the Club to be run more professionally and profitably. The reforms propose sweeping changes in structure, personnel and practices at St. James Park. A share issue designed to bring in more money, and overhaul of the current Board structure, a new ticketing price policy and an increase in the playing budget.

The author of the report was also quoted in another column in the same paper on the same day, saying;

> I am pleased that I am going to be here to see the plan through. I get more joy out of implementing things rather than just planning them.

Immediately before these events, the CVA was discharged. There had been disputation throughout the period leading up to it from creditors who continued to think that the eventual settlement figure of 7.2 pence in the pound (the eventual settlement figure), could and should have been higher. In the view of the Board, even before the changes in personnel, it was a unanimous view that several of the payments represented expenditure made during the previous administration that had been reckless in the extreme. Possibly the worst example was the £112,022.00 owed to Seatbookers for a computerized ticket sales system that was never installed or used, but there were others that were equally bizarre. The Supervisor's abstract of receipts and payments still makes for uncomfortable reading, and the eventual payments for legal fees and Supervisor's fee totalled nearly £58,000.

The Trust Board spent an enormous amount of time and effort during this period trying to deliver a constitution which would better reflect the needs of an organization that now had upwards of 3000 members. The protracted discussions produced a version which was intended to prompt the Board into extensions of its function and the introduction of several new parts of the organization. Ultimately, these discussions were to introduce two aspects of policy that were to affect the efficiency and working of the Trust Board. The first was a change of Trustee tenure from 12 to 8 years (and subsequently to 6) and the eventual introduction of a Trustee Code of Conduct aimed at discouraging ongoing debate by Trustees in open forums. Indeed in two later related cases, in 2010 and 2012, Trustees were to be firstly suspended from the Board for a period of three months, and in the second to resign, feeling that in view of promises that were made in his election manifesto his position was untenable.

The eventual changes were summarized in an article which appeared in 'Supporters Direct' in March 2007.[9] In all 12 aims for the Trust were laid out under the headings Governance, Membership, Communications and Fundraising. Of interest, with regard to the future 'health' of the Trust were:

> (4) To develop and maintain a governance framework as the Club's majority shareholder in cooperation with the Club.
>
> ...
>
> (9) To set a financial structure that provides more long-term funding for projects.
>
> ...
>
> (12) To enhance the long term financial security of Exeter City AFC Ltd by moving the company status to that that of a CIC (Community Interest Company) and moving the Trust to full ownership of Exeter City AFC Ltd by the Company undertaking a new share issue.

During the protracted discussions about these plans, the Club had another change of manager, with Alex Inglethorpe moving to take charge of Tottenham Hotspur Youth Team. The appointment of his replacement, Paul Tisdale (previously in charge of Team Bath – a side that made history by being the first university team to make the first round of the F.A. Cup since the nineteenth century), further emphasized the growing schism between the Club and Trust Board as the majority vote in his appointment was made by a non-Board member who was the Director of football. In the event, the Club Board were exonerated in their decision by three seasons of football which probably represents the most successful period in the Club's history. Two appearances at Wembley in successive years, followed by promotion back to the Football League and a subsequent promotion to League One, meant that the Trust Board was lulled into relative inactivity with the security of growing attendances and increasing membership of the Trust. By the end of season 2007–2008, the Club Board had also grown in size with members of the Board of Society being convinced that the acquisition of specific skills on the Club Board would be a positive, even though it meant a diminution of the power of the Trust Directors on the Club Board, which further eroded the ability of the Trust to directly control decisions made in its name by the Board. The new Club Board members had, in the main, little background in the ethos and original aims of the Trust.

The growing divide between the two Boards is illustrated by correspondence that took place during the Trust Board's discussions with the administrators of the Community Interest Company organization. The Trust Board instigated fact-finding investigations with a view to possibly changing the status of the organization from an Independent Provident Society to that of a Community Interest Company (CIC). The discussions by the Trust Board involved a discussion with Supporters Direct and also the solicitors Bates, Wells & Braithwaite. It was proposed to hold a Trust meeting to lay out the issues for members. It elicited the following email from a Club Board member[10] circulated to a number of those involved, including Supporters Direct:

How many more times do I have to say that?

(1) It is not the Trust's decision about converting the Club to a CIC.
(2) There are far more tricky and linked issues to solve as part of this.

If we are truly to benefit the Club as a whole, not one part of what seems to be someone's tangential agenda.

If you knew the risks you were putting the Club at by behaving in the way you are over this I would hope you would think again. If I/We need to make a public statement to make this clear, I will.

In early 2008, the members of the Trust Board were circulated with a discussion paper written by one of the Trustees.[11] It laid out, under five headings, a rationale with regard to future management of the Club. These were 'Context for Change - The current role of the Chairman of the Football Club - A future role for the Chairman of the Football Club - Role of Trustees as Club Board Directors - Way forward'.[12] In itself its content was fairly non-contentious. It laid out as future roles:

• Responsibility for overall strategy.
• Producing a 5-year and annual business plan in partnership with the Directors.

- Working in partnership with the Chairman of the BOS (with) regard to strategy.
- Acting as a figurehead for the Football Club.

However, the document went on to lay out that the Club should have an Independent Chair, the rationale being explained thus:

> The reason that I am proposing an independent Chair is that I feel we need to look for skill sets outside the conventional football world, namely experience in business and strategic development, an understanding of human resources, finance, and if possible previous experience of the role on non-executive role/directorship, accountability and reporting to shareholders. *Ideally someone with experience of partnership working including knowledge and experience of the public sector.* [author's italics]

What the document proposed was (however inadvertently) to further reduce the influence of the Board of Society and Trustees. It also brought to a head a simmering situation in which the chair of the Trust, as Chair of the Club was made to feel undervalued and unwelcome (especially on match days) by the Club Board. The situation was discussed in full at a meeting of the Trust in early July 2008. It focused on a Board meeting held on 30 June 2008 where, as the minutes relate (and the events were verified by another Director)[13]:

> She was subjected to a verbal attack … with the strong implication that that there was the need for a new Chair, especially now that we are back in the Football League. The discussion covered aspects of the 'establishment' resistance to Trust ownership and female directors.

The eventual outcome was a meeting on 7 July 2008 with a view to establishing a framework for a 'Joint Board Arrangement'. The summary document, written by one of two Trust Board members, is explicit about the reasons for the need for a joint board. It notes[14]:

> It was agreed that there is currently an unsatisfactory atmosphere between the Boards and members discussed some issues that have caused concerns in recent times. It was agreed that for the SJBC to succeed there is a need to build a climate of mutual trust, confidence and respect between the two boards and their members.

In the next paragraph, the document notes:

> BOS rules and the links between the BOS Chair and the Chair of the football club were reviewed, and the difficulties associated with the joint position that is placed on one person was considered. Clearly the current situation is far from ideal and there needs to be work on identifying alternative arrangements *which may be beneficial to the Trust, Club and individual workloads.* (Authors italics)

These events ultimately led to the resignation of the Chair, and replacement by a new Chair who also attempted a 'streamlining' of the working of the Trust Board by setting up working parties, nominally independent of Chair's control, and inaugurated bimonthly meetings to notionally draw together the strands of those working groups.

At the same time, a group worked towards the introduction of an independent chair for the Club Board. When the appointment was agreed and made it was not with the unanimous approval of the Board of Society. The individual appointed had many of the attributes laid out above, but had not until that time been either a member of the Trust, or apparently had much interest in the ethos and ideas that lay behind the supporter ownership model, and as a former civil servant was brought in on the basis of expertise in project-managing. In the event, it again weakened the power of the Trust Board in relation to the Club Board.

By the time of the elections to the Trust Board in 2011, several of the longer standing members were either ineligible to stand again for the Trust Board or had decided that the conditions under which they were being forced to operate, especially the 'Chatham House Rules' that were imposed on the Trust Board, made continuing membership difficult to the point of impossibility. This situation was further exacerbated by potential candidates having their attempted nominations ruled to be invalid. Indeed in 2012 no less than four candidates were debarred by failing to comply with the requirements of the rules. It was also noticeable that the Chair of the Club failed to turn up to either the Annual General Meeting or the subsequent General Meeting, despite it being a requirement of the rules of the Trust that they should attend.

The aim of this paper has been threefold; Firstly, it has aimed to view ways in which the basic Trust management model has been adapted, adopted and modified in usage, and ways in which it has mutated over a period of 10 years. Secondly, to provide an overview of what has been achieved, abandoned and altered within the structure of the club since 2003. Thirdly, the difficult conclusion attempts to provide a meaningful personal overview of the current reality of the Trust management model in practice at Exeter City Football Club.

That the Club survives 10 years after its near demise and has regained its place in the lower reaches of the Football League is testimony to an enormous amount of effort and hard work that has been expended. That it survived the financial crisis that surrounded its last decade of the pre-Trust control period owes a great deal to substantial fundraising, but possibly as much to the success in the FA Cup in 2004–2005. It seems unlikely that without the pay days that the competition provided the position could have become as stable as it did in that period.

Whether the Trust model that was envisaged by the 211 members who decided to change the aims of the Trust to 'owning' the Club bears any relationship to the model as it now operates is much more doubtful. The model that was proposed in the initial constitution was a one-size-fits-all one that laid out a legal framework to work within, but also had legal and practical facets that never quite fitted a football club dragging around so much historical 'baggage'. There are several exemplars that should be mentioned here. Firstly, the shareholding issue has never been resolved. Notwithstanding the changes brought about as a result of the 2011 Companies Act, there are still over 200 individual shareholders who have never been asked to contribute anything to the Club whilst the organization that holds just over 50% of the shareholding has contributed about £1 million to sustain the Club. Nor, to date, has there been any meaningful attempt to utilize shares held in what is termed the suspense account, or raise money through a share issue as was suggested in the 2006 plan. The Club Board has consistently shown a marked reluctance to discuss this situation or to engage meaningfully with planning for such a scheme.

The original Trust members might also have difficulty in reconciling the way that the 'football' side of the Club has taken a dominant role in determining issues such as expenditure and planning, whilst at the same time failing to provide a template for progress, with a feeling that there is little vision about matters of deep concern to the fans, especially with regard to the social context in which the Club exists and its wider position within the communities with which it interacts. Thus whilst there has been constant expenditure on pitch quality, the playing squad and attempts to resolve the ongoing issue of an ageing stadium infrastructure, there has been little improvement that might have been expected within a fans' owned Club.

Thus, communication with the fan base has remained poor, the commercial arm of the Club, especially, has failed to solve many of the issues associated with merchandise which has often been of poor quality, with issues of availability an ongoing problem through a series of suppliers, which has extended to the Club shop. Other pressing issues have been regarded as the preserve of the Trust, and whilst the Club Board has paid lip service to the notion of fan ownership they have done little to inculcate some of the matters recognized in the summary report of *The Social and Community Value of Football*,[15] such as:

- Professional and accessible ticketing,
- club history and culture projects, and
- events, festivals and flag days to help reinforce these social and cultural attachments.

As has been noted, it is unfortunate that the current Club Board has moved away from drawing its members from within the Trust membership, and has over the last seven years decreased (whether intentionally or not) the power of the Trust Board by increasing the number of members so that the Trust cannot, without difficulty, within the Board structure, impose its own views and values.

It has also been noticeable that several roles within the Club hierarchy have grown without much evident input from the Trust Board. Thus, the current (acting?) CEO does not appear to have either a job description, or apparently any mechanism by which his performance can be judged and managed. Nor had the Board of Society (at least until 2011) made any attempt to introduce targets and objectives for Club Board members, and it is notable that the Director with responsibility for Human Resources was unpaid, whilst salaries for the CEO, the club Manager and the Director of Football (who is not a member of the Club Board) have been decided within the Club Board structure. These matters are of particular concern against a back-drop of falling revenue and growing expectations, all the more so against the changing nature of the financial relationship between the Trust and the Club.

From the point of view of Trust members, this is perhaps the most visible shift in the changing nature of how the Club is run. For the first eight years of the Trust majority ownership HMRC questioned, for each financial year, the relationship between the accruing 'loans' made by the Trust to the Club and also the nature of the sum in question. This was satisfied by an annual 'letter of comfort' given by the Trust to the accountants stating that the nature of the loan meant that it would not be recalled. As this 'loan' approached £1 m further payments have been turned, by the Board, without wider consultation with the membership, into 'contributions'. This change has increased unease within a group of Trust members that this meant a sea change in future relationships, especially at a time when the Trust has been conferring over increasing minimum payments for membership.

After 10 years of Trust ownership, it is also evident that the imperatives that drove the early Trust members to seek ways of supporting, then owning, the Club, and putting in place a structure that would enable this to happen, are being replaced by a group of supporters who have little understanding of these early motives, nor much interest in being involved, other than peripherally, in running the Trust. For the most part, their yardsticks are the success that was achieved by the Club with two successive promotions and whether the team on the field plays attractive 'winning' football.

For many fans, this is perceived as a lack of judgement, and a move away from the initial aims and objectives of the Trust as manifested in 2003. There is also a growing imbalance between the ordinary fans and those presently running the Club. Where the reasons for this lie, and whether that fracture is a permanent one is for future writers on the subject, with further knowledge, to determine. With an increasing paucity of attractive, winning football, especially at home, there are calls (mainly in the social media) for an injection of cash into the club and its infrastructure ('the white knight syndrome' that Exeter City so clearly doesn't have) and a dissatisfaction in apparently being unable to bring through its own players from the youth scheme in sufficient numbers to continue being a 'selling' club. As yet these calls are from a minority of members and fans and they have yet to manifest themselves in a full-blown howl of criticism such as there was during the year of the previous management, but the recent resignation of three more Trust Board members does suggest that questions need to be asked to redress the balance between the Trust and those running the Club.

The advantage of 40 years of watching and supporting Exeter City Football Club is the knowledge that, like so many other lower league and non-league clubs, there will be troughs and depressions, vagaries and pitfalls, and mixed in with them, times of inordinate joy, pleasure and ecstasy. Ten years ago, Exeter City Football Club had the opportunity to shape a future free from the whims, personal preferences and personal machinations of a single owner. To date, that initial surge of hope has been replaced by the stark reality of funding lower league football and also a host of missed opportunities to permanently build something that was better placed to provide for the aims of those who founded the Trust. That it appears not to have yet done so is down to a mixture of mistakes, lack of judgement and an apparent unwillingness to grapple with some of the more difficult to solve, and indeed as yet unresolved, issues that still haunt the Club after 10 years.

Disclosure statement

No potential conflict of interest was reported by the author.

Notes

1. Exeter City Supporters Trust Website: 'Our History'.
2. FA Compliance Report: Football Association/Exeter City Football Club, 2003, Internal Document.
3. Minutes of Extraordinary Meeting of Exeter City Trust, 18 February 2003, held at St. James Centre ECFC.
4. Exeter City Supporters Trust Website 'Our History'.
5. Minutes of the Exeter City Board meeting, 18 November 2004. Paper circulated to Board Members.
6. Michie, Oughton, and Walters, *The State of the Game – The Corporate Governance of Football Clubs* (Deloitte/Birkbeck Football Governance Research Centre, 2006), 58.
7. Football Association Compliance Unit Report, 2005. Internal Document; The issues and recommendations here are published under the terms contained in 1.7 of the introduction of the report 24.05. This acknowledges that the Directors 'shall be entitled to deal with any information of the Club which may be contained in this report in such a manner as is deemed appropriate'.

8. Exeter Express and Echo Saturday 4 February 2006, 62.
9. Supporters Direct, *The Supporters Trust Initiative* 2, March 5, 2007, 6–7.
10. EMail from ECFC Director Paul Morrish to various parties. Author's personal copy.
11. Morrish – Undated email – Personal copy of email circulated by Morrish ECFC Director.
12. T. Badcock, 'An Alternative Club Board Model – A Discussion Paper', 10 June 2008.
13. Exeter City Football Club Supporters Trust Board minutes. Reference B 08/025, 18 May 2008.
14. Exeter City Football Club Supporters Trust Memo; 'Progress Report on the Standing Joint Board Arrangement 7 July 2008'.
15. Supporters Direct: *The Social and Community Value of Football, Summary Report*, 16 June 2010.

References

Exeter City Supporters Trust. 'Our History'. http://ecfcst.org.uk/about-the-trust/our-history/.
Michie, J., C. Oughton, and G. Walters. *The State of the Game: The Corporate Governance of Football Clubs 2006* (Research Paper no. 3). London: Deloitte/Birkbeck Football Governance Research Centre, 2006.
Supporters Direct. *The Supporters Trust Initiative* Issue 2, March 2007.
Supporters Direct. *The Social and Community Value of Football: Summary Report*. June 2010.

Fighting strategic homophobia in football

Roy Krøvel

Homophobia among certain men could be understood as a reactionary form of social resilience, insofar as such resilience can work against adaptation and social transformation. Resilience is again closely related to the concept of 'sustainability'. Many fans position the expression of negativity towards gays as a heroic struggle against 'political correctness' and in defence of freedom of thought and speech. But it should also be seen as a strategic action to manipulate the feelings of opponents in order to win. In a time of global hyper commodification, the paramount goal of winning stimulates strategic actions that contribute to shaping norms and values.

Introduction

Why is it so difficult in Norway to eradicate homophobia in football? Among many football fans in this country, a public display of negativity towards homosexuality is still not uncommon. This is particularly puzzling when seen in relation to other sectors of Norwegian society, including some other sports. The persistence of negative attitudes towards male homosexuality among certain male football fans hints at causes with deep sociocultural roots. It is also an indicator of how football has played an important role in producing and reproducing negative attitudes towards male homosexuality.[1] Internationally, several studies of football fans have found that these attitudes are rapidly shifting and[2] only a minority of fans now express homophobic views.[3] Cleland highlights the important changes that have been taking place since 1990, but also stresses the need for continued efforts to support homosexual players.[4]

Little research has been done, however, to understand how and why negative attitudes and homophobia still seem to be reproduced by some Norwegian football fans. This article contributes to a deeper understanding of the reproduction of negative attitudes towards homosexuals in football by investigating media and football fan communication online. The research builds first on quantitative methodologies in order to analyse trends in online discourses on homosexuality, before moving on to critically examining the evolving discourse of anti-homosexuality among football fans online.

By focusing on fan communication online, the article connects with previous studies which have found that the anonymity of the Internet permits certain men to employ a homophobic and sexist discourse.[5]

Literature review and background

The sustainability discourse draws on ecosophy and ecology and owes much to deep ecologists such as Arne Næss and Sigmund Kvaløy.[6] For Næss and Kvaløy 'sustainability' was closely related to diversity and resilience. The term, however, has increasingly come to mean exploiting natural and human resources while maintaining a supposed balance. The term has thus gradually become associated with a conservationist or conservative discourse of anthropocentric exploitation of resources in order to maintain a supposed status quo. In this article I understand 'sustainability' not as 'conservation' but, rather, as closely related to radical perspectives on 'resilience'. Greater resilience is associated with the ability to self-organise, and associated with social learning as part of a process of adaptation and transformation.[7]

In the heat of the moment, football fans can be heard hurling all kinds of abuse at opponents and their fans. Some of it will probably be found to be shocking by an unknowing passer-by. Most of it, however, should not be taken at face value, but should rather be seen as a form of ritual acted out in the carnivalesque atmosphere of the football ground.[8] From a carnivalesque perspective, abuse aimed at opponents is used asa tool for subversion and liberation from the dominant norms of communication and style.

There is an inherent danger in taking football fans too seriously. In fact, a recent study of fans of British association football found homophobia to be rapidly decreasing.[9] Nonetheless, we need to recognise that homosexuals have over the years been subjected to all kinds of exclusion, discrimination and violence in a myriad ways.[10] The current backlash against homosexuality in countries as diverse as Jamaica, Uganda, Russia and India demonstrates just how deeply rooted negative attitudes against homosexuality are in many societies and cultures.[11]

This article employs a critical realist perspective on homosexuality, drawing in particular on Bhaskar[12] and Sayer.[13] From a critical realist perspective, a social phenomenon (for instance, homosexuality) can be real even though it is not a visible part of a particular society's discourse. While some political leaders find it opportune to claim that 'we don't have homosexuals' here, this should not be taken to mean that homosexuality does not exist. It should rather be interpreted as yet another attempt to make homosexuality invisible.[14] Critical realists insist that a reality exists outside and independently from our discourse about it, 'while fully acknowledging that the only access we have to this reality lies along the spiralling path of appropriate dialogue or conversation between the knower and the thing known'.[15] Structural violence, for instance, can make a real phenomenon invisible.

Following Bhaskar's advice to start discourse analysis from the identification of a social problem, this article starts from the assumption that the apparent invisibility of male homosexual footballers is a social problem. Football is the most popular sport among Norwegians. Approximately 10% of the population is registered with the Football Association of Norway. When close to 500,000 Norwegians play football regularly, it should be safe to assume that thousands belong to sexual minorities. Quite a few female footballers have come out of the closet, plus one or two male players in the lower divisions, but no male players in the top divisions have made such a move. Some structural mechanism must be in play to exclude and discriminate against sexual minorities in men's football.

A growing body of literature helps us to understand some of these culturally embedded structural mechanisms that have historically functioned to exclude, discriminate and make homosexuals invisible in Norway.[16] At least two structural mechanisms must be considered in order to understand this aspect of Norwegian football: on the one hand, stereotypes and negative attitudes that tend to make football an unattractive or unpleasant place for homosexuals which causes gay players leave football; on the other hand, mechanisms that tend to discourage homosexuals from being open about their sexual preferences.

Anthropological research on gender and homosexuality has highlighted the diverse and intricate ways that gender and sexuality are shaped by cultural processes. Homosexuality and homophobia are visible in different ways in different societies.[17] Thus, negative attitudes and homophobia should be understood in their particular historical and sociocultural context. In this article, then, I set the interpretation of recent expressions of negativity towards homosexuals in Norway within a Norwegian framework with its particular social and cultural environments, in addition to interpreting such expressions as contributors to the production of a Norwegian social and cultural environment.

Compared to other countries, Norway can be considered a relatively liberal country. This does not mean that homosexuality is, or has always been, accepted. There is a long tradition of discrimination and exclusion of homosexuality in Norway, as is evident in the large number of recently published life stories and biographies of gay activists.[18] According to some media studies, however, important changes have taken place over the last two or three decades: 'Whereas before they [the attitudes of discrimination and exclusion of homosexuality] were totally absent from the media, they are being regularly featured in contemporary media'.[19] A majority of Norwegians, for example, no longer openly express negative attitudes towardshomosexuals.[20] However, men tend to have a more negative perception of sexual minorities – particularly of men who have sex with men – than do women. A similar split is visible in sport itself. No Norwegian top sportsmen have come out as gay, whereas a significant number of female world-class athletes have done so. Marketing research demonstrates beyond doubt that coming out of the closet for these women athletes has not had a negative effect on their popularity or market value.

Although the carnivalesque aspect of fan culture must be considered when trying to understand abusive taunts against the opposition, other possibilities should also be assessed. A range of researchers employ Baudrillard's radical postmodernism to explore 'cultural identities within the context of consumerism and intensive media simulation'.[21] Research on emergent trends in fan culture can similarly be grounded in critical perspectives on consumerism and the rapidly expanding global economy of football, for instance as proposed by Adorno and Habermas.[22] Habermas contends that modern sports can have profound influence over the ethical and moral dimensions of our social lives. According to this author, modern sport inspires strategic action that undermines mutual understanding between social agents, thus 'entailing one agent manipulating others, as if they were mere objects to be treated instrumentally'.[23] Other researchers have built on Adorno to critically examine modern sport as it has 'become debauched as it is subsumed to the logic of the marketplace'.[24]

A particularly interesting phenomenon in this regard is the development of parallel discourses on ethics. While the opponents are judged by one set of norms and values, a privileged position is consciously or unconsciously sought for oneself or one self's community. Doidge, for instance, has demonstrated how inter club rivalry is fuelling player abuse and racism in Italian football.[25] African footballers in particular have become targets of abuse from rival supporters as fans adapt to an increasingly multicultural environment. Racist taunts from fans, however, should not be uncritically taken as expressions of racism. The same fans who in one moment shout racist abuses against an opponent can in the next celebrate the brilliance of one of their 'own' African players. The action is strategic in the sense that it is intended to hurt and, thus, manipulate the feelings of particular players on the opposing team, with the intention of negatively affecting their performance.

This type of abuse puts affected players in a bind. A player who complains will run the risk of revealing that the abuse is having an effect on his or her performance. According to Butler, 'linguistic injury appears to be the effect not only of the words by which one is addressed but the mode of address itself, a mode – a disposition or conventional bearing – that interpellates and constitutes a subject'. 'To be injured by speech is to suffer a loss of context, that is, not to know where you are'.[26]

While some of these theoretical perspectives might look grim, the article also builds on earlier research on Norwegian football fans which has demonstrated that communities of fans do have the potential to react and adapt to global flows by 'questioning borders of identity and community, inviting in new members and reconstructing imagined communities, while facilitating the de-ethnicisation of the local community'.[27] Norwegian football fans have sometimes been first movers as local communities react and adapt to a changing environment.[28]

Methodology

This article builds on results produced mainly through qualitative research, although the first step of the research was to produce a statistical overview of some trends in the public debate on football and homosexuality. This part of the research, however, is intended to indicate some main trends in the discourse on homosexuality in Norway. First, using the World Values Survey, an online database on 'values and cultural changes in societies all over the world',[29] I produced a data-set on Norwegian attitudes on homosexuality from 1982 to 2007, in addition to a comparative data-set on attitudes on homosexuality between 57 countries in 2006/2007. In the quantitative part of the research, Retriever, a Norwegian media survey service, is employed to search for keywords in newspapers and online media over the last 30 years. The keywords identified were 'homosexuality', 'homosexuality and football', 'minorities and football', 'racism and football', 'homophobia' and 'homophobia and football' (the search was performed in Norwegian).These two quantitative methodologies helped to produce an understanding of sociocultural change in the perception of homosexuality in Norway.

The next step was to select a few particularly interesting recent media articles that triggered online debates on homosexuality and football. Based on the quantitative part of the study, 12 articles published online were selected: '– De er redde for å bli Norges første fotball-homo' (on TV2.no), 'Ut av fotballboblen' (*Bergens Tidende*), 'Lettere å stå frem som homofil fotballspiller' (*Aftenposten*), 'Hylles for at han står frem som homo – Premier League' (*VG*), 'Homofile i fotballen' (fotball.no – Norges Fotballforbund), 'Hitzlsperger synes synd på Alex etter homo-utspill' (*VG*), 'Fotball-support' (*LLH*), 'Fotball – homofobiens siste skanse' (*Bergens Tidende*), 'Flertall av fotballfans vil støtte homofile spillere' (forskning.no), 'Flere homofile topp-fotballspillere' (Gaysir.no), 'Er én av svært få åpent homofile fotballspillere' (Ringblad_files) and 'Eg likar ikkje football' (Norsk Skoleforum). The selection was not meant to be representative. It contained a diversity of media outlets: the main Norwegian commercial television channel (TV2); the largest online newspapers (vg.no and aftenposten.no); a major regional newspaper (*Bergens Tidende*); online sites for national gay and homosexual organisations (gaysir.no and LLH); and a site dedicated to science news (forskning.no). The purpose was to capture the greatest possible variety of arguments and counter arguments in the current debate among football fans.

Each of these articles triggered a diversity of responses from readers. The main purpose of this part of the research was to analyse the arguments made by readers in the commentary fields and see if and how the arguments formed patterns relating to each other. The third step of the research was a close reading of online debates among fans of Vålerenga and Rosenborg, two of the most popular clubs in Norway. We will return to these disputes in more detail later. In total, approximately 700 individual contributions to these debates were studied.

Shifting values and attitudes

The World Values Survey documents development and change in a large number of values and beliefs in 87 countries from 1981 to the present. The survey indicates significant changes in attitudes regarding homosexuality. In Norway, the changes have been more radical than in most other countries. In 2006 (the most recently published survey), only in Sweden, Andorra and Slovenia did respondents have a more tolerant view of homosexuality than in Norway. Forty-four per cent of Norwegians found homosexuality 'always justifiable' while 6% answered 'never justifiable'. According to the World Values Survey, then, negative attitudes against homosexuals are still held by a significant number of people in Norway, but significantly fewer than in France, Great Britain, USA, Spain and other countries with which Norway is often compared. More importantly, Norwegians expressed a considerably more liberal view of homosexuality after 1990.

In the early 1980s, things looked different. A large majority of Norwegians held negative attitudes about homosexuals, with a mere 19% finding homosexuality 'always justifiable'. According to the World Values Survey, negative attitudes dominated throughout the 1980s, but changed markedly between 1990 and 1996 when, for the first time, more respondents answered that homosexuality was 'always justifiable' than 'never justifiable'. A cultural change had happened, quite abruptly, over a few years in the 1990s, from predominantly negative to positive views of homosexuality.

The shift in attitudes is even more marked in the media discourse on homosexuality. Until the early 1970s, 'invisibility' dominated, and only a handful of newspaper articles mentioned the issue at all – and when they did the context was almost always negative.

However, the media should not be seen as merely reflecting values and attitudes in society. The relationship is much more complex than that. Most Norwegians, for instance, did not personally know openly gay men or women. What they knew or believed to know about homosexuality was mainly built on second-hand sources such as the media. From this perspective, the media coverage from the mid-1970s is interesting as it perhaps contains the seed that later contributed to the shift in values and attitudes. For the first time, openly homosexual men and women were sometimes represented as fully human with intelligence, knowledge, feelings, dreams, successful careers and so on. They certainly paid a high price for coming out of the closet, as is well documented in a number of autobiographies from this period. Nonetheless, from a media studies perspective, it is notable to see a new media discourse appearing, at least as a possibility for framing homosexuality: gays and lesbians as 'normal' or 'just like you and me'. A key aspect of many of the articles from the 1970s and 1980s is precisely to represent gays and lesbians as 'not so different after all'. This was, for many Norwegians, the first time they had encountered information and knowledge that made it possible to reflexively reconsider values and attitudes regarding homosexuality.

The emergent frame of homosexuality as 'normal' was followed by the emergence of another and gradually more important frame: the anti-discrimination frame. It is noteworthy, however, that the media discourse about discrimination and the stigmatisation of gay and lesbians gained momentum much later than the struggle against the discrimination of women and ethnic minorities.

These struggles were also played out in football. The struggle to end discrimination against women in football had already begun in earnest in the 1970s and was still visible in the media discourse throughout the 1990s and later. In the 1990s, a similar type of discourse, this time against racism, developed both inside and outside football. A new term, 'homophobia', started to appear regularly in the Norwegian media in the mid-1980s in the context of growing public concern about HIV and Aids. It was mainly used, however, by activists and public intellectuals who sought to counteract a possible backlash against gay men. For instance, six articles in two leading national newspapers (*VG* and *Aftenposten*) had already used the term 'homophobia' by 1984. It is a sign of a deeper shift in the media discourse which was to come a few years later.

Gradually, more and more of the discourse on homosexuality came to be framed as struggle against discrimination, exclusion and violence against gays and lesbians. Negative attitudes towards gay and lesbians became news in themselves. From 1996 to 2014, I found 496 newspaper articles employing the term 'homophobia' to discuss discrimination and the exclusion of gay and lesbians in football. Every third article in Norwegian newspapers that used the term 'homophobia' related to football.

These, then, are some of the overall trends in the values and attitudes towards homosexuality found in Norway over the last decades. This historical sociocultural context is necessary to make sense of the resilience of anti-gay attitudes in football.

Emergent structures of negative attitudes

A qualitative analysis of homosexuality and football, focusing on texts and debates, can contribute to a deeper insight into the persistent homophobia. First, a paradox needs to be discussed: on the one hand, a large number of texts refer to various types of displays of negative attitudes towards homosexuality – for instance abusive taunts during games or posts online. Some also implicitly display such feelings in the online debates among fans. On the other hand, very few fans are willing to support their negative attitudes by presenting arguments.

In the fans' discourse, then, displays of negative attitudes towards homosexuality in football are found in numerous ways, but seldom in the form of deliberate argumentation. A few examples will help to clarify this point. First, on several occasions players in the Premier League acted out emotions in a way that could be or was interpreted as anti-gay. In one incident a high-profile player responded to abuse from fans of the opposing team by making gestures usually understood to mean 'homos' – here with disparaging intent. Both fans and the media well understood the intended meaning. The player, however, later denied having had negative opinions about gays and lesbians and said it had not been his intention to offend gays or lesbians by making those particular gestures. Nonetheless, the gestures, as interpreted by the audience and the media alike, built on a historically situated understanding of homosexuality. In this particular understanding, calling someone 'homo' was interpreted as an insult.

Another example is from the online forum Kjernen, an independent group of supporter of Rosenborg. In 2011, a public debate broke out after some Rosenborg fans shouted 'homo' to a Molde player. Juliee commented:

> What is going on? Many are criticising Kjernen in Adressa[30] and in other debate forums. I feel that Kjernenis creating a good atmosphere, and people should accept a few 'naughty' comments and proclamations. I see nothing wrong in shouting 'I hate Molde city', or in something as innocent as 'homo'.

In this and a large number of similar comments, supporters implicitly employed arguments inspired by the gay and lesbian movement. Many in that movement have struggled to 'take back' or reclaim the term 'homo', and many young homosexuals are proud to identify themselves as such, sending a message that there is nothing shameful in it. From such a perspective, Juliee could be right to say that the word 'homo' has been emptied of negative connotations. Or, as Juliee puts it rhetorically: 'Is it now also wrong to shout 'hetero'?'

From a critical realist perspective, words like 'homo' do not contain fixed or essential meanings, but are socially constructed. 'Homo' can indeed convey different meanings, depending on the situation and the sociocultural context of sender and receiver. The online reactions to the use of 'homo' in this specific context indicate that many football fans, drawing on their particular horizons of knowledge, do interpret this particular use of 'homo' as loaded with negative connotation. The majority of responses indicated that most fans understood the use of 'homo' in this context as an attempt to upset or offend players in the opposite team – as Andreas J. put it: 'Calling player "homo" is just sad'.[31]

The two views discussed above are not necessarily mutually exclusive. In football, it is possible to imagine someone who does not have 'anything against homosexuals' using the term 'homo' strategically to achieve a certain goal, for example, contributing to the victory of their home team. In this case 'homo' can be used to psych out opponents because it is expected to evoke memories of earlier stigmatisation and abuse, which in turn can cause or awake negative feelings. The many meanings of 'homo' are not only those that are socially constructed here and now by those present at the moment of communication, but are also embedded in historically situated structures of meaning. The meanings we make today of 'homo' are structured by a sociocultural history of meanings.

A similar example is found in a dispute among members of Klanen; supporters of Vålerenga, after a jury of 'prominent lesbians and gays' awarded Klanen the prize 'hetero of the year' at the 'Gay Gala 2011'. Klanen won the award for, *inter alia*, wielding a rainbow flag bearing the slogan 'all colours are beautiful' at Vålerenga matches.[32] 'Ronny La Rock' responded to a news item about the award: 'Well, well. What to say? Not "fucking gay", in any case'.[33] 'Cyrus' follows up: 'I can say something, Ronny... At least better to be "hetero of the year" than "homo of the year". OK, so now it's out there☺.' Ronny again: 'Heh heh. I totally agree with that!'

In this opening salvo, we already get a glimpse of two recurrent themes in the debates on homosexuality among football fans: first, value hierarchies – hetero is better than homo; second, the pleasure of saying what ought not to be said. It is as if Ronny and Cyrus are already looking forward to the many angry replies they know will be coming. 'Loco' is critical: 'In what way is it better?' ('hetero' better than 'homo'). 'Lame Duck' is one of several who want to explain why 'hetero' is better: 'In today's society "homosexuality" is related to something negative. Not much negativity is connected to "heterosexuality" … You can like it or hate it. But it is a reality'. Lame Duck is quick to mention that 'one of his best friends' is homosexual. 'Ronny La Rock' also claims to have 'homosexual friends' who don't mind his finding homosexuality 'distasteful'.

In many of the anti-gay posts online we see a similar pattern in which the authors position themselves in contrast and opposition to anticipated counter arguments. In order to better understand the emergent homophobic discourse, we first need to explore a couple of the most common and effective counter arguments against homophobia in football.

Criticising homophobia to construct an inclusive community

'Oslo 3' responds furiously to the negative comments on homosexuality on www.kla nen.no: 'Yes, we are the club for all, and I mean ALL.'[34] A large number of comments are posted online in support of an inclusive community with no discrimination based on race, gender or sexual preferences. Andreas J., referring to the dispute over anti-gay taunts from Rosenborg supporters against Molde players, states: 'What if someone from Rosenborg was gay and learns that some members of Kjernen use it to intimidate one of the players we hate the most? How would he then feel about coming out? And what if someone in Kjernen is gay? How easy will it then be for him to be himself?'[35]

I have previously published articles on how Klanen and Kjernen deal with racism, ethnic stereotypes and religious discrimination.[36] In one instance, negative comments on a player with an African background in another team were met with arguments relating those comments to a player with a similar background in the supporter's own team. If such comments about African-Norwegians in opposing teams were to be accepted, they must also be accepted when made about 'our' players, the counterarguments went on. But negative comments on the background and identity of 'our' players cannot be accepted because they will hurt someone we feel for. Therefore, according to the emerging consensus among supporters of the teams I studied, 'we' cannot make such comments about 'them' either.

This process can be seen, drawing on Archer, as a collective reflexive dialogue on the universality of norms and values.[37] It demonstrates that communities of supporters sometimes do have the capacity to critically examine norms and values in order to reconstruct and adapt them to a new context. In these examples, the role model, preferably a player from the team the supporters follow plays a pivotal part in the process of reconstructing norms and values. What would he [the player in these examples] feel? Departing from this question which calls for empathy and reflection, supporters have been seen transcending the local and partisan, rewriting narratives of belonging and reimagining communities and boundaries.

In these cases, this line of argumentation which leads to a reconstruction of norms of values, overcame all opposition and ended up virtually without opposition. The hegemonic view among these supporters embraces ethnic diversity and tolerance although it does not mean that there is no racism among football fans in Norway today. The disputes on homosexuality stand in stark contrast, however, to the inclusive discourse on ethnic minorities and diversity. One explanation for this difference is the lack of openly gay players in male football. While calls for empathy and solidarity with players affected by racist taunts could be related to someone known and cherished, the calls for empathy with possibly homosexual players continued to be abstract and distant, and for that reason appealing to empathy with gay players did not have the strength to unleash a similar reflexive dialogue on the existing norms and values regarding homosexuality.

Positioning homophobia as a struggle to uphold the freedom of expression

Those who defend homophobic taunts respond to their critics by defending it as a legitimate way of expressing true and real feelings. According to many, such taunts happen spontaneously and should not be judged by the same standards as carefully considered statements. Typical arguments are: 'This is only the way I feel'; 'You can't be blamed for the way you feel'; 'This is just who I am'. With characteristic irony, one member of Kjernen writes: 'And in the terraces, the lack of common courtesy is revealed in a number of ways. I propose that someone takes this seriously and educates the members in the correct ways to act out behaviour'.[38]

This line of argument builds on the notion that feelings are natural and spontaneous – they come from inside, and need to be expressed impulsively. Feelings and emotions locked up inside will sooner or later lead to emotional or psychological problems.

However, another dimension appears a little later in the dispute: the 'rights' of those who belong to the minority that 'hates homosexuality'. 'Ronny La Rock' complains about politicians who want to make people change their minds about racism and homophobia. 'Why should anyone be happy because Tin Tin, Barbar and Pippi Longstocking will be sued for racism?' He places the dispute on homophobic taunts within a meta-narrative where it is no longer tolerated to use words like 'negro' or 'dago'. Others blame an omnipresent 'political correctness'. In a fascinating change of roles, 'Ronny La Rock' reminds other members of Klanen that Vålerenga is the club for everybody, including 'those who hate homosexuality'.

The explicit statements of hatred have led the editors of the online forum to exclude 'Ronny La Rock' which, again, leads to a fresh debate. 'Usbenga' notes the paradox in excluding someone for expressing the opinion that homosexuality should not be tolerated. According to Usbenga, something that began with arguments in favour of tolerance ended up in intolerance. For this reason, according to supporters, homophobia must be accepted in order to guarantee diversity of thought and freedom of expression.

It is perhaps best understood as a parody of the parodies recommended by Judith Butler to resist and subvert the power structures which regulate our lives. In this case, however, it is not the minorities that seek to ridicule normative cultural expressions and performances, but homophobes who ridicule the argument of diversity by employing it against those who want to stop discrimination, exclusion and abuse.

The meanings of homophobia

Football supporters can be the first members of local communities to embrace change and reconstruct norms and values – for instance to integrate migrants and newcomers. However, as homophobia in football demonstrates, they can also be the last. The question remains: why football?

Many Norwegian fans do not express any negativity towards homosexuality. In fact, most fans seem to support the inclusion of gays and lesbians in football, and reject the taunts and statements that gays and lesbians are likely to experience as anti-gay. These supporters, however, belong to a subculture with its own normative cultural expressions and performances. It is, to a large extent, socially constructed as a contrast to the 'imagined docile majority', the majority of people who are seen as living conventional lives. The members of Klanen and Kjernen understand fan culture as different, untamed, unconventional, uncontrollable, rebellious, spontaneous, expressive and passionate. Consequently, fans should be expected to be naughty, and to use language that others may find inappropriate and offensive.

In this article, I have shown that a significant shift in norms and values regarding homosexuality in Norwegian society has taken place since the 1990s. Nowadays, negative attitudes against homosexuals are seldom expressed publicly, while a number of respected public figures have come out of the closet. Football seems to be the last bastion of resistance where a significant subculture of homophobia continues openly to reproduce a homophobic discourse.

I have argued that this discourse, while claiming to be spontaneous and non-deliberate, builds on and contributes to reconstructing historically produced structures of homophobia. From studies of collective resilience, we know that resistance to change can sometimes succeed in impeding adaptation to change and social transformation. Collective resilience can hinder necessary action and produce a social reaction. In this case, the subculture of football fandom is sometimes seen as being in opposition to hegemonic social norms and values. Shocking behaviour, including homophobic taunts, contributes to producing identities and a community imagined to be untamed by power structures and 'political correctness'. Reflection on the issue of homophobia reveals the reasons a critical approach to 'sustainability' is necessary. Many other ecophilosophers continued to advocate 'non-violence' and to emphasise social harmony. Kvaløy, in contrast, argued that the conflict model of social change should guide activism: 'I'm all for polarisation. That's the only way we get deeper discussions'.[39] Resilience studies have also demonstrated that collective processes of autonomous organising and self-learning have sometimes led to the breakdown in cascades of existing structures of norms and values.[40] In the case of homophobia, the counter arguments have not succeeded in the same way and to the same degree as in the case of racism. This is most likely due to the lack of role models which hinders feelings of empathy and global solidarity.[41]

Another urgent question for research is related to the conditions in football and football fandom that make the reproduction of homophobia possible. I would suggest that Adorno and Habermas did anticipate some of the current troubles in football in their critique of modern sport subsumed under a capitalist logic. Today, more than ever, winning is the ultimate goal that will bring both pride and money in professional football. Players and fans alike are tempted to break norms and regulations if this is seen to further the campaign to subdue the opponent.

A large number of fans in this study claim to have nothing against homosexuals, claiming to have a number of homosexual friends. They argue that homophobic taunts are part of a strategic communication that will psych out the opponent, a device that can be used against the opposition. Others have previously noted that some men use strategic sexism to sustain masculinity, or strategic racism 'to turn the race to their advantage'.[42]

While the large majority of supporters continue to struggle for a more inclusive fan culture, some football fans have found a space where they can reproduce oppressive power structures and coldly try to use them to help their team to win.

Disclosure statement

No potential conflict of interest was reported by the author.

Notes

1. Caudwell, '"Does Your Boyfriend Know You're Here?" The Spatiality of Homophobia in Men's Football Culture in the UK'; Free and Hughson, 'Settling Accounts with Hooligans: Gender Blindness in Football Supporter Subculture Research'.
2. Anderson, 'Masculinities and Sexualities in Sport and Physical Cultures: Three Decades of Evolving Research'.
3. Campbell et al., 'Sport Fans' Impressions of Gay Male Athletes'; Kian et al., 'Homophobic and Sexist yet Uncontested: Examining Football Fan Postings on Internet Message Boards'; Cashmore and Cleland, 'Fans, Homophobia and Masculinities in Association Football: Evidence of a More Inclusive Environment'; and Cashmore and Cleland, 'Glasswing Butterflies: Gay Professional Football Players and Their Culture'.
4. Cleland, 'Association Football and the Representation of Homosexuality by the Print Media: A Case Study of Anton Hysen'.
5. Kian et al., 'Homophobic and Sexist yet Uncontested'; Cashmore and Cleland, 'Fans, Homophobia and Masculinities in Association Football'; Cleland, 'Discussing Homosexuality on Association Football Fan Message Boards: A Changing Cultural Context'.
6. Nielsen et al., *A New Agenda for Sustainability*; Bhaskar, Naess and Høyer, *Ecophilosophy in a World of Crisis: Critical Realism and the Nordic Contributions*.
7. Krøvel, 'The Role of Conflict in Producing Alternative Social Imaginations of the Future'.
8. Brown, *Fanatics: Power, Identity and Fandom in Football*; Giulianotti, 'Football and the Politics of Carnival: An Ethnographic Study of Scottish Fans in Sweden'.
9. Cashmore and Cleland, 'Fans, Homophobia and Masculinities in Association Football: Evidence of a More Inclusive Environment'.
10. Mondimore, *A Natural History of Homosexuality*; Halperin, *How to Do the History of Homosexuality*; Duberman, Vicinus, and Chauncey, *Hidden from History: Reclaiming the Gay and Lesbian Past*; Miller, *Out of the Past: Gay and Lesbian History from 1869 to the Present*; Aldrich, *Gay Life and Culture: A World History*; and Abelove, Barale and Halperin, *The Lesbian and Gay Studies Reader*.
11. Itaborahy, *State-Sponsored Homophobia. A World Survey of Laws Criminalising Same-Sex Sexual Acts between Consenting Adults*, ILGA Report (The International Lesbian, Gay, Bisexual, Trans and Intersex Association); Chiu, Blankenship and Burris, 'Gender-Based Violence, Criminal Law Enforcement and HIV: Overview of the Evidence and Case Studies of Positive Practices', *Working paper prepared for the Third Meeting of the Technical Advisory Group of the Global Commission on HIV and the Law*.
12. Bhaskar, *Scientific Realism and Human Emancipation*.
13. Sayer, *Why Things Matter to People: Social Science, Values and Ethical Life*.

14. Baks and Malecek, 'Synopsis on Homophobia and Discrimination on Sexual Orientation in Sport'.
15. Wright quoted in Allen, *Ernan Mcmullin and Critical Realism in the Science-Theology Dialogue*, 7.
16. Jordåen, 'Frå Synd Til Sjukdom?: Konstruksjonen Av Mannleg Homoseksualitet I Norge, 1886–1950' (Hovedoppgave i historie, Universitetet i Bergen, 2003); Kristiansen, 'Kjærlighetskarusellen: Eldre Homoseksuelle Menns Livsfortellinger Og Livsløp I Norge'; and Stenvoll, *Politisk Argumentasjon: En Analyse Av Norske Stort-ingsdebatter Om Seksualitet Og Reproduksjon 1945–2001*, Rapport (Rokkansenteret: Trykt Utg.).
17. Gutmann, 'Trafficking in Men: The Anthropology of Masculinity'; Boellstorff, 'Queer Studies in the House of Anthropology'; Parker, 'Masculinity, Femininity, and Homosex-uality'; and Pharr, *Homophobia: A Weapon of Sexism*; Anderson, *Forestilte Fellesskap*.
18. Eide, 'Bekjennelser Og Kompromisser. Homofile/Lesbiske/Skeive Medieerfaringer', *Norsk medietidsskrift* 21, no. 3 (Forthcoming); Kristiansen, *Masker Og Motstand – Dis-kré Homoliv I Norge 1920–1970*.
19. Johnsen, 'Hyllet Etter "Vielse": En Studie Av Homofile I Populærjournalistikken'; Mühleisen and Røthing, *Norske Seksualiteter*.
20. Anderssen and Slåtten, 'Holdninger Til Lesbiske Kvinner, Homofile Menn, Bifile Kvinner Og Menn Og Transpersoner (Lhbtpersoner). En Landsomfattende Spørreun-dersøkelse'.
21. Giulianotti, *Sport and Modern Social Theorists*, 226.
22. 'Introduction', in *Sport and Modern Social Theorists*, ed. Giulianotti; Morgan, 'Habermas on Sports: Social Theory from a Moral Perspective', ibid., ed. Giulianotti.
23. Edgar, 'Sport as Strategic Action: A Habermasian Perspective'.
24. Sewart, 'The Commodification of Sport'.
25. Doidge, '"If You Jump up and Down, Balotelli Dies": Racism and Player Abuse in Italian Football'.
26. Butler, *Excitable Speech: A Politics of the Performative*, 4.
27. Krøvel, 'New Media and Identity among Fans of a Norwegian Football Club'.
28. 'Communicating in Search of Understanding. A Case Study of Fans, Supporters and Islam', in *We Love to Hate Each Other: Mediated Football Fan Culture*, ed. Roy Krøvel and Thore Roksvold.
29. World Values Survey, 'World Values Survey. The World's Most Comprehensive Investi-gation of Political and Sociocultural Change'.
30. A local newspaper.
31. J. Andreas, 09.05.2011 .
32. Ola Nymo Trulsen, 'Vålerenga-Klanen Er «Årets Hetero»,' NRK.
33. The ensuing debate can be accessed on http://forum.klanen.no/archive/index.php/t-25171.html.
34. http://forum.klanen.no/archive/index.php/t-25171.html.
35. J. Andreas, 'Title of Weblog'.
36. Krøvel, 'New Media and Identity among Fans of a Norwegian Football Club'; 'Com-municating in Search of Understanding. A Case Study of Fans, Supporters and Islam'.
37. Archer, *Conversations About Reflexivity*.
38. fettgeiser, 'Re: Bortetur: M***** – Rbk [Re: Bolgebah]', Kjernen, http://www.kjer nen.com/forum/ubbthreads.php/ubb/showflat/Number/214558/fpart/16.
39. Orton, *Conflict and Marxism in Deep Ecology*, Green Web.
40. Grove, 'On Resilience Politics: From Transformation to Subversion'; Goldstein, 'Collaborating for Transformative Resilience', in *Collaborative Resilience: Moving through Crisis to Opportunity*.
41. Bhaskar, *Scientific Realism and Human Emancipation*.
42. Haney-López, *Dog Whistle Politics: How Coded Racial Appeals Have Reinvented Racism and Wrecked the Middle Class*, 48.

References

Abelove, Henry, Michèle Aina Barale, and David M. Halperin. *The Lesbian and Gay Studies Reader*. London: Taylor & Francis, 2012.

Aldrich, Robert. *Gay Life and Culture: A World History*. London: Thames & Hudson, 2006.

Allen, Paul Laurence. *Ernan Mcmullin and Critical Realism in the Science-Theology Dialogue* [in English]. Aldershot [u.a.]: Ashgate, 2006.

Anderson, Benedict. *Forestilte Fellesskap*. Oslo: Spartacus Forlag, 1996.

Anderson, Eric. 'Masculinities and Sexualities in Sport and Physical Cultures: Three Decades of Evolving Research.' *Journal of Homosexuality* 58, no. 5 (2011): 565–78.

Anderssen, Norman, and Hilde Slåtten. *Holdninger Til Lesbiske Kvinner, Homofile Menn, Bifile Kvinner Og Menn Og Transpersoner (Lhbtpersoner). En Landsomfattende Spørre-undersøkelse*. Bergen: Avdeling for samfunnspsykologi, Universitetet i Bergen, 2008.

Andreas, J. *Re: Bortetur: M***** – Rbk [Re: Bengal]*. Ed. Kjernen. Trondheim: Kjernen, 2011.

Edgar, Andrew. 'Sport as Strategic Action: A Habermasian Perspective.' *Sport, Ethics and Philosophy* 1, no. 1 (2007): 33–46.

Archer, Margaret S. *Conversations About Reflexivity*. Oxon: Taylor & Francis, 2009.

Baks, Ben, and Sabine Malecek. *Synpsis on Homophobia and Discrimination on Sexual Orientation in Sport*. Amsterdam: Amsterdam European Gay and Lesbian Sports Federation, 2004.

Bhaskar, Roy *Scientific Realism and Human Emancipation*. London: Routledge, 2009.

Bhaskar, Roy, Petter Naess, and Karl Georg Høyer. *Ecophilosophy in a World of Crisis: Critical Realism and the Nordic Contributions*. London: Taylor & Francis, 2011.

Boellstorff, Tom. 'Queer Studies in the House of Anthropology'. *Annual Review of Anthropology* 36 (2007): 17–35.

Brown, Adam. *Fanatics: Power, Identity and Fandom in Football*. London: Routledge, 2002.

Butler, Judith. *Excitable Speech: A Politics of the Performative*. New York: Routledge, 1997.

Campbell, Jamonn, Denise Cothren, Ross Rogers, Lindsay Kistler, Anne Osowski, Nathan Greenauer, and Christian End. 'Sport Fans' Impressions of Gay Male Athletes.' *Journal of Homosexuality* 58, no. 5 (2011): 597–607.

Cashmore, Ellis, and Jamie Cleland. 'Fans, homophobia and masculinities in association football: evidence of a more inclusive environment'. *The British Journal of Sociology* 63, no. 2 (2012): 370–87.

Caudwell, Jayne '"Does Your Boyfriend Know You're Here?" The Spatiality of Homophobia in Men's Football Culture in the UK'. *Leisure Studies* 30, no. 2 (2011): 123–38.

Cleland, Jamie. 'Discussing Homosexuality on Association Football Fan Message Boards: A Changing Cultural Context'. *International Review for the Sociology of Sport* 50, no. 2 Published online before print February 18, 2013 (2013): 125–40.

Cleland, Jamie 'Association Football and the Representation of Homosexuality by the Print Media: A Case Study of Anton Hysén'. [In English.] *Journal of Homosexuality* 61, no. 9 (2014): 1269–87.

Cashmore, Ellis, and Jamie Cleland. 'Glasswing Butterflies: Gay Professional Football Players and Their Culture'. *Journal of Sport & Social Issues* 35, no. 4 (2011): 420–36.

Doidge, Mark. '"If You Jump up and Down, Balotelli Dies": Racism and Player Abuse in Italian Football'. *International Review for the Sociology of Sport* 50, no. 3 (March 2013): 249–64.

Duberman, Martin B., Martha Vicinus, and George Chauncey. *Hidden from History: Reclaiming the Gay and Lesbian Past*. New York: Penguin Group, 1990.

Eide, Elisabeth. 'Bekjennelser og kompromisser: Homofile/lesbiske/skeive medieerfaringer [Confessions and compromises: Gays / lesbians / queer media experiences]'. *Norsk Medietidsskrift* 21, no. 3 (2014), 209–25.

fettgeiser. 'Re: Bortetur: M***** – Rbk [Re: Bolgebah]'. Kjernen. http://www.kjer nen.com/forum/ubbthreads.php/ubb/showflat/Number/214558/fpart/16.

Free, Marcus, and John Hughson. 'Settling Accounts with Hooligans: Gender Blindness in Football Supporter Subculture Research'. *Men and Masculinities* 6, no. 2 (2003): 136–55.

Kian, Edward M., Galen Clavio, John Vincent, and Stephanie D. Shaw. 'Homophobic and Sexist yet Uncontested: Examining Football Fan Postings on Internet Message Boards.' *Journal of Homosexuality* 58, no. 5 (2011): 680–99.

Giulianotti, Richard. 'Football and the Politics of Carnival: An Ethnographic Study of Scottish Fans in Sweden'. *International Review for the Sociology of Sport* 30, no. 2 (1995): 191–220.

Giulianotti, Richard. *Sport and Modern Social Theorists*. New York: Palgrave Macmillan, 2004.

Giulianotti, Richard. 'Introduction'. In *Sport and Modern Social Theorists*, ed. Richard Giulianotti, 1–9. New York: Palgrave Macmillan, 2004.

Goldstein, Bruce Evan. 'Collaborating for Transformative Resilience'. In *Collaborative Resilience: Moving through Crisis to Opportunity*, ed. Bruce Evan Goldstein, 339–58. Cambridge: MIT Press, 2012.

Grove, Kevin. 'On Resilience Politics: From Transformation to Subversion'. *Resilience* 1, no. 2 (2013): 146–53.

Gutmann, Matthew C. 'Trafficking in Men: The Anthropology of Masculinity'. *Annual Review of Anthropology* 26 (1997): 385–409.

Halperin, David M. *How to Do the History of Homosexuality*. Chicago: University of Chicago Press, 2004.

Haney-López, Ian. *Dog Whistle Politics: How Coded Racial Appeals Have Reinvented Racism and Wrecked the Middle Class* [in English]. New York: Oxford University Press. 2014.

Itaborahy, Lucas Paoli. *State-sponsored Homophobia. A World Survey of Laws Criminalising Same-sex Sexual Acts between Consenting Adults*. ILGA Report. The International Lesbian, Gay, Bisexual, Trans and Intersex Association, 2012

Chiu, Jessica, Kim Blankenship, and Scott Burris. 'Gender-Based Violence, Criminal Law Enforcement and Hiv: Overview of the Evidence and Case Studies of Positive Practices'. *Working paper prepared for the Third Meeting of the Technical Advisory Group of the Global Commission on HIV and the Law*. New York: Global mmission on HIV and the Law. United Nations Development Programme, 2011.

Johnsen, Jørgen Thune. 'Hyllet etter "vielse": En studie av homofile i populærjournalistikken' [Celebrated after gay "marriage": A study of homosexuals in popular journalism]. Master thesis, The University of Bergen, 2011.

Jordåen, Runar. 'Frå synd til sjukdom?: Konstruksjonen av mannleg homoseksualitet i Norge, 1886–1950' [From sin to disease?: Construction of male homosexuality in Norway, 1886-1950]. Hovedoppgave i historie, Universitetet i Bergen, 2003.

Kristiansen, Hans W. *Kjærlighetskarusellen: Eldre homoseksuelle menns livsfortellinger og livsløp i Norge* [The Love Carousel: Older homosexual men's life stories and lives in Norway]. Oslo: Sosialantropologisk institutt, Universitetet i Oslo, 2004.

Kristiansen, Hans W. *Masker og motstand – Diskré homoliv i Norge* [Masks and Resistance - Dicrete gay life in Norway]. Oslo: Unipub, 2008.

Krøvel, Roy. 'New Media and Identity among Fans of a Norwegian Football Club'. *First Monday* 17, no. 5 (2012).

Krøvel, Roy. 'The Role of Conflict in Producing Alternative Social Imaginations of the Future'. *M/C Journal* 16, no. 5 (2013).

Krøvel, Roy. 'Communicating in Search of Understanding. A Case Study of Fans, Supporters and Islam'. In *We Love to Hate Each Other: Mediated Football Fan Culture*, ed. Roy Krøvel and Thore Roksvold, 249–64. Gøteborg: Nordim, 2012.

Miller, Neil. *Out of the Past: Gay and Lesbian History from 1869 to the Present*, New York: Vintage Books, 1995.

Mondimore, F.M. *A Natural History of Homosexuality*. Baltimore: Johns Hopkins University Press, 1996.

Morgan, William J. 'Habermas on Sports: Social Theory from a Moral Perspective'. In *Sport and Modern Social Theorists*, ed. Richard Giulianotti, 173–86. Basingstoke: Palgrave, 2004.

Mühleisen, Wenche, and Åse Røthing. *Norske Seksualiteter*, Oslo: Cappelen Akademisk, 2009.

Nielsen, Kurt Aagaard Bo Elling, Erling Jelsøe, and Maria Figueroa. *A New Agenda for Sustainability*. Burlington, VT: Ashgate Publishing, 2012.

Orton, David. *Conflict and Marxism in Deep Ecology*. Green Web. http://home.ca.inter.net/~greenweb/Conflict_and_Marxism_in_Deep_Ecology.html.

Parker, Richard. 'Masculinity, Femininity, and Homosexuality'. *Journal of Homosexuality* 11, no. 3–4 (1986): 155–63.

Pharr, Suzanne. *Homophobia: A Weapon of Sexism*. Berkeley, CA: Chardon Press, 1997.

Sayer, R. Andrew. *Why Things Matter to People: Social Science, Values and Ethical Life*. Cambridge: Cambridge University Press, 2011.

Sewart, John J. 'The Commodification of Sport'. *International Review for the Sociology of Sport* 22, no. 3 (1987): 171–92.

Stenvoll, Dag. *Politisk argumentasjon: En analyse av norske stortingsdebatter om seksualitet og reproduksjon* [Political argumentation: An analisis of Norwegian Parliamentary Debates on Sexuality and Reproduction]. Rapport (Rokkansenteret: Trykt Utg.). Bergen: Stein Rokkan senter for flerfaglige samfunnsstudier, 2003.

Trulsen, Ola Nymo. 'Vålerenga-Klanen Er «Årets Hetero»'. NRK. http://www.nrk.no/kultur/vif-klanen-hedra-av-homsene-1.7454002.

World Values Survey. *World Values Survey. The World's Most Comprehensive Investigation of Political and Sociocultural Change*. The World Values Survey Association. Accessed September 1, 2014.

Sustaining health improvement activities delivered in English professional football clubs using evaluation: a short communication

Andy Pringle, Daniel Parnell, Zoe Rutherford, Jim McKenna, Stephen Zwolinsky and Jackie Hargreaves

It has been suggested that football and communities are inextricably linked. Healthy lifestyles are an important component in maintaining the sustainability of local communities, not least, because a convincing evidence base supports the holistic benefits that can be derived from health-enhancing behaviours, such as regular physical activity. As such, efforts to promote health improvement through sport and physical activity include those interventions delivered in professional sporting settings. Johnman and colleagues (Johnman and Mackie, 'The Beautiful Game') have heralded sports clubs as important venues for the delivery of health improvement interventions for a range of groups across local communities. This includes health improvement activities delivered in professional football club community schemes. While exemplary practice shows how health improvement programmes can be implemented and evaluated, our experience and engagement with professional football club community schemes supports the notion that more needs to be undertaken to help clubs develop monitoring and evaluation strategies in order to assess the impact of their health improvement programmes. In our short communication, we share our plans for helping two professional football clubs develop their monitoring and evaluation strategies for their community health promotion programmes. Potential outcomes emerging from this process are twofold. (1) To help club community schemes in-build and sustain monitoring and evaluation practices within their future health improvement provision. (2) To use the impact and process outcomes emerging from programme evaluations, to successfully secure the necessary resources to sustain future health improvement activities for their local communities. Outcomes emerging from this study will be of interest to football clubs and evaluators alike, as they seek to develop evaluation strategies for their health improvement programmes.

Introduction

Johnman and colleagues have heralded sports clubs as important venues for the delivery of health improvement interventions for a range of groups across local communities.[1] This includes health improvement activities delivered in professional football club community schemes. While good practice shows how health improvement programmes can be evaluated,[2] our experience and engagement with professional football clubs supports the notion that more needs to be done to help clubs develop monitoring and evaluation strategies in order to assess the impact of their health improvement pro-grammes. In our short communication, we share our plans for helping the community trusts at two professional football clubs to develop their monitoring and evaluation strategies to sustain their health promotion programmes for their local communities.

Background

Healthy and physically active lifestyles are an important component in maintaining the sustainability of local communities, not least because it allows individuals to both maintain and improve their health and well-being holistically.[3] Chronic health conditions such as cancer, cardiovascular disease, diabetes and chronic respiratory disease are now grouped together in public health terms as 'non-communicable dis-eases' (NCDs).[4] NCDs are thought to be responsible for 36 million deaths world-wide each year and evidence shows that around 9 million of these occur before the age of 60.[5] Modifiable lifestyle risk factors underpinning NCDs include physical (in)activity, poor diet, smoking and the harmful use of alcohol.[6] These behaviours can bring about metabolic/physiological changes that increase the risk of developing NCDs including, elevated blood pressure, overweight/obesity, hyperglycaemia and hyperlipidaemia.[7] However, even relatively small changes in these modifiable life-style risk factors can produce substantial health benefits,[8] nevertheless, eliciting and sustaining long-term positive change in these behaviours remains problematic from a public health perspective. At the heart of many of these conditions, is physical (in) activity, where a convincing evidence base supports the role of a physically active lifestyle in the prevention and management of a range of chronic conditions.[9] It is then no surprise that the delivery of healthy and physically active lifestyles through health improvement activities is an important part of health policy.[10] Despite such efforts, the 'health of the nation' remains a cause for concern[11]; as does the need to effectively intervene with health improvement opportunities, including those involv-ing the promotion of sport and physical activity.[12]

With those thoughts in mind, a leading Public Health body, the Royal Society for Public Health, have recently suggested that the

> settings in which we live, offer huge opportunities and threats to our health. Address-ing the social determinants of health is vital to improving population health and reduc-ing health inequalities, and utilising a settings based approach to health provides a way to promote, improve and protect health and tackle health inequalities.[13]

Further, interventions that create and strengthen a diverse natural social network, increase the availability of social support and reduce negative interactions are thought to be a 'best buy' for public health.[14] Therefore, as football and community settings are thought to be inextricably linked,[15] and with health and lifestyle inter-vention of uppermost importance,[16] recreational and professional football settings offer one way for connecting individuals and communities with health improvement opportunities.[17] This not only includes priority groups from across the life course (*children/young people, adults and older adults*),[18] but also those groups who have been labelled 'hard to engage' or 'unreached' (*including, men, substance users and individuals who do not access conventional health services*).[19]

Indeed, the appeal of sporting clubs has been heralded as having important potential global appeal in public health terms.[20] As a result, locating health improve-ment programmes within professional football clubs offers both participants and providers with an attractive proposition and a setting for reaching communities with health behavioural change programmes.[21] The reasons appear to be multifaceted and include the reach of the activity itself (i.e. the *football//sport*), the affiliation of individuals to their football club, the venue of delivery and processes by which health programmes are packaged and delivered.[22] Moreover, it should be noted that the appeal of football clubs as settings for health improvement extends to fans, non-fans and in some cases, those who are not interested in football,[23] thus supporting the potential reach suggested by Johnman, Mackie and Sim.[24]

The importance of selecting the most appropriate settings for reaching individuals with health improvement opportunities takes on an added importance when the current fiscal climate is considered. Reductions in funding for health services[25] and local authority-led sport[26] mean there is not only increased competition on those football clubs attempting to secure funding, but arguably a heightened need to demonstrate how such resources are being used effectively and efficiently. In demonstrating such an impact, the requirement to evaluate has never been more important.[27] This is not only about demonstrating the impact and the process by which programmes have their effect,[28] but also securing the necessary resources to help sustain effective programmes once the initial 'start up' funding has become extinct.[29]

Notwithstanding existing good practice in both research and evaluation,[30] our experience of reviewing funding applications for football-led health improvement programmes and dialogue/interaction with clubs, led us to conclude, that more needs to be undertaken to help some football clubs community schemes develop effective and workable evaluation strategies. In doing so, ceasing the potential to demonstrate the impact of their programmes and the ability to secure resources to sustain their provision in this area, and this provides the 'raison detre' for our study. We feel that this paper will be of interest to our colleagues in professional football club community schemes that face the prospect of developing and implementing evaluation strategies either independently or in partnership evaluation arrangements with their 'local evaluators'.[31] Moreover, our paper compliments the available guidance that helps to shape evaluation strategies and which provides important practical advice and considerations for those working in this important area.[32]

Funding context

In providing the context to our work, we provide the following information and background. Subsequent to an internal funding call to develop sustainable practice in local communities from the Higher Education Innovation Fund (HEIF) and with the support of the Leeds Beckett University Enterprise Team, our researchers were successful in securing funding of around £10,000. Our funding proposal outlined how we would use the resources secured to: (1) help professional football clubs develop effective (*valid, reliable and practical evaluation strategies*) for their health improvement programmes and (2) help sustain the future delivery of effective health improvement programmes offered by professional football clubs to their local communities. While we received funding to support the work described here, there are examples where we have performed similar evaluations using institutional resources and for the purposes of research and investigation.[33] As such, this raises the possibility that clubs might work with their local university department or other local evaluators in a similar fashion.

Intervention context

As part of our existing partnerships, we are in this example, working with the community trusts of two professional clubs located in the English East Midlands, where we have been developing evaluation strategies for their health improvement programmes. We use the following sections to introduce the clubs, examples of their health improvement programmes and examples of their evaluation needs. Our first club is Burton Albion FC, where our collaboration with their Community Trust extends several years through co-author Parnell. Examples of earlier outcomes emerging from this partnership have been published elsewhere.[34] Our second partner is Notts County in the Community (*the community arm of Notts County Football Club*), where our previous alliance extends through co-author Rutherford. Examples of outcomes emerging from this alliance have similarly been published elsewhere in the literature.[35] Both of these organizations are registered charities and are attached to their respective professional football clubs. In both cases, programmes are packaged and delivered using all the branding of the football clubs and we offer some examples of the interventions being delivered and how they aspired to meet the needs of participants in local and neighbouring communities.

Understanding the importance of promoting physical activity across the lifespan, we provide three examples from Burton Albion. Our first example 'Head for Goal' aims to promote positive mental well-being for young adult men 16–24 years, through a weekly programme of football delivered at local community venues.[36] Secondly, 'Golden Goal' is a programme of physical and social activity delivered for 'older-adults' 55 years and older.[37] Thirdly, the club have an extensive physical education and school sport programme that delivers an extended school curriculum for young people.[38] Similarly at Notts County interventions are delivered across the lifespan. Firstly, recognizing the increase and impact of overweight and obesity as a health improvement issue, the Notts County's, 'Motivate' programme offers both adult men and women with a programme of weight management classes. Activities are delivered by club coaches and nutritionists in local community venues within the City of Nottingham. Secondly, continuing with the adult population, 'Energise' is an example of an on-site, 18-week workplace health and well-being programme, delivered to employees during lunch breaks and evenings, using safe, effective and enjoyable physical activity. Activity sessions are delivered by FITC's experienced coaches. Thirdly, recognizing the importance of the health of young adult men, 'On The Ball', is a health improvement programme that has engaged over 250 young men over the last five years. The programme provides weekly football sessions for a core of 40 participants who continue to activity sessions at a local community facility. In both clubs, the need to evaluate impact and process outcomes was fundamental to demonstrating intervention effect and for sustaining health improvement provision in the future.

Our team has worked with both clubs to establish how sustainable and workable evaluation strategies can be developed and implemented for their health improvement programmes. In describing this process, we have used components of 'intervention mapping' as an organizing framework.[39] Intervention mapping is an iterative process that has been used for planning and implementing health improvement programmes and their evaluations. We have used elements of this framework to both organize and report the development and implementation processes (i.e. *evaluation needs, planning and implementation*) that we put in place when developing the monitoring and evaluation strategies for health improvement programmes.

Evaluation needs and planning

Through our collaborations, the two participating clubs expressed the need for support with the development of their monitoring and evaluation strategies. Following existing practices for developing evaluation strategies of health improvement programmes of this nature,[40] our evaluation team met the management at the respective clubs to discuss their current projects and their monitoring and evaluation activities. This included the project outcomes, current monitoring and evaluation processes, barriers to performing evaluation activity, service delivery arrangements and the stakeholders involved in the interventions. Following this, a second meeting was set up with the practitioners specifically involved in the delivery of interventions described previously (i.e. *the coaches*).These discussions also considered future funding targets and shared partnership opportunities, alongside broader engagement with the club's stakeholders through their local steering groups. During these discussions, staff expressed their 'evaluation needs'. While these were not all prevalent in our two clubs, examples of the type of 'needs' which emerged included capacity (i.e. *time to procure and develop evaluation protocols, collect analyse and report data*), commitment (i.e. *pressures on staff to deliver interventions leaving less time for evaluation activities*) and capability (i.e. *skills to develop evaluation methodologies and instrumentation, implementing data protection protocols, obtain research ethics clearance and develop protocols for collecting and analysing data and interpreting and writing up findings/results from evaluations*).[41] Using information from these discussions, the research team developed evaluation strategies, which were bespoke to the respective interventions and provided support to help address some of the needs expressed by staff. These were prepared with the purpose of measuring and evidencing the impact of the respective health improvement programmes.

Staff at the clubs, also highlighted the need to demonstrate how programmes' impacted on the health profiles of local priority groups. For adult programmes, we advised on the following impact outcomes which have been used in the evaluation of community-based health improvement programmes, including those delivered in football-led settings.[42] These measures included, the collection of the following data and helped to establish the reach of programmes: Demographic profiles, (*including age, gender, ethnicity and post-code*); affiliation to football/or football clubs (i.e. *football fan, non-fan, fan of host club, fan of other clubs*); if the activity adopted was new or replacement activity (i.e. *if the adopted physical activity programme was a substitute or a brand new activity*) and lifestyle profiles (including *physical activity, healthy eating, smoking, alcohol and body mass index*).These were supplemented by general measures of health status used elsewhere in the literature[43] along with use and uptake of primary health care services (i.e. consulting GP/Primary Care Services), as appropriate.[44]

Our experience of collecting this information – pre–post-intervention – has been helpful in: (1) building up a profile of the reach of programmes when recruiting local populations, including 'priority groups' and their baseline health profiles and (2) confirming the extent to which such provisions have been effective in facilitating 'change' in health status/profiles. In our two examples, measures were adapted to suit the target audience; including young people, older people or those constituents who are known to experience difficulties engaging evaluations.[45] Along with these adapted measures, instrumentation and protocols were developed that were more suited for securing data on impact outcomes among these groups (i.e. *when assessing changes in the PA levels of young people*). Moreover, the basic service level evaluation described above can be supplemented with additional evaluation activities as required by particular clubs. For instance, where appropriate, the self-report measures outlined can be supplemented with objective measures to assess impact outcomes. Supported by trained researchers, we have been able to offer specific cardiovascular fitness tests; tests for functional capacity; accelerometry to assess the frequency, intensity and duration of physical activity being performed; measurements of overweight/obesity and cardiovascular risk (e.g. *waist circumference, % body fatness, blood pressure and cholesterol*).[46]

In our discussions, staff expressed the value of (1) obtaining insights into how interventions have an impact and (2) the participant's perspectives of engaging programmes. With those thoughts in mind, participant case studies are often required within funding applications and/or reports to funders, as well in the preparation of publicity for programmes. As such, and in order to investigate the process by which interventions achieve their impact outcomes,[47] we raised the feasibility of performing interviews with key stakeholders involved in the interventions. In doing so, we aspire to secure the perspectives of the key participants involved in the interventions. This is being undertaken using procedures adopted for process evaluations in football-led health improvement programmes[48] and national community physical activity programmes.[49] However, by way of example, interviews or focus groups aspired to investigate participant's experiences of attending interventions and what key design factors were important in facilitating 'change' across the behavioural continuum. That is, what key design characteristics (i.e. *the programme offered, the process of delivery, the promotions and publicity used, the place and people involved in the delivery and the price of the programme*) were important/less important in helping people *learn about, start, stick* and *retrial* interventions as appropriate.[50] Prior to any data collection, the research team secured university research ethics clearance for the evaluation activities to take place.

Following the development of the evaluation packages, the research team also organized project specific training days in order to build capacity within existing practitioners at club level who would become 'leads for evaluation'. This training typically lasted one day and was delivered on site and in advance of the evaluations commencing. The training covered a range of topics including ethics, consent (i.e. *informing participants of their rights when engaging evaluations*), data protection (i.e. *keeping evaluation data secure*), administration of the instrumentation (i.e. *how to introduce the evaluation to participants and collect data*) and handling of the data (i.e. *setting up spread sheets for inputting evaluation data*) as performed in evaluations of football-based health improvement programmes.[51] The research team provided ongoing support through meetings, phone calls and/or video calls up during data collection and quality assurance checks of the data were performed at regular intervals. As is standard practice in guidance[52] and prior to the commencement of data collection, instrumentation was piloted and the application of instrumentation practiced in line with public health guidance on evaluation.[53]

Evaluation implementation

On commencement of the interventions, a member of the research team attended and supported baseline data collection in a collaborative and supportive way to ensure correct techniques were being performed. In line with guidance issued elsewhere,[54] regular communications took place between the research team and the 'lead evaluator' (*at the club*) and this continued throughout the lifespan of the health improvement project, as recommended elsewhere.[55] Furthermore, in line with evaluation needs expressed by the staff, the research team would later provide analysis and reports on the data collected. Using a framework from the literature,[56] our participating clubs have the opportunity to utilize the impacts of their respective evaluation activities in a number of ways. Firstly, from a formative perspective, clubs can identify and take remedial action on parts of the programme which are not working as well and actions can be taken to refine provisions. Similarly, evaluations provide an opportunity to confirm which parts of the intervention are working effectively and the reasons for this. Secondly, where appropriate, clubs have the opportunity to develop knowledge and the necessary skills and expertise to in-build/procure monitoring and evaluation activities as part of their future practice. Thirdly, from an ethical perspective, to establish if interventions are effective and that individuals are experiencing the anticipated benefits of attending health improvement programmes. Finally, sustainability, to use the impacts emerging from these evaluations to make the case to local commissioners/national funding agencies to sustain future provisions. Given the competition for scarce public health resources, the outcomes emerging from well thought out evaluation designs have the potential to make a convincing case for future funding, a key evaluation need expressed by staff in the clubs.

Conclusion

We set out to outline the importance of helping professional football club/community schemes sustain their health improvement interventions through effective, acceptable and adaptable evaluation strategies. As the programme of work develops, we aim to disseminate detailed findings of the effect of the respective programmes, how these health improvement provisions were implemented, along with reports on how evaluation outcomes were used to sustain existing/develop new health improvement programmes and the associated evaluation strategies.

Acknowledgements

In preparing this manuscript, the authors are most grateful to the staff at the community trusts of Burton Albion FC and Notts County FC, as well as Leeds Beckett University and the Higher Education Innovation Fund who provided the resources for this work to be undertaken.

Disclosure statement

No potential conflict of interest was reported by the authors.

Notes

1. Johnman and Mackie, 'The Beautiful Game'.
2. Curran, 'Understanding the Barriers to, and Impact of Men's Engagement in Physical Activity and Health Related Behaviours'; Hunt et al., 'A Gender sensitised Weight Loss and Healthy Living Programme for Overweight and Obese Men Delivered by Scottish Premier League Football Clubs (FFIT): A Pragmatic Randomised Controlled Trial'; and Rutherford et al., 'Motivate'.

3. DH, *Start Active Stay Active.*
4. WHO, *Scaling up Action Against Non-communicable Diseases: How Much Will It Cost?*
5. WHO, *From Burden to 'Best Buys': Reducing the Economic Impact of Non-communicable Diseases in Low- and Middle Income Countries.*
6. Zwolinsky et al., 'Optimizing Lifestyles for Men Regarded as "Hard-to-Reach" Through Top-Flight Football/Soccer Clubs'.
7. WHO, *From Burden to 'Best Buys': Reducing the Economic Impact of Non-communicable Diseases in Low- and Middle Income Countries.*
8. Clark, 'The Multiple Challenges of Multiple Morbidities, Lawder, Is the Scottish Population Living Dangerously?'; King, 'Turning Back the Clock'; and Nilsen, Bakke, and Gallefoss, 'Effects of Lifestyle Intervention in Persons at Risk from Type 2 Diabetes Mellitus'.
9. DH, *At Least Five a Week*; DH, *Start Active Stay Active.*
10. DH, *Start Active Stay Active.*
11. DH, *Healthy Lives Healthy People*, 2011.
12. DCMS, *Getting More People Playing Sport*; DH, *Start Active Stay Active.*
13. RSPH, *Annual Conference and Awards.*
14. Cohen, 'Social Relationships and Health'.
15. Parnell and Richardson, 'Introduction'.
16. DH, *Start Active Stay Active*; DH, *Healthy Lives Healthy People.*
17. Hunt et al., 'A Gender sensitised Weight Loss and Healthy Living Programme for Overweight and Obese Men Delivered by Scottish Premier League Football Clubs (FFIT): A Pragmatic Randomised Controlled Trial'; Pringle and Sayers, 'It's a Goal: Basing a Community Psychiatric Nursing Service in a Local Football Stadium'.
18. Parnell et al., 'Football in the Community Schemes', Pringle et al., 'Health Improvement for Men and Hard-to-Engage-Men Delivered in English Premier League Football Clubs'; and Rutherford et al., 'Motivate'.
19. Curran, 'Understanding the Barriers to, and Impact of Men's Engagement in Physical Activity and Health Related Behaviours'; Pringle et al., 'Health Improvement for Men and Hard-to-Engage-Men Delivered in English Premier League Football Clubs'.
20. Johnman and Mackie, 'The Beautiful Game'.
21. Parnell et al., 'Football in the Community Schemes'; Pringle et al., 'Health Improvement for Men and Hard-to-Engage-Men Delivered in English Premier League Football Clubs'; and Rutherford et al., 'Motivate'.
22. Pringle et al., 'The Pre-adoption, Demographic and Health Profiles of Men Participating in a Programme of Men's Health Delivered in English Premier League Football Clubs'.
23. Pringle et al., 'Health Improvement for Men and Hard-to-Engage-Men Delivered in English Premier League Football Clubs'; Robertson et al., 'It's Fun, Fitness, Football Really.'
24. Johnman and Mackie, 'The Beautiful Game'.
25. Black, 'Can England's NHS Survive?'
26. Association of Public Service Excellence, Local authority Sport and Recreation Services in England: Where Next?
27. Pringle et al., 'Assessing the Impact of Football-based Health Improvement Programmes: Stay Onside, Avoid own Goals and Score with the Evaluation!'
28. Glasgow et al., 'Evaluating the Impact of Public Health Interventions'.
29. Dugdill and Stratton, *Evaluating Sport and Physical Activity Interventions*; Pringle et al., 'Assessing the Impact of Football-based Health Improvement Programmes: Stay Onside, Avoid own Goals and Score with the Evaluation!'
30. Curran, 'Understanding the Barriers to, and Impact of Men's Engagement in Physical Activity and Health Related Behaviours'; Hunt et al., 'A Gender sensitised Weight Loss and Healthy Living Programme for Overweight and Obese Men Delivered by Scottish Premier League Football Clubs (FFIT): A Pragmatic Randomised Controlled Trial'; and Rutherford et al., 'Motivate'.
31. Pringle et al., 'Assessing the Impact of Football-based Health Improvement Programmes: Stay Onside, Avoid Own Goals and Score with the Evaluation!'

32. CRI National Evaluation of LEAP, Dugdill and Stratton, *Evaluating Sport and Physical Activity Interventions*; National Obesity Observatory, *Standard Evaluation Framework for Physical Activity Intervention*; and Pringle et al., 'Assessing the Impact of Football-based Health Improvement Programmes: Stay Onside, Avoid own Goals and Score with the Evaluation!'
33. Pringle et al., 'Effect of a Health-improvement Pilot Programme for Older Adults Delivered by a Professional Football Club: the Burton Albion Case Study'.
34. Ibid.
35. Rutherford et al., 'Motivate'.
36. Burton Albion, 'Head for Goal'.
37. Pringle et al., 'Effect of a Health-improvement Pilot Programme for Older Adults Delivered by a Professional Football Club: the Burton Albion Case Study.
38. Burton Albion Community Trust, *Schools and Education*.
39. Ransdell et al., 'Developing Effective Physical Activity Programmes'.
40. Pringle et al., 'Assessing the Impact of Football-based Health Improvement Programmes: Stay Onside, Avoid own Goals and Score with the Evaluation!'
41. Ibid.; Pringle et al., 'Qualitative Perspectives on Evaluability of Community Physical Activity Interventions'.
42. Pringle et al., 'Assessing the Impact of Football-based Health Improvement Programmes: Stay Onside, Avoid own Goals and Score with the Evaluation!'
43. The 12-Item Short form survey from the RAND Medical Outcome Study.
44. Zwolinsky et al., 'Optimizing Lifestyles for Men Regarded as "Hard-to-Reach" Through Top-Fight Football/Soccer Clubs'.
45. Sport England, *Learning from LEAP*.
46. Rutherford et al., 'Motivate'.
47. Glasgow et al., 'Evaluating the Impact of Public Health Interventions'.
48. Pringle et al., 'Health Improvement for Men and Hard-to-Engage-Men Delivered in English Premier League Football Clubs'; Robertson et al., 'It's Fun, Fitness, Football Really'.
49. CRI National Evaluation of LEAP.
50. Glasgow et al., 'Evaluating the Impact of Public Health Interventions'; Pringle et al., 'Delivering Men's Health Interventions in English Premier League Football Clubs: Key Design Characteristics'.
51. Pringle et al., 'Health Improvement for Men and Hard-to-Engage-Men Delivered in English Premier League Football Clubs'.
52. Pringle et al., 'Assessing the Impact of Football-based Health Improvement Programmes: Stay Onside, Avoid own Goals and Score with the Evaluation!'
53. Sport England, *Learning from LEAP*.
54. Ibid.
55. Dugdill and Stratton, *Evaluating Sport and Physical Activity Interventions*; Sport England, *Learning from LEAP*; and Pringle et al., 'Assessing the Impact of Football-based Health Improvement Programmes: Stay Onside, Avoid own Goals and Score with the Evaluation!'
56. Pringle et al., 'Assessing the Impact of Football-based Health Improvement Programmes: Stay Onside, Avoid own Goals and Score with the Evaluation!'

References

Black, N. 'Can England's NHS Survive?' *New England Journal of Medicine* 369 (2013): 1–3. http://www.nejm.org/doi/full/10.1056/NEJMp1305771 (accessed September 9, 2013).
Burton Albion. 'Head for Goal'. http://burtonalbioncommunitytrust.co.uk/courses/387/ (accessed June 14, 2014).
Burton Albion Community Trust. *Schools and Education*. http://burtonalbioncommunitytrust.co.uk/about-schools-education/ (accessed June 6, 2014).
Carnegie Research Institute (Leeds Metropolitan University) with Matrix RCL and Ipsos MORI. *National Evaluation of LEAP: A Final Report on the Local Exercise Action Pilots*. London: Department of Health, 2007. http://www.dh.gov.uk/en/Publicationsand

statistics/Publications/PublicationsPolicy-AndGuidance/DH_073600 (accessed September 24, 2013).

Clark, N. 'The Multiple Challenges of Multiple Morbidities'. *Health Education and Behaviour* 38 (2011): 219–21.

Cohen, S. 'Social Relationships and Health'. *American Psychologist* 59 (2004): 676–84.

Curran, K. 'Understanding the Barriers to, and Impact of Men's Engagement in Physical Activity and Health Related Behaviours: An Examination of an English Premier League Football in the Community Men's Health Programme'. PhD diss., Liverpool John Moores University, 2013.

Department of Culture Media and Sport. *Getting More People Playing Sport*. London: DCMS, 2014.

Department of Health. *At Least Five a Week: Evidence on the Impact of Physical Activity and Its Relationship to Health. A Report by the Chief Medical Officer*. London: Crown, 2004.

Department of Health. *Healthy Lives Healthy People*. London: Crown, 2011.

Department of Health. *Start Active, Stay Active: A Report on Physical Activity for Health from the Four Home Countries Chief Medical Officers*. London: Crown, 2011. http://www.dh.gov.uk/prod_consum_dh/groups/dh_digitalassets/documents/digitalasset/dh_128210.pdf (accessed September 24, 2013).

Dugdill, L., and G. Stratton. *Evaluating Sport and Physical Activity Interventions: A Guide for Practitioners*. University of Salford, 2013. http://usir.salford.ac.uk/3148/1/Dugdill_and_Stratton_2007.pdf (accessed September 24, 2013).

Excellence. 'Local Authority Sport and Recreation Services in England: Where Next?' http://www.apse.org.uk/apse/index.cfm/research/current-research-programme/local-authority-sport-and-recreation-services-in-england-where-next/local-authority-sport-and-recreation-services-in-england-where-next/ (accessed June 6, 2014).

Glasgow, R., T. Vogt, and S. Boles. 'Evaluating the Impact of Public Health Interventions: The REAIM Framework'. *American Journal of Public Health* 89 (1999): 1323–7.

Hunt, K., S. Wyke, C. Gray, A. Anderson, A. Brady, C. Bunn, Donnan, P. et al. 'A Gender-Sensitised Weight Loss and Healthy Living Programme for Overweight and Obese Men Delivered by Scottish Premier League Football Clubs (FFIT): A Pragmatic Randomised Controlled Trial'. *The Lancet* 383 (2014): 1211–24.

Johnman, C., F. Sim, and P. Mackie. 'The Beautiful Game'. *Public Health* 127 (2013). http://www.publichealthjrnl.com/article/PIIS0033350613002448/fulltext (accessed September 10, 2013).

King, D., A. Mainous, and M. Geesey. 'Turning Back the Clock: Adopting a Healthy Lifestyle in Middle Age'. *American Journal of Medicine* 120 (2007): 598–603.

Lawder, R., O. Harding, D. Stockton, C. Fischbacher, D. Brewster, J. Chalmers, A. Finlayson, and D. Conway. 'Is the Scottish Population Living Dangerously? Prevalence of Multiple Risk Factors: the Scottish Health Survey 2003'. *BMC Public Health* 10 (2010): 330. http://www.biomedcentral.com/1471-2458/10/330.

National Obesity Observatory. *Standard Evaluation Framework for Physical Activity Interventions*. London: National Obesity Observatory, 2012. http://www.noo.org.uk/uploads/doc/vid_16722_SEF_PA.pdf (accessed February 20, 2014).

Nilsen, V., P. Bakke, and F. Gallefoss. 'Effects of Lifestyle Intervention in Persons at Risk from Type 2 Diabetes Mellitus – Results from a Randomised Controlled Trial'. *BMC Public Health* 11 (2011): 893. http://www.biomedcentral.com/1471-2458/11/893.

Parnell, D., and D. Richardson. 'Introduction'. *Soccer and Society* 15 (2014): 823–8.

Parnell, D., G. Stratton, and B. Drust, and D. Richardson. 'Football in the Community Schemes: Exploring the Effectiveness of an Intervention in Promoting Positive Healthful Behaviour Change'. *Soccer and Society* 14 (2013): 35–51.

Pringle, A., J. Hargreaves, L. Lozano, J. McKenna, and S. Zwolinsky. 'Assessing the Impact of Football-Based Health Improvement Programmes: Stay Onside, Avoid Own Goals and Score with the Evaluation!' *Soccer and Society* 15 (2014): 970–87.

Pringle, A., J. McKenna, E. Whatley, and N. Gilson. 'Qualitative Perspectives on Evaluability of Community Physical Activity Interventions'. From Education to Application: Sport, Exercise and Health Proceedings of the British Association of Sport & Exercise Science

Meeting, Wolverhampton University, Leeds, UK, British Association of Sport & Exercise Science, September 11–13, 2006.

Pringle, A., D. Parnell, S. Zwolinsky, J. Hargreaves, and J McKenna. 'Effect of a Health Improvement Pilot Programme for Older Adults Delivered by a Professional Football Club: the Burton Albion Case Study'. *Soccer and Society* 15 (2014): 902–18.

Pringle, A., and P. Sayers. 'It's a Goal: Basing a Community Psychiatric Nursing Service in a Local Football Stadium'. *The Journal of the Royal Society for the Promotion of Health* 124 (2004): 234–8.

Pringle, A., S. Zwolinsky, J. McKenna, A. Daly-Smith, S. Robertson, and A. White. 'Health Improvement for Men and Hard-to-Engage-Men Delivered in English Premier League Football Clubs'. *Health Education Research* 29 (2014): 503–20.

Pringle, A., S. Zwolinsky, J. McKenna, A. Smith, S. Robertson, and A. White. 'Delivering Men's Health Interventions in English Premier League football Clubs: Key Design Characteristics'. *Public Health* 127 (2013): 716–26.

Pringle, A., S. Zwolinsky, A. Smith, S. Robertson, J. McKenna, and A. White. 'The Pre-Adoption Demographic and Health Profiles of Men Participating in a Programme of Men's Health Delivered in English Premier League Football Clubs'. *Public Health* 125 (2011): 411–6.

Ransdell, L., M. Dinger, J. Huberty, and K. Miller. 'Planning and Evaluating Physical Activity Programmes. Developing Effective Physical Activity Programmes. Champaign, Illinois. *Human Kinetics* (2009): 13–21.

Robertson, S., S. Zwolinsky, A. Pringle, J. McKenna, A. Daly-Smith, and A. White. '"It is Fun, Fitness, Football Really": A Process Evaluation of a Football Based Health Improvement Intervention for Men'. *Qualitative Research in Sport, Exercise and Health* 5 (2013): 419–39.

Royal Society for Public Health. *Annual Conference and Awards. Healthy settings and Developing Wellbeing in the Community.* London: Royal Society for Public Health, 2014. https://www.rsph.org.uk/en/courses-conferences-and-events/index.cfm/annualconference (accessed June 6, 2014).

Rutherford, Z., S. Seymour-Smith, C. Matthews, J. Wilcox, B. Gough, D. Parnell, and A. Pringle. 'Motivate: The Effect of a Football in the Community Delivered Weight Loss Programme on Over 35 year old Men and Women's Cardiovascular Risk Factors'. *Soccer and Society* 15 (2014): 951–69.

Sport England. *Learning from LEAP*. London: Sport England, 2006.

'The 12 Item Short Form Survey from the RAND Medical Outcome Study'. http://www.rand.org/health/surveys_tools/mos/mos_core_12item.html (accessed June 15, 2014).

World Health Organization. *From Burden to "Best Buys": Reducing the Economic Impact of Non-Communicable Diseases in Low- and Middle-Income Countries.* Geneva, Switzerland: World Health Organization, 2011.

World Health Organization. *Scaling Up Action Against Non-Communicable Diseases: How Much Will it Cost?* Geneva, Switzerland: World Health Organization, 2011.

Zwolinsky, S., A. Pringle, A. White, A. Smith, S. Robertson, and J. McKenna. 'Optimizing Lifestyles for Men Regarded as "Hard-to-Reach" Through Top-Flight Football/Soccer Clubs'. *Health Education Research* 28 (2013): 405–13.

Football and its communities: the celebration of Manchester United FC's Ability Suite

Juan Luis Paramio-Salcines, Phil Downs and John Grady

Manchester United FC (MUFC), in collaboration with their disabled supporters' organization MUDSA (Manchester United Disabled Supporters Association), has demonstrated a long-term organizational commitment and contribution to disability issues and promoting accessibility. The purpose of this 'case study' is to make theoretical sense of the origin, implementation and evaluation of an innovative and unconventional facility and service, the Ability Suite and analyse its effects on enhancing the customer service and experience for supporters with disabilities at MUFC on match and non-match days, as well as to the Manchester community over the period 2003–2013. Despite ad hoc improvements by some clubs, the Ability Suite remains a unique facility and service for supporters with disabilities which provides MUFC with a competitive advantage over most clubs within the main leagues in Europe. Findings show that the Ability Suite is an essential part of the club's commitment to inclusivity and accessibility that fully integrates accessibility in its daily operations and interactions with fans. This raises issues of leadership, shared vision and Corporate Social Responsibility of all members of MUFC from middle and senior management to all the daily operational aspects of MUDSA as key factors to the effective implementation of this unique facility and service. The case concludes by forecasting how the Ability Suite will continue to serve the needs of disabled supporters in the near future and exploring how key findings from this case might be transferable to other clubs.

Introduction

On 5 April 2003, a unique and distinctive facility and service for supporters with disabilities, the so-called *Ability Suite,* was officially launched by one of the top football clubs in the world, Manchester United FC (MUFC) in collaboration with their disabled supporters' organization MUDSA (Manchester United Disabled Supporters Association). This innovative facility and service for supporters with disabilities demonstrates the long-term organizational commitment of MUFC to diversity and inclusion that goes beyond rhetoric and legislation,[1] as well as illustrating the club's Corporate Social Responsibility (CSR) towards an important group of stakeholders.[2]

Most of disability legislation on access to sport facilities including stadia emphasizes 'minimum standards' based on quantitative aspects of services and facilities.

This legislation typically has fundamental limitations, as it does not take into account the quality of services and facilities for people with disabilities. Beyond that, this paper argues that providing high-quality service as well as satisfying all customers, including the growing number of people with disabilities,[3] should be part of the agenda of a wide range of service organizations.[4] Past studies in the area of 'football, communities, and sustainability', as this special issue seeks to address, have not received sufficient attention to help understand the unique characteristics and demands from individuals with disabilities as sport consumers and spectators. In a special issue on 'Fooball and Inclusivity', Parnell and Richardson emphasized that:

> 'The relationship between the football club and the community has been inextricably linked. It is this relationship that ensures that, in order for football to continue to flourish, or even to exist, it will forever be indebted to its communities.[5]

In addition, they claimed the need to provide a high level of accessibility to football matches and stadia as well as to welcome a wider range of customers, including individuals with disabilities.

Yet, never before has any other club besides MUFC provided state-of-the-art services to spectators with disabilities (SwD), both to their own supporters and visitors, and their companions who gather at historic Old Trafford stadium on match and non-match days. The Ability Suite represents a significant 'benchmark' example of enhancing the quality service and experience for all types of fans with disabilities attending events at Old Trafford as well as demonstrating the club's approach to CSR. As an example of this paradigm shift in accessibility and disability, the Ability Suite offers an effective operational model that adds value in order to meet the current demands and expectations of people with disabilities attending matches regularly at Old Trafford and to help ensure they enjoy the same match-day experience as able-bodied spectators receive.[6] Analysing the case of the Ability Suite also serves to offer a new way of conceptualizing accessibility and disability at football club level. Beyond that, since inception in 2000, MUFC was also one of the first football clubs in the Premier League to develop a comprehensive outreach programme to address the needs of schoolchildren and adults with disabilities across the Greater Manchester communities as part of their CSR policy.[7]

When MUFC's disabled supporters or supporters from other clubs were asked about their perceptions of the Ability Suite, as appears in *Celebrating 10 years of the Ability Suite 2003–2013*,[8] one of Manchester United's supporter summed up his overall satisfaction with the operation of the Ability Suite by staying:

> I have seen the world as able-bodied and (now) have to live it as a disabled man. Going to the match has helped me to increase my self-confidence and belief. I'd give the Ability Suite 10 out of 10. I also think that because the club shows disabled fans respect by providing them with facilities as least as good as able-bodied fans, this has an impact on the attitudes and actions of the latter.[9]

Similar perceptions can be found in the following statement by a visiting club supporter travelling to Old Trafford to follow his team, Newcastle United:

> The disabled facilities available at your ground (Old Trafford) are better than any venue I've ever been to- and I'm talking about everywhere from the fanciest restaurants to major shopping centres, airports and tourist venues around the world- and I've travelled! ... It is with the utmost sincerity that I offer my thanks and congratulations in organizing such facilities and staffing them with such kind, friendly people.[10]

This study focuses on the analysis of the process that has facilitated such a highly regarded football club as is MUFC to provide an extensive range of high-quality facilities, including the Ability Suite, to their own SwD, which cover all types of disabilities and their companions as well as supporters from the opposing club. The purpose of this 'case study', therefore, is to make theoretical sense of the origin, implementation and evaluation of the Ability Suite and to examine its effects on enhancing the quality service and experience for SwD at club level on match and non-match days as well as to the Manchester local community over the period 2003–2014. In our case study, we sought to answer the following two research questions: (1) What kind of people in professional roles at MUFC have had input in the initial planning, design, implementation and management of the Ability Suite? and (2) What benefits (or potential detriments) has the Ability Suite provided to different stakeholders (such as the club itself, its fans with disabilities and the local community of Manchester) over the last ten years?

In order to address these two research questions, this paper is divided into five parts which explain both the evolution of the Ability Suite and the key drivers behind its long-term success. The paper begins with an explanation of the embryonic stages of this unique facility and service. The second part explains who the instrumental 'key players' were in the initial planning, design and implementation of the Ability Suite. The third part examines the factors that facilitated MUFC's support of this project. The fourth part reviews the management operations of this facility on non-match days and how this has influenced for people of the Manchester community. The paper concludes with some lessons learned and suggestions arising from this case that might inspire and convince other organizations to adopt the long-term successful approach to accessibility and disability implemented by MUFC and MUDSA.

Historical background

At the time, the Ability Suite was opened in April 2003, Manchester United FC was (and still is) one of the most successful professional football clubs in the world in terms of sporting performance (by the number of trophies at national and international levels),[11] financial performance (by 2003 the total financial turnover of the club had reached a record of £173 m. and was the one of the wealthiest club anywhere in the world),[12] and national and international fan support over recent decades.[13] Most of these developments have attracted the attention of academics, business schools and consultant companies.[14] More recently, the long-term and successful management by Sir Alex Ferguson in the club over the last 26 years and his contribution to building a team as well as a club has received detailed analysis.[15] The commitment and contribution of MUFC to disability issues as well as promoting accessibility for their supporters with disabilities has a long history and goes 'beyond and above' legislation. Therefore, both issues have become part of Manchester United's business culture and their overall CSR over the last three decades. Bearing this in mind, the understanding and motivation about how and why accessibility of spectators with disabilities (SwD) and disability has become part of Manchester United's business culture and their overall CSR was recently analysed through the lens of CSR.[16]

Despite extensive evidence of the benefits and services that the Ability Suite has catered to all types of disabled supporters and to Manchester's communities, as the following eloquent comment by a visiting disabled supporter illustrates, surprisingly it has yet to be emulated by many other clubs in Europe.[17]

> I'm a Manchester City season ticket holder and have been to most PL (Premier League) grounds, including Old Trafford several times. …..The way you look after home and visiting disabled supporters I find incredible, and I'm compelled, implored even, to say what a dream it is to visit Old Trafford in a disabled capacity. Your whole operation is just so slick, organized and better than any I have experienced before. The dedicated parking facility, dedicated entrance, dedicated concourse and toilet facilities, basically just removes all the stress one normally encounters when travelling to away grounds. You have plenty of staff on hand always… (and) your disability policy is first class. I'd like to thank the club for this, and please God your generous allocation of free tickets[18] (again incredible) meets my criteria for next season, as win lose or draw, the experience I had all round, and the way your staff from the gate to the stewards to the PR people leaves the rest standing…Thanks again for taking disabled supporters as seriously as the rest, it means a lot and I can vouch that other disabled supporters feel the same way.[19]

Review of literature

Service quality is becoming a significant area of research in sport facility management. As a result, analysis of how the planning and management of stadia and arenas during sporting events can impact on the customer experience and how this applies to ensure a high-quality experience for customer in general or VIP guests in particular start to abound.[20] An examination of recent literature analysing the unique needs of spectators with disabilities (SwD) attending stadia and arenas to follow sporting events, including professional football clubs, in Europe[21] and in the United States[22] reveals that there is more nuanced scholarship and analysis about this managerial issue. It can be argued that there are distinctly different approaches to providing accessibility and accommodation for people with disabilities in football venues throughout Europe and the United States. While American approaches are largely guided by the legal regulations that require facilities to be accessible, European perspectives stress that the event experience should always be at the core, which means putting the fans first.

Anecdotal evidence suggests that the match-day experience for a football fan with a disability still ranges from difficult to thoroughly unpleasant in many stadia in Europe.[23] Increasingly, as accessibility has become a major political issue for UEFA, some European Leagues such as the Premier League and Bundesliga and some individual clubs, notably Manchester United FC, Arsenal,[24] Manchester City and Bayern Munich, are responsive to the needs of this large group of fans and have incorporated accessibility and disability as part of their organization's culture and everyday business operations.[25] Indeed, satisfying all types of customers, including people with disabilities, should be a key component in the football industry as it happens in other service sectors,[26] but no other club besides MUFC has provided this level of extensive services to their fans with disabilities and their companions. The Ability Suite represents, therefore, a non-traditional and innovative way to meet the demands and expectations of SwD at the club level and to local communities.

When explaining the resistance of football clubs to implement other similar facilities at their stadia, it can be argued that while there are still a number of physical barriers to promoting stadium accessibility, there is also a notable resistance by top and middle managers to innovation and change,[27] to the implementation of a project on the same scale as the Ability Suite.[28] In this regard, one reason that might explain this resistance from those managers to the implementation of an inclusive business environment such as a football club's stadium may represent, as Scott-Parker and Zadek[29] clearly contend there is a prevailing feeling in the United Kingdom, that 'most managers, including many in public sector and non-profit organizations, remain unconvinced that people with disabilities can enhance their overall business performance'. Similar sentiments were shared in the Australian tourism industry.[30] Paramio-Salcines et al. have recently sought to prove that fans with disabilities as well as older fans are two new markets segments of sport consumers that the football industry should value as one that makes good business case,[31] but still there is scant empirical evidence to substantiate this aspect in the context of attending football matches as spectators in stadia.

The key issue is whether management theories prove useful in analysing the process of design, implementation and operation management of the Ability Suite by MUFC and MUDSA and also they are useful to explain the factors that could facilitate or inhibit the diffusion of innovations as the Ability Suite represents. Institutional theory has been utilized to examine organizational changes in different sport organizations (e.g., diffusion or resistance of a particular process or structure).[32] Several researchers have offered conceptual frameworks for promoting and managing innovation and changes in all types of organizations, suggesting that innovation as the Ability Suite represents, should be part of any organization's culture and everyday business.[33]

Method

In analysing the efforts of MUFC and MUDSA to meet the needs of disabled supporters through the Ability Suite and its related services, adoption of a case study approach is justified. Case studies serve different purposes such as providing answers and explanations of an under-researched area[34] as well as understanding and interpreting organizational practices like the implementation and operation of the Ability Suite. Trying to help diffuse this knowledge to other academics as well as practitioners, this exploratory study combines a mixed-method approach with three layers: interviews and direct personal communications with Phil Downs, observation of the operation of the Ability Suite at Old Trafford during various sporting events and performing content analysis of documents.[35] In addition, there is much demand for academic-practitioner collaboration in sport organizations as well as in sport management scholarship.[36] As Edwards observes, 'any attempt to conceptualize reflection on professional practice must incorporate the experience of practitioner'.[37]

Before the analysis of this case was conducted, a continuous formal and informal dialogue between of all three researchers who have expertise in the areas of accessibility and disability issues over the last year has contributed to initially define and further refine the areas of interest of this particular case. This included formulation of the research questions, choosing issues that emphasize the uniqueness of the case, data collection and data analysis.

In the same iterative way, the three multi-layer approach analysis as part of this reflective practice process was initially informed by and integrated the long-term practical knowledge of one of the authors, Phil Downs, who was instrumental in the vision, initial planning and implementation of this project from its conception as his role of secretary of MUDSA and in his current role as Disability Liaison Officer over the last three decades.[38] Apart from this, the paper incorporates his own reflection on his daily practice (reflection on action) which has contributed to opening new venues for understanding the managerial implications of this project and help to understand why MUFC implemented the Ability Suite (reflection on action and reflection for action).[39] Moreover, all of the researchers have seen the operation of the Ability Suite at different types of events in recent years (including Old Trafford hosting football matches during the London 2012 Olympics). In addition, a content analysis was performed using a wide array of internal documents produced by the club, Manchester United Foundation and MUDSA, MUDSA's official magazine *Rollin' Reds* and MUDSA *Members' Handbook*, MUFC (http://www.manutd.com/) and MUDSA (http://www.mudsa.org/) websites as well as other documents related to the design and implementation of the Ability Suite for the last decade.[40]

Findings

The multi-method data collection process produced a vast amount of rich data. In analysing the data, several key themes emerged. Those include recognizing the origin of the facility and service, identifying those key individuals who were behind the initial planning and implementation of the Ability Suite, understanding the non-traditional uses of the Ability Suite on non-match days, and realizing the influence on MUFC's disabled fans and the local community. The following section seeks to offer an insight into the key (but not exhaustive) themes that emerged from the data, in order to address the key research questions of this paper.

Embryonic stages of the Ability Suite

When looking in retrospect, it is important to explain key individuals that were behind the initial planning and implementation of this facility and service. Trying to explain the origin of this facility, it could be argued, as John Kay claims, that a successful project as the Ability Suite represents was 'based on a mixture of calculation and opportunism, of vision and experiment'.[41] What is more, though is critical to have a vision as the Ability Suite represents, but also a critical factor is, as Fischer and Rohde emphasize, implementing these ideas as 'the implementation process is generally a project management effort'.[42] The Ability Suite is illustrative of both principles.

Our exploratory research revealed that most of the people pointed to Phil Downs as one of the key people who had the vision, passion and personal commitment at the club level to initiate this innovative project. As stated previously, after the creation of MUDSA in December 1989, Downs has been at the forefront of the development of this organization, which has been also instrumental in the preliminary planning, design, implementation and operation management of all services provided to fans with disabilities over the last three decades. Over the years, the partnership between MUDSA and MUFC has led to building increased confidence through a variety of formal and informal relationships with a 'continuous stakeholder dialogue' between both sides having contributed to the involvement of MUDSA in decision-making processes affecting disabled supporters, such as the building of the Ability Suite. However, there were also other instrumental people in the club's organizational board who made this facility a reality in 2003 and had a personal commitment and responsibility to the project as is explained in the following section.

Manchester United FC has been a pioneer in offering new and enhanced services to all their fans, such as Manchester United satellite channel (MUTV), the launching of the club official website in August 1998 as well as exploring new commercial opportunities.[43] In relation to MUFC's approach to accessibility and disability, the Ability Suite can be considered a successful innovation and still a unique facility and service for fans with disabilities which provides the club a competitive advantage over most clubs within the main leagues in Europe.[44] When Phil Downs was asked if he was aware of similar approaches to the concept of the Ability Suite in other clubs' stadia during the early 2000s, Downs remarked:

> Before the Ability Suite idea came into being some disabled fans had small areas to use on match days but they were very small, and not purpose-built and with no non-match day purpose. In other words, they were simply like small café's ... very small! The two I knew about were at Leeds United and Wolverhampton Wanderers but the Ability Suite idea wasn't going to be anything like those facilities at the other clubs ...

It is important to also recognize and appreciate the state and level of facilities that MUFC offered to their fans with disabilities during the 1980s at Old Trafford (see Table 1), which can be seen in the quote below:

> Wheelchairs users at this time came into the ground through the staff entrance. They then journeyed along the tunnel that passed the players dressing rooms before emerging in front of the current dugout where Sir Alex Ferguson sat for many years. They then took a spot on a specially concreted platform onto which 15–20 wheelchairs were squeezed along with their helpers who stood throughout the match...Those in wheelchairs could not see the touchline on the North/Sir Alex Ferguson stand of the pitch, not the ball if it was below the player's knees on that side of the pitch ... Refreshments facilities were non-existent and any chance of having a brew meant bringing it

Table 1. Historical Evolution of the Implementation of Seats for Wheelchair fans and their companions at Old Trafford over the years.

1980	15–20 wheelchair places
1991 season	37 wheelchair positions with adjacent companion places (during Stretford End redevelopment)
1996 season	70 wheelchair places with adjacent companion places (North Stand three-Tier development)
2000 season	104 wheelchair places with adjacent companion places (East and West Stand developments)
2006 season	120 wheelchair positions with adjacent companion places (NE and NW Quad developments)
2013/2014 season	120 wheelchair positions with adjacent companion places in three wheelchair platforms for general access: (1) 104 wheelchair seats plus adjacent companion places (south-east) (2) 8 wheelchair seats plus adjacent companion places (north-east) (3) 8 wheelchair seats plus adjacent companion places (north-west) (renamed as the Sir Alex Ferguson stand in 2013) In addition, there are 89 wheelchair places (1 place per executive box)

Source: Updated from Downs and Paramio-Salcines, 'Incorporating Accessibility and Disability in the Manchester United Culture and Organization as part of their CSR Policies', 140; Manchester United Disabled Supporters Association (MUDSA), *Celebrating 10 years of the Ability Suite 2003–2013*, 29–32.

yourself! Toilets facilities consisted of the use of toilet in a tiny room used as storage space for cleaning materials. Such facilities were not especially, conducive to creating lasting friendships between disabled fans.[45]

As mentioned previously, the idea behind the Ability Suite was 'based on a mixture of calculation and opportunism, of vision and experiment'.[46] This idea was reinforced by George Johnstone, the MUFC's Building Services Manager over the last 15 years and the man who has overseen massive projects like the expansion of the East and West stands of Old Trafford stadium, the training ground development and, the focus of this paper, the building of the Ability Suite. About the construction process, he stated:

> The Ability Suite wouldn't have happened if the old ticket office wasn't moving ... It was opportunism on my part when I discovered what was about to happen so I lobbied hard with the Group Properties Manager and of course David Gill (the then MUFC's CEO)...The main driver for the Ability Suite was obviously the opportunity in the first place but there was an operational need to move disabled supporters from the concourse area where it was congested and also where the stadium police is!.[47]

During the 1990s, the situation changed slightly when the legal environment in most countries was becoming more orientated towards addressing the issues faced by people with disabilities. This included the United Kingdom's passage of the Disability Discrimination Act (DDA) in 1995. In the same way, the combination of the sporting performance of MUFC in the 1990s contributed to increase the popularity of the club and by extension, this demand has facilitated the upgrading and expansion of certain areas of the stadium over the last two decades. This has also encouraged the longtime joint collaboration between MUDSA and MUFC, which was considered critical to support this unique facility. The emergence of all MUFC's highly regarded disabled supporters' facilities and services, including the Ability Suite, was due to two primary reasons as Downs explained:

> Firstly, one of the main catalysts was the establishment of the first disabled supporters' association in Great Britain and probably in Europe, Manchester United Disabled Supporters Association (MUDSA) in 1989. Secondly, an important part of our study was the willingness of the senior managers of the club at that time to be advised by their disabled supporters in the development of a whole range of facilities and services that would allow disabled people a parity of match-day experience equal to that of those who are non-disabled (personal communication, April 10, 2013).

Before the official launch of the Ability Suite in April 2003, as mentioned above senior managers of MUFC had been reacting positively to Phil Downs and MUDSA's recommendations and requests and showed their long-term commitment and positive, discretionary and responsive CSR approach to their wide range of services for disabled supporters and their companions. As part of this approach, the reader can value the historical evolution of the services for fans using wheelchairs and their companions at Old Trafford since the early 1980 to the present as is summarized in Table 1.

This collaborative work has continued since the early 1980s when Phil Downs initially joined the club.[48] The first event organized by what became MUDSA was the first Christmas Party in 1989 that allowed disabled fans to meet MUFC players and coaches, an idea first proposed by another influential actor, Sir Alex Ferguson's personal assistant Lyn Laffin[49]; an event has grown substantially in relevance over

Table 2.   Operation Management at the Ability Suite on match days and non-match days at the 2013–2014 season.

	Match days	Non-match days
Ability Suite	Hospitality area for pre-, mid- and post-match days Dedicated Ability Team's staffDedicated Entrance to Old Trafford StadiumAdapted Kiosk with a low-level counterFree RefreshmentsSpace for 80 wheelchairs and carers	Seven Annual Events for MUDSA's members and other members of the club <ul><li>Player Questions and Answers Session (January)</li><li>Ten Pin Bowling Challenge (April)</li><li>Carrington Training Ground Visit</li><li>Belle Vue GreyHound Stadium Dogs (July)</li><li>MUDSA AGM (June)</li><li>Annual Dinner (Oct/Nov)</li><li>Christmas Party (December)</li></ul>
	Two TV large screensTwo Accessible Toilets and an additional Eight Accessible Toilets and First Aid Room in the concourse area	Educational and Learning Centre for people of Greater Manchester's communities with MUFC and Trafford College <ul><li>Short educational courses with four computers positions</li></ul> MUFC's internal meetings, delivering courses by MUFC's Foundation

Source: Manchester United Disabled Supporters Association (MUDSA), *Celebrating 10 years of the Ability Suite 2003–2013;* MUDSA. *Members' Handbook Summer 2014.* See also more information on MUDSA's web page at http://www.mudsa.org/.

the last 16 years (see Table 2). As different key actors in the process coincided, the Ability Suite aimed to cover two objectives:

> Firstly, a dedicated match-day lounge for disabled supporters which provides added benefits to disabled supporters plus frees up concourse congestion and secondly, a non-match day Learning Center forming part of the Manchester United FC's Corporate Social Responsibility (CSR) policy. For the latter, the Ability Suite is currently used on non-match days by a local college, Trafford College, in delivering basic skills courses on areas such as health, well-being, communication and confidence building. It is also used by the club to deliver internal training sessions, some focusing on disability awareness.[50]

We felt there was a gap in provision for wheelchair supporters in inclement weather because on some occasions it was really unpleasant sitting on the platform. So, providing proper 'shelter', for want a better description, in those conditions was important because, looking at it operationally, having a lot of wheelchairs in the concourse area wasn't good because we've got the emergency services there and if something happened it could have caused problem. The Ability Suite provided a very good solution to keeping the concourse free, plus providing at its lowest level a 'shelter'. We went beyond that by providing what is effectively a lounge with all its

Table 3. Description of the services and facilities for different kinds of SwD at Old Trafford stadium on match and non-match days at the 2014–2015 season.

Manchester United FC and MUDSA Web contact Disability Liaison Officer	Stadium, Date of Building, Capacity	Seats for different kinds of SwD	Other accessible services	Capacity/seats for fans with disabilities (%)
www.mudsa.org (launched on 1 November 2002)	Old Trafford, 1910, 76,312	General access	Tickets and membership services	76,312/411 = 0.53%
		One hundred and twenty (wheelchairs) in three separate locations		
Phil Downs		South-east (104)	Dedicated phone lines and email addresses to fans with disabilities	
		North-east/north-west (8/8) Overall: 108 home and 12 away (+helpers seating) Twenty-one (+helpers seating) (severe mobility difficulties) Thirteen (+helpers seating) (moderate mobility difficulties) Forty (visually impaired) (+companion seating)	Three hundred parking spaces Hospitality areas *Ability Suite* Ten Accessible toilets 89[a] Suites and Executive Boxes with adjacent accessible toilets New Food, Beverages and Concessions Stands Museum and Tour Centre and Club Store Commentary headsets for visually impaired fans Induction Loop Facilities Services for Assistance Dogs Two Accessible Coaches for away transport	

Source: Updated from Downs and Paramio-Salcines, 'Incorporating Accessibility and Disability in the Manchester United Culture and Organization as part of their CSR Policies', 142. Manchester United Disabled Supporters Association (MUDSA), *Celebrating 10 years of the Ability Suite 2003–2013*; and MUDSA, *Members' Handbook Summer 2014*.
[a]All of the Executives boxes have now been upgraded with external seating, including provision for one wheelchair per box. This effectively adds another 89 wheelchair places to the overall capacity, but this figure is not included in the publicized figure because they cannot be considered 'general access'.

facilities and the contribution we had from Vodafone with the assistive technology together with the idea of using it as a learning facility on non-match days.[51]

In sum, the ambition behind of the Ability Suite was not only to provide good standards of facilities and services for fans with disabilities but also to have the first truly 'VIP area' for disabled fans and their families and companions, exceeding clearly not only the legal requirements but also their needs and expectations and enhancing the quality experience of SwD. Today, the Ability Suite offers, among other services, a dedicated Ability Team's staff, an adapted kiosk with a low counter, space for approximately 80 additional wheelchair fans and carers, 2 large TV screens and overall 10 accessible toilets (see Table 2).

In trying to identify who exerted influence and inspired that this facility came to be named the 'Ability Suite', rather than focusing on the possible negative connotation of the term of 'disability' as might be expected, this service was known as 'Ability Suite' which focuses instead on abilities. As Phil Downs pointed out:

> The term 'Ability Suite' was credited to Manchester United representatives and Vodafone representatives agreeing that Ability Suite was the best option given that the emphasis was always going to be about defining around what people could do rather than what they couldn't do (personal communication, 11th March 2014).

The collaboration between MUFC and MUDSA has gone further over the last three decades and contributed to the implementation of new services and facilities in a continually evolving process of enhancing the level of service quality to their fans with disabilities. As such, in the early 1990s, the East Stand redevelopment contributed to the building of an elevated viewing platform in the south-east corner of the stadium. In 2005, another extension of the stadium increased the overall capacity and fans with disabilities were clearly benefiting after the addition of second tiers to both north-east and north-west of the stadium, creating an additional 16 wheelchair spaces in the process as appears on Table 1.

As most of legislation on stadium accessibility worldwide focuses on quantitative standards, MUFC, in partnership with MUDSA, has also been committed to a continuous and incremental approach to providing an equality of match experience to their SwD. As such, MUFC and MUDSA have gradually implemented other qualitative services and facilities like the Ability Suite, technological improvements like MUDSA's own website[52] (2002), club's radio commentators, induction loop facilities (2006), flat screens at ground level and facilities for visually impaired fans (2007), architectural and managerial services like accessible VIP areas. This extensive level of services has also contributed to clearly enhance the service quality provided to their disabled fans (see Table 3). Today, the area for SwD currently accommodates 120 wheelchair places plus their carers, 42 seats with additional legroom for ambulant fans who have significant mobility issues but do not yet need to use a wheelchair and 36 pairs of tickets for those who simply require easy access seating due to moderate mobility difficulties.[53]

The Suite Dream became a reality. The initial planning, design and implementation of the Ability Suite

What was conceptualized as 'Suite Dreams' at that time, the Ability Suite became a reality in 2003 which also coincided with a coincidental development as the movement of the Old Ticket Office to its current location:

> I (Phil Downs) asked Building Services Manager, George Johnstone about this, I could see that there may be potential for the idea to get off the ground because the concourse area leading into the viewing area directly above was always very congested before the match, especially in bad weather…The area which includes a small police station, is where the emergency services are located it meant that disabled fans might get in the way and be in danger if there was an emergency. So as well as providing a great facility for our members, it felt, it would be an advantage in an operational context for the club.[54]

As one of the influential figures behind this project, Downs, pointed out different key people that were also quite influential in this decision in different ways. From the organization board perspective, the Ability Suite involved an extensive number of departments' working together and also the commitment and support from senior to middle managers of MUFC as well as from other key figures in the club like Sir Alex Ferguson and his personal assistant, Lyn Laffin. At the top management level, David Gill, the former MUFC's Chief Executive at that time was critical for the success of this project.[55] And other figure was Ken Merrett, the then club secretary of MUFC who also approved the concept of the Ability Suite. Our findings also identified the continuous personal commitment and long-time support of Sir Alex Ferguson to all the actions of MUDSA, regarded as the greatest manager in history, including the official launch of the Ability Suite. This raises the issue of leadership as one of the main drivers that contributed to the long-term commitment of MUFC to these issues as part of their CSR approach. Also as different authors[56] emphasize that the support and personal commitment from top managers to the front line people, as the dedicated Ability Suite team who interact with disabled supporters on match days, have had a positive influence to the implementation of the Ability Suite. In particular, the former CEO of MUFC David Gill summarized what the Ability Suite has meant for disabled supporters at club level since its inception:

> The Ability Suite provides a service by being able to pull together a group of people with various different kinds of disability and encouraging them to interact. This is a marvelous felling and to see what has been created is a dream for disabled fans who, as a result, can experience the same level and enjoyment of the beautiful game as everyone else.[57]

Once the whole concept was approved by senior managers as David Gill and Ken Merrett, as mentioned above the involvement of middle managers was identified as critical to facilitate the implementation of the Ability Suite. One of those was George Johnstone,[58] the club's Building Services Manager. Johnstone described how the Ability Suite came to fruition:

> We take particular pride in the Ability Suite. It was a facility we were crying out for and we had talked many times about how to improve things and the Ticket Office move finally gave us the opportunity.[59]

The movement of the old Ticket Office outside of the main building of Old Trafford stadium was critical as it provided the right space to locate the Ability Suite. This unique concept in accommodating the needs of disabled supporters contributed to their safety, comfort and quality of service on match days and also contributed from the operational side to provide additional space for those fans on match days and above all, on non-match days was probably the main distinctive feature of the operation of the Ability Suite. In terms of funding, the Ability Suite costs the remarkable figure of £150,000 (around $238.095) to build.[60] Explaining what funds meant at that time, Downs remarks that

> I think one of the most astonishing things to me was the cost because I really expected (the Ability) to cost a fortune and if I was going to hazard a guess in those days I would have thought £60,000 at the end of the day. In fact it cost £150,000 and the club and Vodafone (one of the main sponsors of the club until recently) jointly funded it. It was exceptional for the club to consider spending that amount of money for their disabled supporters.

When Johnstone was asked what this meant to the club in terms of financial support and level of commitment to supporters with disabilities, he mentioned that:

> I honestly do not think it would have been seen as exceptional on the part of the club. I do not think they would feel they need to be congratulated for doing something out of the ordinary. I think there would have been the view that this is the right thing to do and right time to do it. Obviously, we could have done a much cheaper job but we had a clear view of what could be achieved and we made sure we did it well and the Ability Suite we ended up creating is something, which is truly exceptional.[61]

The Ability Suite on non-match days and its influence on the Manchester Community

As mentioned above, one of the distinctive uses of the Ability Suite is its operation on non-match days and its influence on Manchester United's disabled fans and to the local community. In this endeavour, over the years this facility has been used as an education and learning facility on non-match days which has attracted different partners such as Learn Direct, Ability Net, South Trafford College, Heading for Success and Manchester Metropolitan University, who run a range of courses targeted towards Manchester's local people with disabilities (see Table 2).

Looking back in retrospect, Learn Direct was the first organization that became involved in this collaborative project providing basic skills courses to local people with disabilities. This organization was funded by the Central Government to deliver these courses, but due to financial problems at that time, the Government decided to cut the funding, which negatively affected to the viability of the courses. After that, another organization, the Ability Net, based in Liverpool, came on board offering services for blind people. Later on, MUDSA and MUFC has moved onto a more in-depth partnership with the largest local college at Old Trafford, South Trafford College, who is using the Ability Suite most days of the week and delivers basic skills courses for those people wishing to back into education. This fall into the MUFC's CSR approach and to date, it is unique within football in Great Britain. In addition, the Ability Suite is also used for MUFC's for internal meetings, delivering courses by the Foundation. This facility has become a small-medium size facility with a great flexibility that also allow to generate revenues that could assist to the operation of the facility.

Our findings also revealed that MUFC and MUDSA continue to be at the forefront of innovation by introducing speech 'Read-back' for visually impaired people on each web page and have internet search desks in the Ability Suite. MUDSA is benefiting from a partnership arrangement with a telecoms company who are sponsoring our Ability Suite and other projects that MUDSA has. For example, MUDSA is currently revamping their website, created on 1 November 2002, to 'work smarter' with their members and provide them with more information more quickly. At the time of writing, the MUDSA website has been completely updated. The part of the relationship with the telecom partner that is of interest to them relates to 'Knowledge Transfer'. In this context, 'knowledge transfer' will allow the telecoms company to link into a 'fast track' process where they can assist the football clubs that they are associated with in bringing together good facilities for disabled people in their country. This particular company is heavily involved in developing a 'Humanitarian City' where all kinds of services are available to develop the abilities of disabled people.

What is more, it is worth noting the implementation of a comprehensive outreach programme to address the needs of schoolchildren and adults with disabilities in Greater Manchester communities as part of MUFC's CSR policy.[62] Since its inception in 2000, Manchester United FC was the one of the first football clubs to develop a comprehensive outreach programme that has clearly benefitted an increasing number of children and adults with disabilities engaged in different disability programmes as Ability Counts in the club. Among others, in the 2013–2014 season, 159 disabled players were registered on this programme and 13,780 young children were involved in different programmes delivered by Manchester United Foundation aiming to facilitate their participation in sport, learn life skills and gain the qualifications and leadership experience that will help them into employment.[63]

Future developments and lessons learned from the case of the Ability Suite

Although the Ability Suite can be described as an innovative facility and service for people with disabilities and the local community, there are some relevant aspects of this case study that might inspire other sport organizations to follow and adapt the long-term commitment of MUFC and MUDSA to accessibility and disability. MUFC's 'Ability Suite' represents a significant 'benchmark' example of how a football club can strategically enhance not only the customer experience for a considerable number of fans with disabilities attending events at Old Trafford, but also provide an array of educational and learning opportunities to adults and children with disabilities from Manchester's local community demonstrating a greater commitment and contribution to their local community as part of the club's approach to CSR. Based on the findings of this study and consistent with the studies of Fischer and Rohde, Oke, Johnson and Scholes and Ferlie, Fitzgerald, Wood and Hawkins, it is essential that managers at all levels in sport organizations share the vision as well as a strong personal commitment to any innovation, such as the innovative approach to treating supporters with disabilities.

A key finding of this case study is also that the Ability Suite is part of a long-term incremental approach to increasing inclusivity and accessibility within a CSR framework given the concerted actions taken by MUFC in collaboration with MUDSA over the years. As Phil Downs remarked, one of the key aspects in confronting resistance by managers at all levels in football clubs in Europe is that 'there are no 'quick fix' solutions to the overall subject of disability. Each club or national association needs to consider advancements in this area as part of a strategy that is essentially 'evolution not revolution'.[64] Another theoretical and practical implication of this case is that football venue managers must move beyond 'minimum standards' based on quantitative aspects of services and facilities, and start to consider how to truly enhance the level of service quality offered to their SwD to provide them with an experience equal to that of their able-bodied spectators.

There is a need to develop coherence in implementing and supporting this long-term commitment of senior and middle managers of MUFC in partnership with MUDSA to enhance the level of service quality provided to their SwD and, above all, as Johnson and Scholes remarked, the behaviour of top managers to reinforce strategies to advocate for disability issues and promote accessibility. As noted by David Gill, in his new role as a non-executive director of MUFC, he has stated his intention to continue his commitment to improving facilities for the club's SwD. 'The club remains committed to continuing its healthy, working relationship with MUDSA in order to improve facilities for disabled fans in the future'.[65] As part of the club's ongoing organizational commitment to SwD, MUFC has engaged in discussions about expanding the capacity of the Ability Suite and has approved a 'buggy service' which will transport supporters with walking difficulties from the coach parks to the footprint at Old Trafford. The expansion of the Ability Suite will involve a complete retrofit of an adjacent room which will represent a significant financial commitment in order to enhance the comfort of SwD. Whereas these steps clearly represent further commitment to SwD, it also demonstrates that the inclusive culture within Manchester United has seamlessly continued despite personnel changes at the highest levels of the club.

This case study research establishes theoretical relationships between leadership, shared vision and CSR. This includes all the club's employees, from front line, middle to senior managers, as facilitators of the implementation of an innovative service for SwD at MUFC. The findings of this study indicate that the Ability Suite remains an innovative service for SwD, which provides MUFC with a competitive advantage over most clubs within the main leagues in Europe. This exploratory study provides initial insights that might inspire other sport organizations to adapt MUFC's strategic approach to accessibility and disability.

Acknowledgements

This study is part of the research project titled 'Estudio Comparativo de las Funciones y Competencias del Experto en Accesibilidad Universal en Instalaciones y Eventos Deportivos: Perspectiva Norteamericana y Europea' (*Comparative Study of the Role and Competencies of the Disability Liaison Office on Sport Facilities and Events: North American and European Perspective*) led by Dr. Juan L. Paramio-Salcines, Universidad Autonoma de Madrid with Dr. John Grady, University of South Carolina and funded by the Spanish Bank, Banco de Santander (2ª Convocatoria de Proyectos de Cooperación Interuniversitaria UAM-Banco de Santander con EEUU, 2013–2014).

Disclosure statement

No potential conflict of interest was reported by the authors.

Notes

1. Evidence of this issue in top organizations is provided by Groysberg and Connolly, 'Twenty-four CEOs on Creating Diverse and Inclusive Organizations'. See also Fischer and Rohde, 'Management Resistance to Innovation'; Johnson and Scholes, *Exploring Corporate Strategy*; and Ferlie et al., 'The Nonspread of Innovations: The Mediating Role of Professionals'.

2. See more details at MUDSA, *Celebrating 10 years of the Ability Suite 2003–2013;* MUDSA, *Members' Handbook Summer 2014*; and Downs, Paramio-Salcines, and Grady, 'Celebrating 10 years of Manchester United's Ability Suite: From Organizational Buy-In to Premium Patron Services'.

3. Paramio-Salcines, Grady, and Downs, 'Growing the Football Game: The Increasing Economic and Social Relevance of Older Fans and those with Disabilities in the European Football Industry'; Kitchin, 'Planning and Managing the Stadium Experience'.

4. For a study that focuses on how to plan and manage the match-day experience of supporters with disabilities at Arsenal's Emirates stadium, see Kitchin, 'Planning and Managing the Stadium Experience'. See also Hudson and Hudson, *Customer Service for Hospitality and Tourism*.

5. Parnell and Richardson, 'Introduction', 823.

6. Downs and Paramio-Salcines, 'Incorporating Accessibility and Disability in the Manchester United Culture and Organization as part of their CSR Policies'; Paramio-Salcines, Grady, and Downs, 'Growing the Football Game: The Increasing Economic and Social Relevance of Older Fans and those with Disabilities in the European Football Industry'.

7. See more details of the impact and implications of this programme on children and adults with disabilities on different Manchester communities at Manchester United Foundation. *A Season Review. Taking Manchester United to the Heart of the Community. Impact Report 2012/13;* Manchester United Disabled Supporters Association (MUDSA, *Members' Handbook Summer 2014*).

8. See more details of the organization of the Ability Suite at MUDSA, *Celebrating 10 years of the Ability Suite 2003–2013*. Also Mark Metcalf, who is a football writer and was involved in the production of the above document, wrote a post *Suite Dreams-Facilities for Disabled Fans at Old Trafford*, which explained what this facility and service, means for all fans with disabilities. The reader can find more comments on MUFC and MUDSA's facilities at Level Playing Field. 'Manchester United'.

9. This quote is taken from MUDSA, *Celebrating 10 years of the Ability Suite 2003–2013*, 10.

10. This quote is also taken from MUDSA, *Celebrating 10 years of the Ability Suite 2003–2013*, 17.

11. As Elberse noted, it took Ferguson as a manager of MUFC four years to win the first trophy the Football Association Cup on 12 May 1990 and another three years to win the Premier League title on 2 May 1993. He left MUFC on May 2013 leaving behind a huge and lasting legacy on the club after winning 13 English Premier League titles along with 25 other domestic and international trophies.

12. See more details of the financial performance of the club at 2003 on Perry, 'Manchester United, Brand of Hope and Glory'. At the time of writing, Deloitte's study 'Commercial Breaks' stressed that Manchester United is the second largest club in Europe as measured by financial turnover with €518 m. for the 2013/2014 season.

13. Downs and Paramio-Salcines, 'Incorporating Accessibility and Disability in the Manchester United Culture and Organization as Part of their CSR Policies'.

14. The analysis of Manchester United FC has been noted by a number of academics and practitioners, but particularly see Mellor, 'The Genesis of Manchester United as a National and International "Super-Club", 1958–68'; Andrews, *Manchester United. A Thematic Study*; Szymanski, 'Why Manchester United is so Successful'; Johnson and Scholes, *Exploring Corporate Strategy*; Perry, 'Manchester United, Brand of Hope and Glory'; Brown, "Not for Sale'? The Destruction and Reformation of Football Communities in the Glazer Takeover of Manchester United' explored the background, fan culture and opposition of club's fans to the corporate takeover of the club by the Glazer's family or Deloitte, 'Commercial Breaks Football Money League'. In terms of fan support, Mellor suggested that level of national and global support of Manchester United that the club gained in the 1960s linked to their financial strength have been critical to understand their present recognition. On this issue, a global football survey carried out by market research agency, Kantar, reported that 659 million people follow Manchester United, regarded as the world's most popular club worldwide. As part of their global reach, 71 million are in America, 90 million are in Europe, 173 million are in Africa and the Middle East and finally 325 million are in Asia.

15. See a much detail analysis of the managerial implications on Sir Alex Ferguson's case on Elberse, 'Ferguson's Formula'.
16. Downs and Paramio-Salcines, 'Incorporating Accessibility and Disability in the Manchester United Culture and Organization as Part of their CSR Policies'.
17. Only a Premier League club like Arsenal has tried to replicate the concept of the Ability Suite by offering a disabled supporter's lounge in the Learning Centre adjacent to the Emirates stadium before a match. See http://www.arsenal.com/news/community-news/ arsenal-fc-celebrates-equality-and-diversity. Similarly, a League One club like Wolverhampton Wanderers officially opened a new Disabled Lounge on 31 July 2013 at their Molineux stadium.
18. With regard to the influence of offering free tickets on the experience of fans with disabilities, according to Phil Downs, 'any influence relating to the "complimentary" tickets would be negligible in impact because the demand will always be there whether the club charge or not'. It is also worth noting that as the Centre for Access to Football in Europe (CAFÉ) stated, there is a lack of uniformity in the existing management systems for SwD when attending large sporting events across Europe. In the case of Manchester United and as part of their long-term commitment to their SwD there is a clear policy with respect to the ticketing management policy for their own SwD as well as for visiting supporters (see more details at 'Disabled Supporters' Information Booklet 2013/14').
19. This comment was sent by a Manchester City fan to MUDSA by email after the match between Manchester United FC and Manchester City, held on Tuesday 25 March 2014.
20. For example, see Kitchin, 'Planning and Managing the Stadium Experience'.
21. See, for example, Downs and Paramio-Salcines, 'Incorporating Accessibility and Disability in the Manchester United Culture and Organization as part of their CSR Policies'; Kitchin, 'Planning and Managing the Stadium Experience'; Paramio-Salcines and Kitchin, 'Institutional Perspectives on the Implementation of Disability Legislation and Services for Spectators with Disabilities in European Professional Football'; Paramio, Campos, and Buraimo, 'Promoting Accessibility for Fans with Disabilities to European Stadia and Arenas: An Holistic Journey Sequence Approach'; and Paramio-Salcines, Grady, and Downs, 'Growing the Football Game: The Increasing Economic and Social Relevance of Older Fans and those with Disabilities in the European Football Industry'.
22. See, for example, a much more detailed discussion of different legislations on disability and accessibility in countries including Australia, the United States, United Kingdom, Germany and Spain and their impact on the stadium experience for those people with disabilities when attending all types of events on Grady and Paramio-Salcines, 'Global Disability Laws and their Impact on the Stadium Experience'; Grady and James, 'Understanding the Needs of Spectators with Disabilities Attending Sporting Events'.
23. For a much detailed review of the existing level of accessibility at facilities and services provided by the main football stadia clubs in England, Germany and Spain, see Paramio, Campos, and Buraimo, 'Promoting Accessibility for Fans with Disabilities to European Stadia and Arenas: An Holistic Journey Sequence Approach'.
24. For a fuller discussion of the approach of a club like Arsenal to their supporters with disabilities in their new Emirates stadium, see Kitchin, 'Planning and Managing the Stadium Experience'.
25. Paramio-Salcines, Grady, and Downs, 'Growing the Football Game: The Increasing Economic and Social Relevance of Older Fans and those with Disabilities in the European football Industry'.
26. See Grady, 'Accessibility doesn't Happen by Itself: An Interview with Betty Siegel, J.D., Director of The Kennedy Center Accessibility Program' for a detailed analysis of how Betty Siegel, the Director of one of the most relevant cultural art centres, the Kennedy Center, in the United States has incorporated the accessibility to their business operations. Grady and Ohlin, 'Equal Access to Hospitality Services for Guests with Mobility Impairments under the Americans with Disabilities Act: Implications for the Hospitality Industry'; Hudson and Hudson, *Customer Service for Hospitality and Tourism* for a much detail analysis of how to provide quality service in hospitality and tourism services.

27. For a review of the influence of top and middle managers on the implementation of strategies in organizations, see Fischer and Rohde, 'Management Resistance to Innovation'; Oke, 'Barriers to Innovation Management in Service Companies'; Johnson and Scholes, *Exploring Corporate Strategy*; and Ferlie et al., 'The Nonspread of Innovations: The Mediating Role of Professionals'.
28. See Downs and Paramio Salcines, 'Incorporating Accessibility and Disability in the Manchester United Culture and Organization as part of their CSR Policies'; Paramio-Salcines, Grady, and Downs, 'Growing the Football Game: The Increasing Economic and Social Relevance of Older Fans and those with Disabilities in the European Football Industry'.
29. Scott-Parker and Zadek, 'Managing Diversity: A Key Factor in Improving Efficiency, Productivity, and Overall Business Success'.
30. Rice, 'Universal Management: A Proposal to Change the Direction of Accessibility Management in the Australian Tourism Industry to create Benefits for all Australians and Visitors to Australia'; Patterson, Darcy, and Mönninghoff, 'Attitudes and Experiences of Tourism Operators in Northern Australia towards People with Disabilities'.
31. Paramio-Salcines, Grady, and Downs, 'Growing the Football Game: The Increasing Economic and Social Relevance of Older Fans and those with Disabilities in the European Football Industry'.
32. Authors like Washington and Patterson call for more frequent contributions between institutional theory and sport management studies. The reader can find more studies on the use of this theoretical framework on O'Brien and Slack, (analysis of the newly English Rugby Union); Southall et al., (analysis of the 2006 National Collegiate Athletic Association Division I Men's Basketball Tournament); Paramio-Salcines and Kitchin, (analysis of implementation of disability legislation and provision of disability services within the three main professional football leagues and their clubs in Europe).
33. See, for example, Fischer and Rohde, 'Management Resistance to Innovation', 11; Oke, 'Barriers to Innovation Management in Service Companies'; Groysberg and Connolly, 'Twenty-Four CEOs on Creating Diverse and Inclusive Organizations'; Johnson and Scholes. *Exploring Corporate Strategy*; and Ferlie et al., 'The Nonspread of Innovations: The Mediating Role of Professionals'.
34. Yin, *Case Study Research: Design and Methods*; Stake, 'Case Studies'.
35. See Edwards and Skinner, *Qualitative Research in Sport Management*; Edwards, 'Reflective Practice in Sport Management'; Stake, 'Case Studies'; Yin, *Case Study Research: Design and Methods*; and Veal and Darcy, *Sport Studies and Sport Management. A Practical Guide*.
36. There are a plethora of authors that advocate this demanded collaboration between academics and practitioners in all types of organizations, including sports organizations. See, for instance, Bartunek, 'Academic-Practitioner Collaboration need not Require Joint or Relevant Research: Toward a Relational Scholarship of Integration'; Cohen, 'The Very Separate Worlds of Academic and Practitioners Publications in Human Resource Management: Reasons for the Divide and Concrete Solutions for Bridging the Gap'; Rynes, 'Let´s Create a Tipping Point: What Academics and Practitioners can Do, Alone and Together'; Rynes, Giluk, and Brown, 'The Very Separate Worlds of Academic and Practitioner Publications in Human Resource Management: Implications for Evidence-Based Management'. On the sport management area, some authors imply this collaboration, see Edwards, 'Reflective Practice in Sport Management'; Costa, 'The Status and Future of Sport Management: A Delphi Study'; and Edwards and Skinner, *Qualitative Research in Sport Management*; and Frisby et al., 'Putting "Participatory" into Participatory Forms of Action Research'.
37. Edwards, 'Reflective Practice in Sport Management', 76.
38. At this point, it is important to present to the reader a brief profile of one of the authors who is also one of the most significant practitioners in the area of accessibility at football stadia in England. With almost 40 years of experience of wheelchair user in addition to 20 years of operational expertise at one of the largest stadium, Old Trafford, Phil Downs (Member of the British Empire, MBE, since 2004, for services to disabled people) is the Secretary of the Manchester United Disabled Supporters Association (MUDSA) and has served as the Disability Liaison Officer at Manchester United

Football Club since 1989. In this professional role, he is responsible for day-to-day operations regarding accessibility at Old Trafford stadium. Considered a pioneer in the area of providing access for people with disabilities in England, Downs is the former Secretary of the National Association of Disabled Supporters (now Level Playing Field) and was instrumental in drafting England's 'Accessible Stadia' guide. See more details of his contribution to promote disability and accessibility at club level stadia in England and in Europe on Downs and Paramio-Salcines, 'Incorporating Accessibility and Disability in the Manchester United Culture and Organization as part of their CSR Policies'; and Paramio, Campos, and Buraimo, 'Promoting Accessibility for Fans with Disabilities to European Stadia and Arenas: An Holistic Journey Sequence Approach'.

39. See more details on this approach on Edwards, 'Reflective Practice in Sport Management'; Edwards and Skinner, *Qualitative Research in Sport Management*, 154.
40. The reader may find more details on the following documents at MUDSA, 'For the Club. Phil chats with George Johnstone'; MUDSA, *Disability Supporters Information Booklet 2013/2014*; MUDSA, *Celebrating 10 years of the Ability Suite 2003–2013*; MUDSA. *Members' Handbook Summer 2014*; Manchester United Foundation. *A Season Review. Taking Manchester United to the Heart of the Community. Impact Report 2012/13*; and Downs, 'Joining Forces'.
41. Kay, *Foundations of Corporate Success*, 8.
42. Fischer and Rohde, 'Management Resistance to Innovation', 97. Also Westerbeek and Smith, *Business Leadership and the Lessons from Sport* emphasize that one of the lessons from sport that could be applied to any business environment is that teamwork is a critical factor for success.
43. Perry, 'Manchester United, Brand of Hope and Glory'.
44. Downs, 'Joining Forces'; Paramio, Campos, and Buraimo, 'Promoting Accessibility for Fans with Disabilities to European Stadia and Arenas: An Holistic Journey Sequence Approach'; and Downs and Paramio-Salcines, 'Incorporating Accessibility and Disability in the Manchester United Culture and Organization as Part of their CSR Policies'.
45. MUDSA, *Celebrating 10 years of the Ability Suite 2003–2013*, 20.
46. Kay, *Foundations of Corporate Success*, 8.
47. MUDSA, 'For the Club. Phil chats with George Johnstone', 19.
48. Downs and Paramio-Salcines, 'Incorporating Accessibility and Disability in the Manchester United Culture and Organization as part of their CSR Policies'; MUDSA, *Celebrating 10 years of the Ability Suite 2003–2013*, 20.
49. MUDSA, *Celebrating 10 years of the Ability Suite 2003–2013*, 23.
50. Downs and Paramio-Salcines, 'Incorporating Accessibility and Disability in the Manchester United Culture and Organization as part of their CSR Policies', 140.
51. MUDSA, 'For the Club. Phil chats with George Johnstone', 20–1.
52. www.mudsa.org.
53. MUDSA, *Celebrating 10 years of the Ability Suite 2003–2013*, 30.
54. See Phil Downs statement in MUDSA, *Celebrating 10 years of the Ability Suite 2003–2013*, 7.
55. In the summer 2013, David Gill stepped down from the position of chief executive at Manchester United FC and chairman of Manchester United Foundation and was replaced by this deputy John Shiels.
56. Fischer and Rohde, 'Management Resistance to Innovation'; Oke, 'Barriers to Innovation Management in Service Companies'; Johnson and Scholes, *Exploring Corporate Strategy*.
57. MUDSA, *Celebrating 10 years of the Ability Suite 2003–2013*, 7.
58. At the time of writing, George Johnstone was retired from his duties at the club level.
59. MUDSA, 'For the Club. Phil chats with George Johnstone', 19.
60. Downs and Paramio-Salcines, 'Incorporating Accessibility and Disability in the Manchester United Culture and Organization as part of their CSR Policies'.
61. MUDSA, 'For the Club. Phil chats with George Johnstone', 20.
62. As part of their CSR approach, the Premier League itself and football clubs at the Premier League as the case of MUFC are implementing programmes to make a positive social difference to the local communities in which the clubs are located. See Anagnostopoulos, 'Getting the Tactics Right. Implementing CSR in English Football'.

63. See more details of the impact and implications of this programme on children and adults with disabilities on different local communities at Manchester United Foundation, *A Season Review. Taking Manchester United to the Heart of the Community. Impact Report 2012/13;* MUDSA, *Members' Handbook Summer 2014.*
64. Paramio, Campos, and Buraimo, 'Promoting Accessibility for Fans with Disabilities to European Stadia and Arenas: An Holistic Journey Sequence Approach', 371.
65. MUDSA, *Celebrating 10 years of the Ability Suite 2003–2013*, 19.

References

Anagnostopoulos, C. 'Getting the Tactics Right. Implementing CSR in English Football'. In *Routledge Handbook of Sport and Corporate Social Responsibility*, ed. Paramio-Salcines, J. Babiak, and G. Walters, 91–104. London: Routledge, 2013.

Andrews, D., ed. *Manchester United. A Thematic Study.* Oxfordshire: Routledge, 2006.

Arsenal FC. 'Arsenal FC Celebrates Equality and Diversity'. http://www.arsenal.com/news/community-news/arsenal-fc-celebrates-equality-and-diversity.

Bartunek, J. 'Academic-practitioner Collaboration Need Not Require Joint or Relevant Research: Toward a Relational Scholarship of Integration'. *Academy of Management Journal* 50, no. 6 (2007): 1323–33.

Brown, A. '"Not for Sale"? The Destruction and Reformation of Football Communities in the Glazer Takeover of Manchester United'. *Soccer & Society* 8, no. 8 (2007): 614–35.

Centre for Access to Football in Europe (CAFÉ). 'Center for Access to Football in Europe. Proof of Disability Research Project-2013'. http://www.cafefootball.eu/en/news/cafe-proof-disability-research-project-final-report-announced.

Cohen, D. 'The Very Separate Worlds of Academic and Practitioner Publications in Human Resource Management: Reasons for The Divide and Concrete Solutions for Bridging the Gap'. *Academy of Management Journal* 50, no. 5 (2007): 1013–9.

Costa, C. 'The Status and Future of Sport Management: A Delphi Study'. *Journal of Sport Management* 19 (2005): 117–42.

Deloitte. *Commercial Breaks Football Money League.* Manchester: Deloitte Sport Business Group, 2015.

Downs, P. 'Joining Forces'. *Gazetta* 9 (2006): 3.

Downs, P, J. Paramio-Salcines, and J. Grady. 'Celebrating 10 years of Manchester United's Ability Suite: From Organizational Buy-In to Premium Patron Services'. Paper presented at the 2014 Kennedy Center LEAD Conference, Chicago, USA, August 1–4, 2014.

Downs, P and J. Paramio-Salcines. 'Incorporating Accessibility and Disability in the Manchester United Culture and Organization as part of their CSR Policies'. In *Routledge Handbook of Sport and Corporate Social Responsibility*, ed. J Paramio-Salcines, K. Babiak, and G. Walters, 135–46. London: Routledge, 2013.

Edwards, A. 'Reflective Practice in Sport Management'. *Sport Management Review* 2, no. 1 (1999): 67–81.

Edwards, A., and J. Skinner. *Qualitative Research in Sport Management.* Oxford: BH Elsevier, 2009.

Elberse, A. 'Ferguson's Formula'. *Harvard Business Review* 91, no. 10 (2013): 116–25.

Ferlie, E., L. Fitzgerald. M. Wood, and C. Hawkins 'The Nonspread of Innovations: The Mediating Role of Professionals'. *Academy of Management Journal* 48, no. 1 (2005): 117–34.

Fischer, B., and M. Rohde. 'Management Resistance to Innovation'. *American Journal of Management* 13, no. 1 (2013): 93–9.

Frisby, W., C. Reid. S. Millar, and L. Hoeber. 'Putting "Participatory" into Participatory forms of Action Research'. *Journal of Sport Management* 19 (2005): 367–86.

Grady, J. 'Accessibility doesn't Happen by Itself: An Interview with Betty Siegel, J.D., Director of The Kennedy Center Accessibility Program'. *Journal of Venue and Event Management* 2, no. 2 (2010): 69–73.

Grady, J., and J. James 'Understanding the Needs of Spectators with Disabilities attending Sporting Events'. *Journal of Venue and Entertainment Management* 4, no. 2 (2013): 47–62.

Grady, J., and J. Ohlin. 'Equal Access to Hospitality Services for Guests with Mobility Impairments under the Americans with Disabilities Act: Implications for the Hospitality Industry'. *International Journal of Hospitality Management* 28 (2009): 161–9.

Grady, J., and J. Paramio-Salcines. 'Global Disability Laws and their Impact on the Stadium Experience'. Paper presented at Sport Entertainment &Venues Tomorrow (SEVT) Conference, Columbia, SC, USA, November 20–22, 2013.

Groysberg, B., and K. Connolly. 'Great Leaders who make the mix work'. *Harvard Business Review* 91, no. 9 (2013): 69–76.

Hudson, S., and L. Hudson. *Customer Service for Hospitality and Tourism.* Oxford: Goodfellow, 2013.

Johnson, G., and K. Scholes. *Exploring Corporate Strategy.* London: Prentice Hall, 2001.

Kay, J. *Foundations of Corporate Success.* Oxford: Oxford University Press, 1993.

Kitchin, P. 'Planning and Managing the Stadium Experience'. In *Managing Sport Business: An Introduction*, ed. L. Trenberth and D. Hassan, 350–66. London: Routledge, 2011.

Level Playing Field. 'Manchester United'. London. Level Playing Field. http://www.levelplay ingfield.org.uk/clubs/manchester-united.

Manchester United Disabled Supporters Association (MUDSA). 'For the Club. Phil chats with George Johnstone'. *Rollin' Reds* 16, no. 3 (2013):18–9.

Manchester United Disabled Supporters Association (MUDSA). *Disability Supporters Information Booklet 2013/2014.* Manchester: MUDSA, Manchester United FC, 2013.

Manchester United Disabled Supporters Association (MUDSA). *'Celebrating 10 years of the Ability Suite 2003-2013'.* Manchester: MUDSA, Manchester United FC, 2014.

Manchester United Disabled Supporters Association (MUDSA). *Members' Handbook Summer 2014.* Manchester: MUDSA, Manchester United FC, 2014.

Manchester United Foundation *A Season Review. Taking Manchester United to the Heart of the Community. Impact Report 2012/13.* Manchester: Manchester United Foundation, 2013.

Mellor, G. 'The Genesis of Manchester United as a National and International 'Super-club', 1958–68'. *Soccer & Society* 1, no. 2 (2000): 151–66.

Metcalf, M. 'Suite Dreams-Facilities for Disabled Fans at Old Trafford'. 18 December 2013. http://writemark.blogspot.com.es/2013/12/suite-dreams-facilities-for-disabled.html.

O'Brien, D, and T. Slack. 'The Emergence of a Professional Logic in English Rugby Union: The Role of Isomorphic and Diffusion Processes'. *Journal of Sport Management* 18 (2004):13–39.

Oke, A. 'Barriers to innovation management in service companies'. *Journal of Change Management* 4, no. 1 (2004): 31–44.

Paramio, J, C. Campos, and B. Buraimo. 'Promoting Accessibility for Fans with Disabilities to European Stadia and Arenas: An Holistic Journey Sequence Approach'. In *Managing Sport Business: An Introduction*, ed. L Trenberth and D. Hassan, 267–88. London: Routledge, 2011.

Paramio-Salcines, J, J. Grady, and P. Downs. 'Growing the Football Game: The Increasing Economic and Social relevance of Older Fans and those with Disabilities in the European Football Industry'. *Soccer & Society* 15, no. 6 (2014): 864–82.

Paramio-Salcines, J., and P. Kitchin. 'Institutional Perspectives on the Implementation of Disability Legislation and Services for Spectators with Disabilities in European Professional Football'. *Sport Management Review* 16, no. 3 (2013): 337–48.

Parnell, D., and D. Richardson. 'Introduction'. *Soccer & Society* 15, no. 6 (2014): 823–7.

Patterson, I. S. Darcy, and M. Mönninghoff. 'Attitudes and experiences of tourism operators in Northern Australia towards people with disabilities'. *World Leisure Journal* 54, no. 3 (2012): 215–29.

Perry, B. 'Manchester United, Brand of Hope and Glory'. In *Exploring Corporate Strategy, Texts and Cases*, ed. G Johnson, K. Scholes, and R. Whittington, 217–22. London: Prentice Hall, 2005.

Rice, P. 'Universal Management: A Proposal to Change the Direction of Accessibility Management in the Australian Tourism Industry to create Benefits for all Australians and Visitors to Australia'. *The Review of Disability Studies: An International Journal* 2, no. 2 (2006): 64–79.

Rynes, S. 'Let's Create a Tipping Point: What Academics and Practitioners can do, Alone and Together'. *Academy of Management Journal* 50 (2007): 1046–54.

Rynes, S.T., T. Giluk, and K. Brown. 'The Very Separate Worlds of Academic and Practitioner Periodicals in Human Resource Management: Implications for Evidence-based Management'. *Academy of Management Journal* 50 (2007): 987–1008.

Scott-Parker, S., and S. Zadek. 'Managing Diversity: A Key Factor in Improving Efficiency, Productivity, and Overall Business Success'. *Journal of Vocational Rehabilitation* 16 (2001): 119–23.

Southall, R., M. Nagel, J. Amis, and C. Southall. 'A Method to March Madness? Institutional Logics and the 2006 National Collegiate Athletic Association Division I Men's Basketball Tournament'. *Journal of Sport Management* 22 (2008): 677–700.

Sport Industry Group. 'Man United Named Most Popular Club'. http://www.sportindustry. biz/news/view/11126/man-utd-named-most-popular-club.

Stake, R. 'Case Studies'. In *Handbook of Qualitative Research*, ed. N Denzin and Y. Lincoln, 236–47. Thousand Oaks, CA: Sage, 1994.

Szymanski, S. 'Why is Manchester United So Successful?'. *Business Strategy Review* 9, no. 4 (1998): 47–54.

Veal, A., and S. Darcy. *Sport Studies and Sport Management. A Practical Guide*. London: Routledge, 2014.

Washington, M., and K. Patterson. 'Hostile Takeover or Joint Venture: Connections between Institutional Theory and Sport Management Research'. *Sport Management Review* 14, no. 1 (2011): 1–12.

Westerbeek, H., and A. Smith. *Business Leadership and the Lessons from Sport*, New York: Palgrave Macmillan, 2005.

Yin, R. *Case Study Research: Design and Methods*. 3rd ed. Thousand Oaks, CA: Sage, 2003.

Index

INDEX

Lightning Source UK Ltd.
Milton Keynes UK
UKHW031005210420
361997UK00014B/3306

9 780367 229849